Serving Hispanic, Latine, and Latinx Students in Academic Libraries

This book is number five in the Series on
Critical Race Studies and Multiculturalism in LIS,
Rose L. Chou and Annie Pho, Series Editors

Serving Hispanic, Latine, and Latinx Students in Academic Libraries

Sommer Browning and Isabel Soto-Luna

Library Juice Press
Sacramento, CA

Published in 2023 by Library Juice Press.

Litwin Books
PO Box 188784
Sacramento, CA 95818

http://litwinbooks.com/

This book is printed on acid-free paper.

Publisher's Cataloging in Publication

Names: Browning, Sommer, editor. | Soto-Luna, M. Isabel, editor.
Title: Serving Hispanic Latine and Latinx students in academic libraries / Sommer Browning and M.
    Isabel Soto-Luna, editors.
Description: Sacramento, CA : Library Juice Press, 2023. | Series: Critical race studies and
    multiculturalism in LIS ; 5. | Includes bibliographical references and index.
Identifiers: LCCN 2023945578 | ISBN 9781634001373 (acid-free paper)
Subjects: LCSH: Academic libraries – Services to Hispanic Americans. | Hispanic Americans and
    libraries. | Hispanic Americans – Information services. | Hispanic Americans -- Archives.
Classification: LCC 711.92.H56 S47 2023 | DDC 027.6/3--dc23
LC record available at https://lccn.loc.gov/2023945578

Contents

Introduction

Isabel Soto-Luna and Sommer Browning

In researching the library literature, we found a dearth of books focused on the academic library experience of Latine students. This was surprising to us because there are hundreds of academic libraries serving millions of Hispanic and Latinx students across the country. This is especially evident in the growing number of Hispanic-Serving Institutions (HSIs). HSIs are federally designated colleges and universities with over 25% of their undergraduate full-time students identifying as Hispanic. According to the Hispanic Association of Colleges and Universities (HACU), as of 2021–2022 there were 572 such institutions, with 400 more designated as emerging HSIs. But there are many more institutions of higher education with large Latine populations that do not have the HSI designation. These are institutions of all kinds—community colleges, research-centered institutions, trade colleges, tribal colleges. But as Taveras Rivera, Ortiz Rodriguez, and Arocho state in their introduction to chapter 12, "Centro Library and Archives Bring Resources for Students and Educators in Hispanic Serving Institutions," just because institutions are designated as HSIs—or enroll lots of Latine students—doesn't mean that they are making visible changes to their missions or visions.

Sommer works for a library that serves over 40,000 students, with over 25% identifying as Latine or Hispanic. While we have diversity and equity statements included in our strategic plan, our collection development guidelines, and our vision statements, what do we do for Latine students specifically? We celebrate Latinx Heritage Month, periodically create new materials lists on the undocumented student experience or other issues related to the Latine community, translate some of our webpages into Spanish but that's about it. Considering, too, that our campus was created in the 1970s through a city approved bond measure that displaced hundreds of mostly Hispanic families and businesses, doing the minimum feels unjust. For Sommer, this was a great motivation to create this book. What are other libraries doing? What can we do? Where do we start?

Sommer reached out to the dean at one of the HSIs in Colorado and was connected with Isabel Soto-Luna, a Visiting Assistant Professor at an HSI and new librarian. They hadn't met prior to starting this project but in spite of their very different experiences with publishing, their backgrounds, their length in the profession, and many other things, they found that they shared values around diversity, equity, and inclusion. Those shared values were kept front and center throughout the entire process of putting this book together.

The same can be said of the book's contributors. These authors come from all over the country, have a variety of backgrounds, and work in all kinds of institutions. But they have one important thing in common, they are all making visible changes to their programs, services, or philosophies in order to serve their Latine students the best way they can.

The book is divided into four sections. Section 1 is called "Foundations" and begins with Isabel Soto-Luna's chapter on terminology and specifically the evolution and meanings of the words Latine, Latinx, and Hispanic. The three other chapters in this section are also foundational in that they share three different ways of engaging Latine students. Niki S. Fullmer and Brittany Paloma Fiedler present a comprehensive survey they administered to 15 Latine students about their perceptions of academic libraries, and share specific ways their library can improve its relationship with them. In chapter three, Sally Najera Romero, Elizabeth V. Hernandez, and Alyssa V. Loera work to directly improve that relationship through creative and welcoming Latinx Heritage Month library programming. Lisa Cruces and Jess Williams, in the final chapter of the section, explore theories of care work and authenticity and how these concepts inform their first-generation committees, undergraduate instruction, and the student employment experience.

"Decolonizing Information Literacy" is the title of Section 2 and it focuses on approaches to information literacy that honor and highlight Latine experience. Elizabeth Teoli-Thomason and Alejandra Méndez Irizarry discuss how their library meets the particular needs of their community college students in an online environment. Rosemarie Rodriguez explores the way zines can engage students and allow them to share their expertise while creating knowledge for others to use. In chapter seven, Stephanie B. Fletcher, Beronica Avila, Jill Bambenek, and Molly Mansfield describe a collaborative Día de los Muertos celebration that engaged students in the library in multifaceted ways.

Actively and methodically building inclusive collections that represent Latine student experience is the focus of Section 3, "Establishing and Growing Representative Collections." Despite budget and staffing challenges, the library workers in these chapters have prioritized increasing the diversity of their collections. Anthony Davis Jr. has done this with a focus on donations and collaborations with outside organizations. In Caitlin Archer-Helke's chapter, the author describes a journey of personal education that forged a decolonial philosophy of collection development, and shares practical advice for anyone building a representative collection. Nelson Santana explores the concept of decolonizing the mind and how his study of theories of decolonization factors into the collection development work he does at Bronx Community College of the City University of New York.

The final section, "Archives, Research, and Heritage," centers three rich archival collections and the ways library workers have incorporated them into their work with their Latine students. The chapter written by Azalea Camacho, Mario H. Ramirez, and Lettycia Terrones highlights Cal State LA library's culturally relevant information literacy efforts as well as a program that engages students in archival practice and primary source analysis through processing the Mervyn M. Dymally Papers. In chapter 12, Elizabeth Taveras Rivera, Raquel M. Ortiz Rodriguez, and Anibal Arocho explore the ways Centro, the Center for Puerto Rican Studies at Hunter College, is integrated in student learning and the curriculum through a cultural ambassadors program, a poster series, and other programs. In the book's final chapter, Sandy Enriquez, Covadonga Lamar Prieto, Rachel Starry, Andrea Hoff, and Krystal Boehlert share their work partnering with Hispanic Studies instructors to create a comprehensive research course for undergraduate students using unpublished manuscripts and other materials in the Tomás Rivera Archive at University of California, Riverside.

It was imperative to us, as the editors, that this book include authors of various backgrounds and experiences. We specifically wanted to amplify the voices of Latine library workers who are doing this work in their libraries. As you will discover, there are many instances of Latine library professionals bringing their own life experience into their work. We believe this is an incredibly important way to create space for Latine students and build community and camaraderie. Through a voluntary and anonymous survey of our authors with a 70% response rate, we found that over 70% of authors identify as Latine, Hispanic, Chicanx, Black, Brown, Asian, and/or Indigenous. We learned that many of the authors in the book are native Spanish speakers and that the majority are first-generation or non-traditional students themselves. Overwhelmingly the chapters are written by authors who identify as female, but the book also includes authors who identify as male and non-binary. We are proud to celebrate the experiences of these library workers. We also want to acknowledge that this book was written and edited during the COVID-19 pandemic, a time when every author and editor was under incredible personal and professional stress, performing duties at their libraries that were not in their job descriptions, and working hard to keep their students and library staff safe. A deep thanks is offered to the books' authors, who on top of it all, took time to write about their experiences and make this book possible.

We hope that you will see yourself, your library, and your students in this book. We hope that these programs, services, and approaches inspire you to further support your Latine students in their educational, professional, and personal goals.

Sommer & Isabel, June 2022

Section 1
Foundations

Hispanic, Latine, Latinx
How Monolithic Terminology Can Amplify and Erase Millions of Voices

Isabel Soto-Luna

Author Statement

Given the personal topic that this book and chapter speak to, this author would like to acknowledge the way in which her positionality could impact this work.

First, this author recognizes that where she works (the University of Nebraska at Omaha (UNO)) and lives (Omaha, NE) occupies the traditional treaty lands of the Omaha (UmoHhoN) and Otoe-Missouria Tribal Nations. This author would also like to acknowledge the Ponca Tribe of Nebraska, the Winnebago Tribe of Nebraska, the Santee Sioux Tribe of Nebraska, and the 170 plus other tribes represented within the Omaha area.

Isabel Soto-Luna identifies as a Mexican American, cis-gendered, brown woman and mother who is an immigrant raised in the United States and whose native language is Spanish. As a non-traditional undergraduate student, Soto-Luna attended a Hispanic Serving Institution in Southern Colorado where she worked as a student archives assistant. She serves as the Business Librarian for Criss Libraries at UNO, and is affiliate faculty for OLLAS, the Office of Latino/Latin American Studies also at UNO.

Lastly, this author recognizes that her preferred use of terminology (such as Latine) is personal and may not reflect the way in which others identify. Personal identity is important, and her intent is simply to use a term that is inclusive of all genders while recognizing the difficulty that Spanish speakers can have with other gender inclusive terms.

Introduction

The use of the term Hispanic in the U.S. has long been used as a catch-all for what is a remarkably diverse group of people. Often incorrectly interchanged with the term Latine, many do not understand why the term, along with others like Latine, and Latinx, is both important and problematic. The way people identify is incredibly personal and can be a result of a variety of experiences.

Hispanics and Latines (the U.S. Census counts these groups as one) make up 18.7% of the U.S. population with non-Hispanic African Americans comprising 12.4% of the population (Jones et al., 2021). While the Census Bureau considers Hispanic and Latine as one group, it does at least recognize that these groups encompass various races and so it distinguishes race as separate, allowing people to acknowledge both their race and Hispanic and/or Latine origins. This is important to know because according to the U.S. Census Bureau, the U.S. saw a decrease in the non-Hispanic white-only population from 63.7% in 2010 to 57.8% in 2020 (US Census Bureau, 2021) and it is forecasted that the Hispanic/Latine population will grow to over 111 million by 2060 (US Census Bureau, 2018). This means that as the population grows, we will see (and are already seeing) a growth in Hispanic and Latine higher ed students.

As academic librarians, it is important that we recognize and understand the differences in these terms and how our students use them, assuming they use them at all. To truly support Hispanic communities, and in the case of HSI students, it is important to know how the use of the term Hispanic in the U.S came about, the misconceptions around it that have caused strife among varying groups, and why this term (and others) can be problematic. In this chapter, I go over a summarized history of the term Hispanic, its use in the United States, and the ways it has both amplified, such as the classification of Hispanic Serving Institutions, and caused erasure among the Central American, Southern American, and Caribbean American people in the United States. I will also go over how some of the terms used in describing these groups of people came to be, the issues that surround them, and some of the political and immigrant complexities that exist within the community.

While this chapter does not in any way pretend that the topics touched on are a comprehensive explanation of Hispanics and Latines in the U.S., it hopefully does give you a primer into the complexities of the community.

Hispanic

History and Use in the United States

Spain, having been part of the Roman Empire, was at one point called Hispania along with the rest of the Iberian Peninsula. As to where the term Hispania itself came from, that is contested. What is not contested is that at some point Hispania turned into España, and Hispanic became symbolic of Spanish speakers. When Spain colonized the Americas, they brought with them their language, culture, and traditions, and imposed them on the Indigenous peoples that existed in these lands. With them they also brought slaves who were also forced to assimilate and become part of the new lands. Today, Spanish is the fourth most spoken language in the world, with only English, Mandarin Chinese, and Hindi used more worldwide (Ethnologue, 2022). In the U.S., however, Spanish is the second most spoken language (US Census Bureau, 2020) with most of the people who speak it originating from somewhere in Latin America (e.g., Central, South, and the Caribbean; US Census Bureau, 2020). Why is this important to know? Because this is part of what has caused the confusion between Latine and Hispanic, the erasure of cultures and races among Latines in the U.S. and throughout the Americas, and the many stereotypes that live on and pit Latines against each other.

So how did the term Hispanic take hold in the U.S.? In her book *Making Hispanics: How Activists, Bureaucrats, and Media Constructed a New American*, G. Cristina Mora (2014) links the use of the term in the U.S. to the census. With this group having previously been classified as white with European ancestry, activists knew that this meant many were not being counted as their own group and therefore could not be accurately represented, they compromised on the term Hispanic, using the Spanish language to group different nationalities and cultures into one ethnic group. This meant businesses and media now had a group they could market to and serve, and a whole new group of people for politicians to pander to, changing the racial and political landscape in the United States (Mora, 2014).

However, this was not the perfect compromise as the term erased the uniqueness of these cultures and the diversity of races and backgrounds that came with these differences, attempting to turn them into a monolith. And by using the term Hispanic, it still put European influence and whiteness front and center, creating the illusion that all Hispanic or Latine people are white, light-skinned, or brown. This perpetuated white-supremacy and continued the erasure of Black and Indigenous peoples. It also completely ignored the different political and immigration relationships that these countries held with the United States, which were important as these had the power to create division and strife among Hispanic and Latine groups.

Part of that strife is the assumption that all Hispanics and Latines are immigrants and that most must be undocumented, forgetting that many were already here when the United States was expanding, especially in the Southwest and Pacific region of the country. A point that Pedro Garza makes in his 2017 Forbes article "Mexicans Didn't Immigrate to America — We've Always Been Here."

Puerto Rico, for example, has been a territory of the United States for a long time and Puerto Ricans were given citizenship with the passing of the Jones–Shafroth Act in 1917, a move that had more to do with politics than the people (Melendez, 2017) and that has not always been to their benefit. If anything, Puerto Ricans have found themselves at a crossroads, where those who live on the island do not possess the same rights as all other U.S. citizens, such as being able to vote in the presidential elections. In fact, many people are not even aware that Puerto Ricans are U.S. Citizens (Dropp & Nyhan, 2017) and are often referred to as immigrants in the media, and sometimes even in academia and published works. This has meant that many Puerto Ricans face the same discrimination as immigrants and are seen as foreigners which in many cases has created an us vs. them mentality between Puerto Ricans and other Hispanic/Latine populations (*Puerto Ricans as Immigrants and Other Misperceptions*, 2018).

People in the U.S. also seem to forget, or perhaps not know if we're giving them the benefit of the doubt, that while Puerto Ricans are not immigrants, there have been different laws for immigration from other countries in Latin America and the Caribbean.

For Cubans, immigration to the U.S. has historically been very different than for those from other countries, starting with the Cuban revolution. In "Balseros, Boteros, and El Bombo: Post-1994 Cuban

Immigration to the United States and the Persistence of Special Treatment," Todd Henken (2005) talks about the history of Cuban immigration and the welcoming reception received by those fleeing from Cuba during the revolution, which included job and housing assistance, job retraining programs, college loans, and "unprecedented exceptions" to residency and citizenship laws. Most of this came from the anti-communist mentality prevalent in the U.S. at the time. Rafters from Cuba found in international waters were allowed blanket refugee status in the U.S., while rafters from other countries, like Haiti, were deported (Henken, 2005). In 1995, there was a change to how rafters were treated when found which resulted in the "Wet Foot Dry Foot Policy" that meant rafters who made it to U.S. soil could stay, but those picked up in international waters would be deported (Daniels, 2017). However, anyone from any other Latin American country still had to go through a lengthy immigration process and many times were discriminated against and treated as criminals. Because Cuban immigrants were political exiles whose properties were seized by the Castro regime, as opposed to economic migrants, were mainly white and middle class, and were granted special immigration status, many Cubans were able to achieve their full potential in the U.S. (Florido, 2017). This is not to say that the plight of Cubans in this country is not legitimate—the horrors and trauma they lived through are very real—but this distinction created a schism between them and other Latines, one that hasn't been helped by the support many Cubans give to conservative politicians who are known for discriminatory policies toward immigrants. In 2016, President Obama ended the "Wet Foot Dry Foot Policy" and Cuba agreed to take back those Cubans with orders of deportation as a result of crimes committed (Daniels, 2017). As a result, many Cubans have been pushed further to the right politically seeing the democratic party as socialist, something which they definitely do not support given their history with Castro, even as many new generations of Cubans born in the U.S. have started supporting liberal ideas (Gonzalez, n.d.).

Mexico, the country where the majority of the Latine population in the U.S comes from (US Census Bureau, 2020), has had a love/hate relationship with the U.S. throughout its history. While there have been wars and political strife between the countries, there has also been cooperation. A recent example of that cooperation when it comes to immigration from Mexico is the Bracero Program. The Bracero Program was a guest worker program that lasted just over two decades between 1942 and 1964 and allowed over four million Mexican agricultural workers to migrate legally as the U.S. found itself short of agricultural workers but with a high demand of agricultural products during World War II (Kosack, 2021). It was based on an agreement between the U.S. government, who initiated conversations, and the Mexican government who had misgivings (Kosack, 2021). The bracero workers were mistreated in various ways including improper housing, and were not given adequate medical care or water while the bosses "insisted that they could treat their workers however they wished, since the bracero contracts were merely a ruse to satisfy public opinion and get Mexico to allow the importation of its workers" (Henderson, 2011, p. 204). The program gave start to the paradoxical want for cheap labor while still having a distaste for immigrants, especially undocumented immigrants (Mize, 2011). Ironically, it was the bad implementation of the program in the U.S. and the blacklists that Mexico could create blocking certain U.S. states and counties from participating in the bracero program based on complaints from the workers, that led to many farmers encouraging undocumented immigration (Hernández, 2006). The hypocrisy, of course, was ignored, and has continued to be ignored. During the two decades that the Bracero Program was in place, another less known companion to it came about, "Operation Wetback." As the Bracero Program was forcing farmers to treat their workers with a small level of decency, farmers from states that had been blacklisted (like Texas) were encouraging undocumented immigration in order to find cheap agricultural labor. At the same time, the U.S. government was painting undocumented and documented workers as criminals, and the women as prostitutes (Ngai, 2014). Under this political climate, "Operation Wetback" began in 1954 with the intention of repatriating undocumented immigrants back to Mexico.

> The construction of the "wetback" as a dangerous and criminal social pathogen fed the general racial stereotype "Mexican." A 1951 study by Lyle Saunders and Olen Leonard, conducted as part of a project sponsored by the Mexican American social scientist and civil rights advocate George I. Sánchez, stated, "No careful distinctions are made between illegal aliens and local citizens of Mexican descent. They are lumped together as 'Mexicans' and the characteristics that are observed among the wetbacks are by extension assigned to the local people." Wetbacks, said one official, were "superficially indistinguishable from Mexicans legally in the United States" (Ngai, 2014, p. 171).

Wetback was, and continues to be a derogatory term for immigrants alluding to undocumented status. The operation ran concurrently with the Braceros Program, and the stereotype of Mexicans as criminals has persisted as can be seen in current political discourse, even when the data shows that this is not true (Ye Hee Lee, 2015).

These are just three examples of the countries from where the largest Hispanic and Latine populations in the United States originate (US Census Bureau, 2020) and the treatment they have received from the U.S. government and its people. Every country in Latin America is treated differently and has different immigration laws that apply to their people. Even though the government has different immigration laws for each country, the Hispanic and Latine population in the U.S. is seen as homogenous and assumptions are made that everyone is from Mexico. While Mexico is the place of origin for most Latines, it is most definitely not the only one (US Census Bureau, 2020). As Maria Cardona (2016) states in her article "Hispanics and Latinos Are Not All Mexicans, but All Deserve Respect:"

> As a Latina woman, I want to hear someone ask me what country I am from instead of assuming I am Mexican, but even more, I need to know that Mexican-Americans and all immigrants are treated fairly as human beings and are not subject to ridicule by misinformed politicians and textbooks. Mexican, Hispanic or Latino—everyone needs to be treated with respect.

The assumptions over the homogeneity of Hispanics and Latines have meant that many cultures, and traditions among the community have been erased or anglicized. Traditions like Dia de los Muertos are celebrated all over Latin America, and yet it is seen as a purely Mexican tradition, one that has lost a lot of meaning in the U.S. In the U.S. many equate it to Halloween and dress up as a Catrina without understanding why these traditions exist and what they mean.

The term Hispanic also left out many countries and communities in Latin America that do not speak Spanish as the main language, including Indigenous peoples within Spanish speaking countries who maintained their language and still speak it today. Statistics show that Bolivia, Guatemala, and Mexico have high numbers of Indigenous Peoples that make up their population, 48%, 43.8%, and 19.4% respectively (Buchholz, Katharina, 2021). Many of these people still speak their native language, 31.9% percent of Bolivians do so as does 49% of the population in Paraguay (Corporación Latinobarómetro, 2018). And of course, you have countries like Brazil, whose official language is Portuguese. Are they any less deserving of the services available to Hispanics in the U.S.?

Using language as the classifier also meant that people from Spain are included with all other Hispanic groups, which has led to controversy. Historically, the term Hispanic in the U.S. has been correlated with people of color (POC), ignoring that Hispanics and Latines comprise all races including whites. And in fact, many Spaniards do not see themselves as Hispanic or Latine. In the study "'I'm Not Spanish, I'm from Spain': Spaniards' Bifurcated Ethnicity and the Boundaries of Whiteness and Hispanic Panethnic Identity," José G. Soto-Marquez writes:

> The daily struggle for a distinct European/white identity was the norm for most Spanish immigrants interviewed in New York City. Yet their national sense of self in Spain never revolved around the common ethnic or racial categories we use in daily American life and on nearly every form we fill out. "Hispanic" was something they might have talked about in relation to language or culture back home, but "Latino" was certainly used only for the millions of South American immigrants who flocked to Spain before the 2008 economic crisis. Many of the interviewees even noted that the pejorative term *sudacas* (a loose Spanish reference to South Americans akin to spics in the United States) was widely used. In effect, most interviewees noted that "racism in Spain was the norm" and that there was tremendous social distance and segregation between Spanish natives and immigrants from Africa, Latin America, Eastern Europe, and South Asia; as Mauricio, a 24-year-old intern at the United Nations, noted in relation to immigrant communities in Spain, "Everybody sticks to themselves; they don't engage much with Spaniards." (2019, p. 90)

While not all Spaniards in the U.S. have this attitude, there have been controversies in the media and among Latine groups about them being considered for major awards under "Latin" categories and being described as people of color. Antonio Banderas found himself in this predicament when he was described as both Latino and a POC during the #OscarsSoWhite controversy (Benavides, 2020). This is just one example of the issues happening around inclusivity of Spaniards with all other Hispanics and Latines. The erasure of colonization and the arguments around "proper Spanish" are two other concerns that could be their own books.

And this is the biggest difference between being Hispanic or Latine, who is and isn't included, and why. Latine encompasses everyone from Latin America, regardless of language but excludes those from Spain as Latin America is comprised of Mexico, Central and South America, and the Caribbean. While most in the community do fall under both categories, the distinction is an important one, as even among Latines there are those who still believe that the language does matter and this has caused many to consider *Latinidad* (Latin-ness) not inclusive enough of Indigenous and Black people in the region. Because of the conflation of Latine with Hispanic, there are also many from Latin America who do not feel comfortable calling themselves Latine.

Hispanic Serving Institutions (HSIs)

While the term Hispanic in the U.S. has caused controversy, the new classification allowed for advocates to ask the government for the creation of programs and services for the Hispanic population in the U.S. including the creation of Hispanic Serving Institutions (HSIs).

According to the Digest of Education Statistics, there were approximately 4.1 million Hispanic students registered at HSIs during the fall of 2020 across 24 states and Puerto Rico (National Center for Education Statistics, 2021). The number of HSIs across the U.S. and Puerto Rico is 569, making up 18% of institutions of higher education with 67% of undergraduate students enrolled at an HSI (Excelencia in Education, 2021).

But unlike Historically Black Colleges and Universities (HBCUs), and many tribal colleges and universities (TCUs), HSIs are relatively new. In the late 70s and early 80s, Hispanic and Latine activists noticed that there were institutions in specific geographical areas of the country that were enrolling a high number of Hispanic/Latin students, but the students' needs were not being met, and they were not as successful as their white peers. In 1986, starting as a grassroots movement, advocates created the Hispanic Association of Colleges and Universities (HACU), coined the term Hispanic Serving Institutions, and became the membership association for HSIs (Santiago, 2006). HACU represented and advocated for these institutions and in 1992 persuaded Congress to recognize the HSI designation and assign federal appropriations towards these institutions (Garcia & Taylor, Morgan, 2017). In 1995, the first appropriation of $12 million dollars was approved by Congress through the "Developing Institutions Program" (Santiago, 2006). This program is also known as Title V.

As opposed to institutions that are created with the intention of serving a specific underrepresented group, like HBCUs and TCUs, HSIs are designated by the U.S. Department of Education and must meet the following requirements:

- is an eligible institution; and

- has an enrollment of undergraduate full-time equivalent students that is at least 25 percent Hispanic students at the end of the award year immediately preceding the date of application. (*Hispanic-Serving Institutions (HSIs) | White House Initiative on Advancing Educational Equity, Excellence, and Economic Opportunity for Hispanics*, n.d.)

In this case, an eligible institution would be one that qualifies as an institution of higher education (*Definition: Eligible Institution from 20 USC § 1101a(a)(2) | LII / Legal Information Institute*, n.d.). Institutions must also go through an application process in which they need to meet the Needy Student qualification:

> At least 50 percent of an institution's degree-seeking students received financial assistance under: the Federal Pell Grant, Federal SEOG, Federal Work Study, or the Federal Perkins Loan Programs. Or, the percentage of an institution's undergraduate degree seeking students who were enrolled at least half-time and received Federal Pell Grants exceeds the average percentage of the same at similar (type and control) institutions. (Department of Education, n.d.)

In their applications, institutions must also calculate their Core Expenses per FTE:

> Core Expenses are regular operational expenditures of postsecondary institutions (excluding auxiliary enterprises, independent operations, and hospital expenses). These are then divided by the FTE (12-month undergraduate enrollment for the academic year). This measure is then compared to the average value for other similar (type and control) institutions. The Core Expenses per FTE measure must be lower than the average for the institutional group. (Department of Education, n.d.)

Even after going through the application process, receiving the HSI designation does not guarantee an institution access to funds, this process merely grants eligibility to apply for the funds, there are other requirements that must be met to receive Title V grant funding.

There are two Title V grants that institutions can apply for, Title V part A is the Developing Hispanic-Serving Institutions (DHSI) Program and its purpose is to:

- To expand educational opportunities for; and improve the academic attainment of Hispanic students; and

- Expand and enhance the academic offerings, program quality, and institutional stability of the colleges and universities that educate the majority of Hispanic students. (*Hispanic-Serving Institutions (HSIs) | White House Initiative on Advancing Educational Equity, Excellence, and Economic Opportunity for Hispanics*, n.d.)

Title V part B is the Promoting Postbaccalaureate Opportunities for Hispanic Americans (PPOHA) Program and this grant is meant to:

- expand postbaccalaureate educational opportunities for, and improve the academic attainment of, Hispanic students; and

- expand the postbaccalaureate academic offerings as well as enhance the program quality in the institutions of higher education that are educating the majority of Hispanic college students and helping large numbers of Hispanic and low-income students complete postsecondary degrees. (*Hispanic-Serving Institutions (HSIs) | White House Initiative on Advancing Educational Equity, Excellence, and Economic Opportunity for Hispanics*, n.d.)

There is also a Title III Part F grant titled Hispanic-Serving Institutions – Science, Technology, Engineering, or Mathematics (HSI STEM) and Articulation Programs and is meant to:

- increase the number of Hispanic and other low-income students attaining degrees in the fields of science, technology, engineering, or mathematics; and

- to develop model transfer and articulation agreements between two-year and four-year institutions in such fields. (*Hispanic-Serving Institutions (HSIs) | White House Initiative on Advancing Educational Equity, Excellence, and Economic Opportunity for Hispanics*, n.d.)

Each of these grants has their own list of requirements for eligibility, and you are competing against other HSIs for the funding. These other requirements make it difficult for many institutions to receive the funding needed to serve their students leaving equity gaps in higher education spending despite the appropriations that Congress designates for HSIs, and having to compete and do all the work of applying for the grants doesn't help. In fact, HACU estimates that HSIs receive only "68 cents for every federal dollar going to all other colleges and universities annually, per student, from all federal funding sources." (Hispanic Association of Colleges and Universities, n.d.)

There are other sources of funding for HSIs, and while difficult to navigate, the designation is a good one to have when handled properly and used in the way it was intended, which is to provide better services, education, and opportunities to Hispanic students. While many institutions that receive the designation do not necessarily put the systems in place to truly support their Hispanic students (these are called Hispanic Enrolling Institutions by some), the benefits to an institution and the students can be very positive.

Hispanic and Latine Identities

Hispanic vs Latino/a, Latinx, Latine, Chicano/a

While we have so far gone over the term Hispanic, its distinction from Latine, and the ways in which it is used the U.S., it is also important to know all of the other terms that you may have heard of but are not familiar with or are unsure of how to use. Knowing why they exist and how some people use them to self-identify, or don't, is important when serving your Hispanic or Latine students. Keep in mind that self-identification is incredibly important, and the definitions below may not hold true for everyone, as the reasons why people identify the way they do are their own and do not need to be quantified.

Latinx – a term created in the U.S. to be inclusive of all gender demographics and especially the LGBTQ+ community. While it has grown in popularity, only about 3% of Hispanics and Latines use it with most being women, skewing younger (under 29), predominantly English-speaking, and being college graduates or have some college experience (Noe-Bustamante et al., 2020). Although the term goes back to the early 2000s, it started being largely popularized in the mid-2010s (Noe-Bustamante et al., 2020), and it has caused debate since. The term is not very well known outside of the U.S.

Latine – another gender-neutral option for Latino/a, replacing the a or o with an e and can be used for other nouns that are gendered (example:

amigues, niñes, etc.) (*Call Me Latine.*, n.d.). It is becoming more prevalent as more prominent figures use this term. Because of its ease of use in both English and Spanish, it is the preferred term for this author.

Afro-Latine – people from Latin America and the Caribbean who are of African descent. It is estimated that approximately 15 times more slaves were taken to Latin America than the U.S. and that about 130 million of their descendants now live there (Gonzalez-Barrera, 2022a). In the U.S., they make up about 2% (6 million) of U.S. adults, although given the fraught nature of race in Latin America and the fact that people mostly self-identify (as they should), these are estimates and hard numbers can be hard to come by (Gonzalez-Barrera, 2022a).

Chicano/a–a term used by those of Mexican descent whose families have been in the U.S. for generations, recently there have been those who are second or third generation immigrants also using the term. The term was popularized during the Civil Rights era when the Chicano Movement was also in full swing. However, there are those who are not of Mexican descent but worked with the Chicano Movement and have fought for the rights of all Latines and therefore identify as or relate to the term Chicano/a (*You Say Chicano, I Say...*, n.d.). For gender inclusive purposes, some will use Chicanx, Chican@, or Chicane.

While these are not all of the terms that can be used to describe the Hispanic and Latine population of the U.S., they are the most recognized and popular in academia and the media. There are arguments for which group terms are preferred by who and why, this author has her own reasons for preferring Latine, but at the end of the day, people's preferences are their own and should be respected. You must also be aware that while these terms can be used for individual identification, some are mostly used for identifying the larger community, and individuals tend to self-identify in very different ways.

Evolving Identities

Most immigrants, 56%, in the U.S. will identify with their country of origin such as Mexican, Colombian, Salvadorian, etc., about 40% of them identify as Hispanic or Latine, and only 4% identify as American (Gonzalez-Barrera, n.d.-b). However, for those who are U.S. born, how they identify changes by generation; about 22% of children of immigrants identify as American, and for third or higher generations that number goes up to 33% (Gonzalez-Barrera, n.d.-b). This tells us that the majority of the Hispanic and Latine population in the U.S. still relate to and connect with their communities and countries of origin no matter how many generations they have been here in the U.S.

What about Hispanics and Latinos in the U.S. who only speak English? Since such an emphasis has been placed on language for the creation of the Hispanic classification, and is often interchanged with Latine, does that mean that you can no longer call yourself Hispanic or Latine if you don't speak Spanish? While the majority of Hispanics and Latines say that's not the case (Lopez, 2016), gatekeeping by Hispanics and Latines who believe that being part of the community means you have to fit within very specific parameters about language and image is very real. In their study ""I Look Mexican, So They Assume I Speak Spanish": Latinx Teacher Candidates' Experiences with Raciolinguistic Policing," Christian Fallas–Escobar, Kathryn Henderson, and Kristen Lindahl (2022) write:

> Repeatedly, as Latinx TCs [teacher candidates] reported, Spanish-speaking Latinx interlocutors assumed they spoke Spanish by virtue of their skin color and reacted with surprise or reproach at realizing otherwise. For instance, in their respective language portraits, Alicia explained, "I have had Hispanics walk up to me thinking I speak Spanish (…) because you look Hispanic, you have to speak Spanish," and Liss accounted that "at work, guests always walk up to me assuming I speak Spanish because I am a very dark-skinned Latina." As they expounded, looking Latinx (understood as having dark skin) makes them subject to raciolinguistic policing, which triggers negative reactions if the expectation for Spanish proficiency is not met. In this regard, Natalia explained that customers at her job react with great surprise at realizing she only speaks English. As she noted in her language portrait, she feels that such customers "judged me by the color of my skin and assumed I spoke Spanish." Nicole echoed this experience in her own language portrait when she explained that "because of my Hispanic heritage, many other Hispanics immediately start talking to me in Spanish and then are shocked when I explain I cannot and always ask 'why??!'"(p. 204)

Even though only 28% of the Hispanic and Latine population in the U.S. say it's necessary to speak Spanish in order to consider yourself part of the community (Lopez, 2016), they do seem to be a very vocal minority.

Race also plays a factor in how Hispanic and Latine people identify. Yes, the grouping of all Hispanic and Latine people has brought about more awareness, benefits, and political power, but mostly to white Hispanics and Latines. In the online article "The Problem with Latinidad," author Miguel Salazar (2019) writes:

> Historically, the forging of this ethnic identity has been understood as a necessity in the face of white supremacy and anti-Mexican Juan Crow laws. In response to recent events, it's been useful for raising awareness of migrant family separations, Washington's insistence on militarizing borders in Mexico and Central America, and mass shooters warning of a "Hispanic invasion" of the United States. Even so, its most vocal critics, who are often young and black or indigenous, have not minced words in their critique of what they see as an exclusionary identity fabricated by—and for the benefit of—white and mestizo elites and the American political class.

In the article, the "journalists, organizers, and thinkers" that Salazar interviews about *Latinidad* argue that the term Latino isn't inclusive of Indigenous and Black people of Latin America (Salazar, 2019) which is one of the many problems of conflating Hispanic and Latine and centering the Spanish language as a measure of how Hispanic or Latine you are. In the process of bringing awareness to the plight of the community, Indigenous and Black voices are being pushed out and lost.

As a result, there has rightfully been a lot of pushback that has resulted in the launching of organizations like Ain't I Latina, "an online destination created by an Afro-Latina for Afro-Latinas. Inspired by the lack of representation in mainstream media, as well as Spanish-language media..." (Ain't I Latina?, n.d.), the International Society of Black Latinos who create "awareness of the existence of people who are of Afro-Latino heritage by honoring our rich and diverse cultures" (*International Society of Black Latinos*, n.d.), and the Afro-Latino Association for Policy & Advocacy, "a non-profit formed to create awareness of the unique cultural impact of Afro-Latinos..." (Afro-Latino Association for Policy and Advocacy, n.d.), to name just a few.

The Hispanic and Latine LGBTQ+ community is another that grapples with issues of self-identity. While the number of self-identifying LGBTQ+ Hispanics and Latinos has grown, this is in part because this group tends to skew younger (Galván, 2022) and are also more likely to have a college education (Wilson et al., 2021). And there have been reports that the Hispanic and Latino community has become more accepting of those who identify as LGBTQ+ (Franco, 2022). However, just because the community is coming out more, growing, and showing signs of acceptance, doesn't mean that they don't face discrimination. It is just the opposite as they are much more likely to be discriminated against than their white LGBTQ+ peers in all aspects including housing, healthcare, jobs, education, etc. (Mahowald, 2021).

There are many other ways in which the identities of the Hispanic and Latine population change over time and generations. Many are moving away from their traditions and becoming more "Americanized," while others are discovering the roots that for various reasons their ancestors gave up.

Conclusion

Like all other ethnic and racial groups in the U.S., the experiences, cultural expressions, language, parent's educational attainment, and familial responsibilities will vary wildly among your students. You will find many who will need a lot of language support, and others who only speak English but want to learn the language of their ancestors to connect with their culture. Many are first-generation students, and others have parents who may have attained education all the way up to graduate degrees. Not stereotyping or making assumptions about your Hispanic or Latine students, just like you wouldn't or shouldn't about any other group, is key.

So, what should you call your Hispanic and Latine students? Ask. Ask your students, reach out to faculty in the appropriate departments (like Chicane/Latine Studies), reach out to student organizations, have conversations with staff. Let them be the ones to tell you and guide you, not just in how they identify, but also in terms what their needs are. You cannot fit your students into a box and expect them to act accordingly. Like all your other students, these are unique individuals with their own needs, experiences, and backgrounds. Some may need more help than others, and some will need no help at all. Your job is to ensure that the resources they need are available, and that you are doing the work of recognizing, in your services, programming, and collections, that this is not a monolithic group but rather a group of individuals. It is up to you to do the work of decolonizing your libraries so that everyone feels welcome.

References

Afro-Latino Association for Policy and Advocacy. (n.d.). *Home*. Retrieved May 19, 2022, from http://afrolatin.org/index.html

Ain't I Latina? (n.d.). About. *Ain't I Latina?* Retrieved May 19, 2022, from http://ain-tilatina.com/about/

Benavides, L. (2020, February 9). Why Labeling Antonio Banderas A "Person of Color" Triggers Such A Backlash. *NPR*. https://www.npr.org/2020/02/09/803809670/why-labeling-antonio-banderas-a-person-of-color-triggers-such-a-backlash

Buchholz, Katharina. (2021). *How Indigenous Are Countries in the Americas?* https://www-statista-com.leo.lib.unomaha.edu/chart/19633/countries-by-indigenous-population-in-the-americas/

Call me Latine. (n.d.). Call Me Latine. Retrieved May 18, 2022, from https://call-melatine.com/

Cardona, M. (2016, October 3). Hispanics and Latinos are not all Mexicans, but all deserve respect. *The Columbia Chronicle*. https://columbiachronicle.com/b79edbd4-8770-11e6-8b7b-c7675ed6e454

Corporación Latinobarómetro. (2018, November 9). *Share of indigenous language speakers Latin America by country 2018*. Statista. https://www-statista-com.leo.lib.unomaha.edu/statistics/1058273/latin-america-share-indigenous-language-speakers-country/

Daniels, L. (2017). The End of Special Treatment for Cubans in the U.S. Immigration System: Consequences and Solutions for Cubans with Final Orders of Removal. *DICKINSON LAW REVIEW, 122*, 35.

Definition: Eligible institution from 20 USC § 1101a(a)(2) | LII / Legal Information Institute. (n.d.). Retrieved May 18, 2022, from https://www.law.cornell.edu/definitions/uscode.php?width=840&height=800&iframe=true&def_id=20-USC-1269006097-984066309&term_occur=999&term_src=title:20:chapter:28:subchapter:V:part:A:section:1101a

Department of Education. (n.d.). *Infographic: How to Determine Institutional Eligibility for Titles III, V, and VII Grants*. Retrieved May 18, 2022, from https://www2.ed.gov/about/offices/list/ope/idues/insteligcht.pdf

Dropp, K., & Nyhan, B. (2017, September 26). Nearly Half of Americans Don't Know Puerto Ricans Are Fellow Citizens. *The New York Times*. https://www.nytimes.com/2017/09/26/upshot/nearly-half-of-americans-dont-know-people-in-puerto-ricoans-are-fellow-citizens.html

Ethnologue. (2022, February 21). *The most spoken languages worldwide in 2022 (by speakers in millions)*. Statista. http://www.statista.com/statistics/266808/the-most-spoken-languages-worldwide/

Excelencia in Education. (2021, April). *Hispanic-Serving Institutions (HSIs): 2019-20 Fact Sheet*. https://files.eric.ed.gov/fulltext/ED614622.pdf

Fallas–Escobar, C., Henderson, K., & Lindahl, K. (2022). "I Look Mexican, So They Assume I Speak Spanish": Latinx Teacher Candidates' Experiences With

Raciolinguistic Policing. *The Modern Language Journal, 106*(1), 196–215. https://doi.org/10.1111/modl.12762

Florido, A. (2017, January 15). End Of "Wet-Foot, Dry-Foot" Means Cubans Can Join Ranks Of "Undocumented." *NPR.* https://www.npr.org/sections/codeswitch/2017/01/15/509895837/end-of-wet-foot-dry-foot-means-cubans-can-join-ranks-of-the-undocumented

Franco, M. E. (2022, March 24). *Latinos are highly accepting of members of LGBTQ community, poll finds.* Axios. https://www.axios.com/2022/03/24/latinos-lgbtq-acceptance

Galván, A. (2022, March 15). *Poll: LGBTQ-identification is higher among Latinos than white or Black American adults.* Axios. https://www.axios.com/2022/03/15/latinos-lgbt-poll-gen-z

Garcia, G. A., & Taylor, Morgan. (2017, September 18). *A closer look at Hispanic-Serving Institutions.* Higher Education Today. https://www.higheredtoday.org/2017/09/18/closer-look-hispanic-serving-institutions/

Gonzalez, H. (n.d.). *How has Cuban immigration changed since the cessation of the Wet Foot/Dry Foot policy? | Immigrant Connect.* Retrieved May 16, 2022, from https://immigrantconnect.medill.northwestern.edu/blog/2019/11/19/how-has-cuban-immigration-changed-since-the-cessation-of-the-wet-foot-dry-foot-policy/

Gonzalez-Barrera, A. (n.d.-b). The ways Hispanics describe their identity vary across immigrant generations. *Pew Research Center.* Retrieved May 18, 2022, from https://www.pewresearch.org/fact-tank/2020/09/24/the-ways-hispanics-describe-their-identity-vary-across-immigrant-generations/

Gonzalez-Barrera, A. (2022a, May 2). About 6 million U.S. adults identify as Afro-Latino. *Pew Research Center.* https://www.pewresearch.org/fact-tank/2022/05/02/about-6-million-u-s-adults-identify-as-afro-latino/

Henderson, T. J. (2011). Bracero blacklists: mexican migration and the unraveling of the Good Neighbor Policy. *Latin Americanist, 55*(4), 199–217. https://doi.org/10.1111/j.1557-203X.2011.01130.x

Henken, T. (2005). Balseros, Boteros, and El Bombo: Post-1994 Cuban immigration to the United States and the persistence of special treatment. *Latino Studies, 3*(3), 393–416. https://doi-org.leo.lib.unomaha.edu/10.1057/palgrave.lst.8600159

Hernández, K. L. (2006). The crimes and consequences of illegal immigration: A Cross-Border examination of Operation Wetback, 1943 to 1954. *The Western Historical Quarterly, 37*(4), 421. https://doi.org/10.2307/25443415

Hispanic Association of Colleges and Universities. (n.d.). *Appropriations for HSIs.* Retrieved May 16, 2022, from https://hacuadvocates.net/hacu/appropriations?0

Hispanic-Serving Institutions (HSIs) | White House initiative on advancing educational equity, excellence, and economic opportunity for Hispanics. (n.d.). Retrieved May 18, 2022, from https://sites.ed.gov/hispanic-initiative/hispanic-serving-institutions-hsis/

International Society of Black Latinos. (n.d.). International Society of Black Latinos. Retrieved May 19, 2022, from https://blacklatinos.com/

Jones, N., Marks, R., Ramirez, R., & RioS-Vargas, M. (2021, August 12). *2020 Census Illuminates Racial and Ethnic Composition of the Country.* Census.Gov. https://www.census.gov/library/stories/2021/08/improved-race-eth-nicity-measures-reveal-united-states-population-much-more-multi-racial.html

Kosack, E. (2021). Guest Worker Programs and Human Capital Investment: The Bracero Program in Mexico, 1942–1964. *Journal of Human Resources, 56*(2), N.PAG-N.PAG. https://doi.org/10.3368/jhr.56.2.0616-8015r2

Lopez, M. H. (2016, February 19). Is speaking Spanish neces-sary to be Hispanic? Most Hispanics say no. *Pew Research Center.* https://www.pewresearch.org/fact-tank/2016/02/19/is-speaking-spanish-necessary-to-be-hispanic-most-hispanics-say-no/

Mahowald, L. (2021, July 29). Hispanic LGBTQ individuals encounter heightened discrimination. *Center for American Progress.* https://www.americanprogress.org/article hispanic-lgbtq-individuals-encounter-heightened-dis-crimination/

Melendez, E. (2017). Comments on the Jones Act and the Grant of U.S. Citizenship to Puerto Ricans. *Centro Journal, 29*(1), 316–327.

Mize, R. L. (2011). Consuming Mexican labor: From the Bracero Program to NAFTA. University of Toronto Press.

Mora, G. C. (2014). *Making Hispanics: How activists, bureaucrats, and media con-structed a new American.* The University of Chicago Press.

National Center for Education Statistics. (2021, December). *Digest of Education Statistics, 2021.* National Center for Education Statistics. https://nces.ed.gov/programs/digest/d21/tables/dt21_312.40.asp?current=yes

Ngai, M. M. (2014). *Impossible subjects: Illegal aliens and the making of modern America* (New paperback edition / with a new forward by the author). Princeton University Press.

Noe-Bustamante, L., Mora, L., & Lopez, M. H. (2020, August 11). About one-in-four U.S. Hispanics have heard of Latinx, but just 3% use it. *Pew Research Center's Hispanic Trends Project.* https://www.pewresearch.org/hispanic/2020/08/11/about-one-in-four-u-s-hispanics-have-heard-of-latinx-but-just-3-use-it/

Puerto Ricans as immigrants and other ,isperceptions. (2018, February 6). Puerto Rico Report. https://www.puertoricoreport.com/puerto-ricans-immigrants-misperceptions/

Salazar, M. (2019, September 16). *The problem with Latinidad.* The Nation. https://www.thenation.com/article/archive/hispanic-heritage-month-latinidad/

Santiago, D. A. (2006). *Inventing Hispanic-erving institutions: The basics.* Excelencia in Education. https://www.edexcelencia.org/research/issue-briefs/inventing-hispanic-serving-institutions-basics

Soto-Márquez, J. G. (2019). "I'm not Spanish, I'm from Spain": Spaniards' bifurcated ethnicity and the boundaries of Whiteness and Hispanic panethnic identity. Sociology of Race and Ethnicity, 5(1), 85–99. https://doi.
org/10.1177/2332649218766388

US Census Bureau. (2018, September 6). Forecast of the Hispanic population of
the United States from 2016 to 2060 (in millions). Statista. http://www.
statista.com/statistics/251238/hispanic-population-of-the-us/

US Census Bureau. (2020). Hispanic population in the U.S. by origin 2019. Statista.
http://www.statista.com/statistics/234852/us-hispanic-population/

US Census Bureau. (2020, September). Languages spoken (at home) other than English in the United States by number of speakers
in 2019. Statista. http://www.statista.com/statistics/183483/
ranking-of-languages-spoken-at-home-in-the-us-in-2008/

US Census Bureau. (2021, August 12). The chance that two people chosen at ran-
dom are of different race or ethnicity groups has increased since 2010.
Census.Gov. https://www.census.gov/library/stories/2021/08/2020-unit-
ed-states-population-more-racially-ethnically-diverse-than-2010.html

Wilson, B. D. M., Mallory, C., Bouton, L., & Choi, S. K. (2021, September). Latinx LGBT
Adults in the US. Williams Institute. https://williamsinstitute.law.ucla.edu/
publications/latinx-lgbt-adults-in-the-us/

Ye Hee Lee, M. (2015, July 8). Analysis | Donald Trump's false comments con-
necting Mexican immigrants and crime. Washington Post. https://
www.washingtonpost.com/news/fact-checker/wp/2015/07/08/don-
ald-trumps-false-comments-connecting-mexican-immigrants-and-crime/

You Say Chicano, I Say...: Code Switch. (n.d.). National Public Radio Retrieved
May 18, 2022, from https://www.npr.org/2019/05/01/718703438/
you-say-chicano-i-say

Is it for Me?
Alienation, Assimilation, and Ambition in Academia

Niki Fullmer
Brittany Paloma Fiedler

Introduction

Even though colleges and universities across the United States are implementing strategies to market their commitment to diversity, equity, and inclusion, students of color, specifically Latinx students, are graduating at a lesser rate than the national average (National Center for Education Statistics, 2019). In the academic librarian profession, only 6% of librarians are Latinx while 71% are white (Sweeney & Schonfeld, 2017). Academia and libraries are historically white, and this fact was recognized by many of the Latinx students who participated in a study conducted at the University of Nevada, Las Vegas, a Hispanic Serving Institution (HSI), in the spring of 2020. During the study, the researchers asked Latinx students questions about their public and school library usage and their perception of the university and its library in relation to their identity. Latinx students knew that academia was not designed for them, and many of the participants discussed their assimilation to the predominant norms and culture of academia and libraries. This chapter outlines and analyzes themes developed from the 15 interviews and provides suggestions to better support Latinx students in academic libraries.

Background

The University of Nevada, Las Vegas (UNLV) is a public, doctoral-granting, R1 university with just over 30,500 students. UNLV is designated as a HSI with 30.9% of students identifying as Hispanic and 10.9% identifying as two or more races (University of Nevada, Las Vegas, 2016). The library of focus in this chapter, UNLV Lied Library, is a five-story building that opened in January 2001 to support the growing UNLV student body and the Las Vegas community. The building was designed to seat over 3,100 students and has 600 computers. The building also houses a tutoring center, makerspace, and graduate student commons. From the survey responses collected from the study, "630 out of 652 (97%) respondents said they visited one of the campus libraries in the last six months and 533 out of 652 (81%) said they visited the university libraries at least once a week" (Fullmer & Fiedler, 2021, 138). UNLV libraries are highly trafficked spaces, with the Lied library being one of the most active buildings on campus. To understand Latinx students' nuanced perspectives and insights about the UNLV libraries, the researchers performed 15 interviews with undergraduate Latinx students who have completed at least one semester of college.

Methodology and Participant Demographics

In this chapter, the researchers built on their previous research in the paper "Past Perception, Present Usage: Latinx Students and Academic Libraries" (Fullmer & Fiedler, 2021). That publication focused on analyzing survey data that consisted of closed-ended questions as well as open comments where participants could share additional thoughts. The researchers were able to obtain an email address list of non-international undergraduate Latinx-identifying students who had completed at least one semester at UNLV from the university's Retention, Progression, Completion Initiatives & Analytics Coordinator in the Student Success Office. Over 600 students completed the survey which contained questions (Appendix A) focused on library usage and their perceptions of library staff during that use. After the students completed the survey, they were provided the option to volunteer for an interview with the researchers. 15 students were selected from a randomized list to be interviewed at the beginning of March 2020. The interview questions appear in Appendix B. At the start of each interview, the researchers introduced themselves as women of color, their educational experiences at both UNLV and predominantly white institutions (PWIs), and explained the inspiration and motivation for the research project. This protocol was established to build a rapport with the participants and create a cultural bond where they would feel open to sharing their thoughts, feelings, and vulnerabilities. The 15 interviews provided nuanced information about the participants' experiences and their feelings as Latinx students in higher education, which was not captured in the initial survey.

With all qualitative data analysis, there is a chance of bias pattern seeking. To limit that, the researchers employed a double coding method utilizing in vivo coding and focused coding. For each coding method, the researchers both coded one interview and reviewed their codes together for intercoder reliability, or the practice of multiple researchers coding data to ensure reliability. In vivo coding is an effective tool during the initial stages of coding for capturing the voice and perspectives of marginalized groups. For this research, it was important to code the participants' actual words in order to understand their "discourse, cultures, and worldviews" (Saldaña, 2021, 138) in relation to higher education and library usage. After the first coding cycle, the researchers adopted focused coding to identify themes from the quotations coded during the in vivo coding process. The researchers developed 29 codes (Appendix C) which are separated into three categories: diversity and representation on campus, library specifics, and library feelings.

To ensure that a variety of Latinx voices were being recognized, the researchers collected demographic data such as employment status, generational college status, regions where the participants or their family were from, emigration period, and English language learning period. The researchers did not seek out specific Latinx survey participants to fill these various demographic categories, but through randomized invitations to participate they were able to collect stories and information from Latinx students with various and intersecting identities. The collected demographic data shows:

- 11 employed (average 30 hours per week) students and four unemployed students
- 11 first generation students, four not first-generation students
- Nine North American or Mexican students, two Central American students, one South American student, two Caribbean students, one Indigenous student (students were able to select all that applied)

- Five students' grandparents or an earlier generation came to the U.S., eight students' parents came to the U.S., and 2 students emigrated to the U.S.

- Eight students spoke both English and another language as their primary languages, one student spoke English only, six students did not learn English at home (the average age to start learning English was age seven)

While the interviews in no way encompass all the experiences and intersecting identities of Latinx students in higher education, these 15 unique perspectives provide valuable insight on how some Latinx students experience academia and libraries.

Feeling Fortunate

One interesting interview theme was the idea of being "fortunate" or "lucky." 73% of interviewed students were employed, which is a substantial difference compared to the national average of 43% (NCES, 2019). One participant said, "I was fortunate enough that at this point in my life, I was able to leave the job, but there are plenty of parents out there that just can't." The unemployed participants felt fortunate that they could attend school without working while the employed participants felt lucky for having less work hours or a flexible schedule. Participants also felt blessed for having familial support of their education. One interviewee said, "Usually if I am home, I do help my mom in chores and things like that, but it's not a responsibility where it's like you have to do it. My mom is really cool about that. She's like, I understand you're tired, you work, you go to school, you have things to do. But if I do have free time, I'll help out as much as I can." Another student noted, "I was lucky because I was able to go to a school where I had family there, like my cousins went there so I wasn't totally alone." For many of the participants, and many students at UNLV (including the authors), the traditional college experience is not one afforded to them. Other interviewees expressed gratitude for learning English early or easily, for emigrating with family members, or for being documented. They were very aware that in the Latinx community in the United States, those things are not guaranteed, and their lives have been easier because they had those benefits. Overall, the participants felt blessed, even though they have much less privilege than a traditional university student.

Diversity and Representation on Campus

From fall 2016 through summer 2019, UNLV's tagline was "Different. Daring. Diverse." Each year UNLV publicizes where it ranks on the U.S. News & World Report list of diverse undergraduate universities (U.S. News & World Report, 2021). In 2021, UNLV tied for most diverse with 66.9% of students identifying as a minority and 30.9% identifying as Latinx) (UNLV, 2021). Thirteen of 15 participants noted the diversity of the university in their interviews, and several referenced the publicity around diversity, which they interpreted as UNLV having legitimate pride in non-white students. Almost all participants used positive language, describing the diversity of UNLV as unique, cool, great, and two even used the word "love." When asked if materials, books, events, and programs in the library reflected their culture, students who said "yes" often referenced the diversity of other students. For example, one student said, "When I went to the Bob Ross [virtual reality painting event], there was a lot of Hispanic people" and another noted, "Yes, [I see my culture reflected in] the other people that show up to the events." Because UNLV is diverse, participants gave the benefit of the doubt to the libraries and "assume[d] that the books here probably reflect the culture because of how many [diverse] people are here" and "I would definitely see that diversity all over campus, including here [in the library]." These students did not have experiences of actually interacting with any part of the library that reflected their culture, but they generously assumed that the diversity must be there even if they have not seen it personally.

Two students did not express positive feelings towards UNLV's diversity. One student felt the official demographics did not match her experience with the student body and noted that she "really had to go out of [her] way to find Latinx students." She, unlike 95% of students at UNLV, lived in a dorm on campus (US News Best Colleges, n.d.). She noted that all her Latinx friends lived off campus and explained that she can only afford the dorms because she saved her money while working in a state where the minimum wage was $15/hour. The other student did not comment on UNLV's diversity at all at any point in his interview. When asked about cultural representation in the library, he noted that "I find it really difficult to find Peruvian representation...the Latino community, to me, having lived here [in the United States] for as long as I have, is synonymous with the Mexican community."

Students also noted the diversity, or lack thereof, in university employees, and described how that affected their experiences on campus. This is particularly noteworthy because UNLV's faculty are much more diverse than average. Nationally, 76% of faculty are white (Davis & Fry, 2019) while at UNLV only 65.2% of tenured and tenure track faculty are white. Unfortunately, only 5.6% of tenure-track faculty are Latinx (very close to the national average of 5%). 8.4% of non-tenure track faculty are Latinx. One participant noted that the first time they had a Latinx professor at their previous institution, "it made [them] really excited about the class itself and all the things we were going to have to read" and when they had a Latinx professor at UNLV "it was the same experience. I was really impassioned about the readings and I loved the professor." Three other interviewees specifically referenced the lack of diversity in their professors. One student lit up when she described the only non-white instructor she had saying, "She's a woman, and she's Latinx, and she's thriving. She's a professor at UNLV. That was really inspirational." The instructor the participant mentioned was a graduate teaching assistant, but many people identify all instructors as professors. She elaborated, saying "You're able to build these relationships with professors that are in your culture, understand your culture...you're able to connect with them." Another student described connecting with an "amazing" teaching assistant in a science class. Even though the instructor was white, she attributed their closeness to gender. The TA was a woman, and the student was one of three women in the class, and the only student who shared a major with the TA. This student also mentioned that her instructors often make jokes that most students laugh at, but she does not understand. She attributed her lack of understanding to her different cultural reference points as a Latina. Finally, one student noted the lack of staff diversity led to the mispronunciation of Latinx students' names at UNLV's graduation ceremonies, which is disrespectful to the students and their families.

Four participants had an interesting perspective on the importance of diverse representation because they saw the benefits in their own jobs. A participant who worked in a school felt that Latinx and Spanish speaking parents were "not afraid to ask questions...speak up more...send emails a lot more." A UNLV student worker said "[my identity] helps a lot because...other students that see you they're like, hey, you know, you're Hispanic...it kind of draws people towards you." Another participant who worked on campus specifically mentioned their identity as a first-generation student and connecting with the first-generation students that they work with. A transgender Latinx person said, "I am as authentic as possible with as many identities as possible, because you never know who you're going to be able to affirm in their own identity" but they also noted that this authenticity can be dangerous and might cost them professional opportunities. Three students used the word "comfortable" when describing working with people with shared identities, and one noted the feeling extends to every space including "at school, teachers, librarians, people in TV shows, doctors and things like that."

Latinx Library Representation

Eight out of 15 participants had experiences with Latinx librarians at some point in their lives, and these were all positive, although the extent of positivity ranged. The most tepid response came from a participant who had an instruction session with the Latina interviewer (although the participant did not initially realize the interviewer was the Latina librarian she described). The participant said the interaction with the interviewer was good, the interviewer made her feel cozy, and she didn't really consider the interviewer's identity in the library classroom (but it is notable that she remembered it). All other participants were more emotional and excited as they described how amazing it was to know Latinx librarians, how safe and comfortable they felt with Latinx public and school librarians, and how welcome their parents felt if the librarians spoke Spanish. Participants with immigrant parents, whether documented or not, always commented on how that identity contributed to the feeling of being welcomed by a Latinx librarian. One participant with an undocumented parent mentioned that their parent would come into the library where Latinx librarians worked but not the other libraries the participant visited.

Fourteen out of 15 participants felt that there would be benefits to working with Latinx or Spanish speaking librarians. Two clarified that they would not personally need the services of Spanish speaking librarians because of their English proficiency (one grew up bilingual, the other learned English at age eleven), but they felt it could be beneficial for others. One wanted to know if the university library was open to the public before she agreed that it would be good. These three students felt UNLV should have Latinx and Spanish speaking librarians not for UNLV students, but for the Las Vegas community, even though most students at the university are locals. This perspective of "[a]cademic and public libraries serv[ing] clearly different purposes" where "the academic library is primarily used to support course work, while the public library is used for cultural support" is also seen in earlier research on Latinx students and libraries (Adkins & Hussey, 2006, 470). This showcases how Latinx students see academic libraries as fulfilling one role while public and school libraries fulfill another. Other participants felt the presence of Latinx librarians would promote diversity, make Latinx students feel more connected, increase a sense of belonging, and create a more welcoming environment. Three students noted that Latinx librarians are more culturally connected to and have more understanding of Latinx students. Two students said that Latinx librarians would have a different perspective from their non-Latinx colleagues. The one student who said no, there would not be any benefits to having a Latinx librarian, clarified that "I really don't see it as a plus or a negative." He went on to explain how his dad is more comfortable speaking in Spanish and always wants to find Spanish speaking people, but the participant felt that after a decade in the United States his dad does have, and should have, enough English proficiency to navigate the world in English. The participant described wanting to rebel against his dad's cultural pride in being Latin American and his dad's desire to connect with other Latinx people in the US.

Because not all Spanish speakers are Latinx, and not all Latinx people speak Spanish, these interview questions asked about students' experiences with "a librarian who was Latinx *or* spoke Spanish" (Appendix B). The students often responded to both parts of the question, particularly if they or their parents spoke Spanish, and no student ever referenced a Spanish speaking librarian who was not Latinx. However, future research would likely benefit from disentangling cultural identity versus language preference and proficiency.

Perceptions and Expectations in Higher Education

None of the 15 students interviewed described any feelings of imposter syndrome, or "the fear of being discovered as a fraud despite their demonstrated talent and achievements in higher education" (Chrousos & Mentis, 2020, p.749), whether they were talking about UNLV or the schools they transferred from (which included community colleges and a private liberal arts college at a predominantly white institution (PWI)). However, interviewees did convey that they knew society and thus educational institutions do not have high expectations for Latinx people. One participant said, "education gives you such a level of dignity back," suggesting that uneducated people have had their dignity taken away. On the other hand, another participant wondered whether education changed anything because "people already think that you're nothing, even when you have [a diploma]." The understanding of society's low expectations spanned from elementary school to university. One student realized that their school librarian "encourag[ing] them to seek knowledge" was unique because "not a lot of poor brown kids are getting that sort of encouragement." Another student, a Latina biology major who frequently referenced both her gender and ethnicity when discussing her experiences, said that the white men in her classes "don't expect you to really perform. They don't really expect you to know what you're talking about."

An AfroLatinx participant said that because he grew up in a very white, nice neighborhood, he had assimilated to being in white spaces and thus knew the white behavioral norms of places like libraries. Nonetheless, he still wondered "if there's space for someone like me to be in academia." Another student used almost the same language: "I just don't feel like academia is for me." They also attributed their socioeconomic status to their feelings in academic libraries saying, "from an economic lens, being poor, you're not accustomed to spaces of grandeur like that." It was disheartening for the researchers to hear that even at a minority majority university in a minority majority city, the students still felt the legacy of higher education that was originally created for upper class white men. Now, it is the responsibility of those within higher education to remove these barriers and create a welcoming community for all students.

Library Resources and Services

Tours and Orientations

UNLV uses campus tours to orient students to the institution, the campus, and the resources available. Thirteen out of 15 participants had gone on a tour as a part of their application or admissions process. Three participants said the tours were helpful and "made it lose the fear of somewhere you've never been and... opened it up to being a free space and an open space for everybody to come in." The participants who had a positive tour experience remarked on the comfortability they felt after the tour was completed. Although the tours are supposed to be standardized, depending on the year, tour guide, or type of tour, many students did not receive adequate information about the library or its services. "Oh my God, yes, that tour was horrible. They made us walk in through the library and they were like, oh well we're just going to cut through the library really quickly just to show you," shared one participant. For others, the only memorable parts were the air conditioning (most orientation tours take place in July and August) and the LASR (Lied Automated Storage and Retrieval) system housed in the library. LASR is located on the first floor near the entrance of the building, which makes it the first stop on the tour, and the only stop if the tour is running behind schedule. None of the interviewed students had utilized LASR in their time at UNLV, but the fact that so many remembered it shows the potential tour guides have in introducing students to resources. Librarians should thoughtfully determine what lasting impression they want students to have about the library. For Latinx students, or students who do not have experience with higher education, the academic library can be an intimidating space, especially because it is so different from more familiar public and school libraries.

Librarians should regularly assess students' takeaways from tours and orientations and consider how they can work with campus partners to better enhance students' understanding of the academic library and its resources. To better situate incoming Latinx students to the library, include information about both resources and personnel, and consider explaining the role the academic library plays in undergraduate research. Based on these findings, UNLV Library worked with the Office of Undergraduate Admissions to reverse the tour directionality, so the first stop is near the Reference and Information Desk, the Technology Help Desk, and the Makerspace, highlighting the people who can help students navigate the resources of the library. Ideally, library orientation is more than just a stop on a campus tour.

According to ¡*Excelencia in Education!,* Latinx students are "much more likely to be first-generation students than other racial/ethnic groups" (Santiago et al., 2019, p. 6). The report also noted that nationally, 44% of Latinx students are the first in their families to attend college. In this study, 73% of interviewed students and 79% of surveyed students were first generation. Therefore, it is also important to make tours available to parents so they can better understand academic library resources and encourage their child to use them. Almost all of the interviewees had memories of visiting or using public libraries with their parents when they were young, so library use seemed to be valued by the interviewees' parents. One student said, "yes, we found, just in general, the [university] library itself was just amazing to see, and my parents were like [excited expression], and I liked that." For libraries to be well utilized by their Latinx student body, they must develop orientations that actively welcome students and clearly explain the library's role. Other ways to introduce students to academic library resources include:

- Drop in tours throughout the first week of the semester when students often have extra time between classes.

- Tabling at outreach events across campus to connect with students who might not regularly be in the campus libraries.

- Presenting to or collaborating with student resource organizations to highlight resources and staff related to their interests.

- Design tours that are led by Spanish speaking guides or have translators for Spanish speakers.

Displays

The main library at UNLV is five stories tall with rotating exhibits on TV monitors, display cabinets, and wall hangings throughout the first three floors. At the time of the interviews, the displays were: "On Water: A Photographer's Life in the Colorado River Basin," "OUT: Documenting the History of Queer Las Vegas," "The Art and Stories of Latinx Graduation Caps at UNLV," and "Paris Dreams, City Scenes: Joel Berman and the Themed Resort." Unfortunately, 11 of the interview participants could not recall ever seeing or engaging with these or any previous exhibits. Three students did recall the ones related to their own identities as Latinx and/or queer people. One participant described that the graduation cap exhibit "made me decide to decorate my cap. And it made me feel like they care about Latinx students." This exhibit was created from research conducted by folklorist Dr. Sheila Bock in collaboration with the UNLV Special Collections & Archives. The few students who interacted with the identity-based displays had positive feelings about them and about the library for choosing to focus on their communities. However, a majority did not interact or see either of them, and no student mentioned the other two displays besides a vague awareness of their existence. "I see art stuff they have in there. I feel like it's small but I've never seen anything there that represents me."

The lack of interaction may be due to the placement of the displays. One student noted, "Like if you go to other floors, it's not there. I don't know, I haven't seen it, so I don't know if it is there." Many participants described selecting one area in the library as their "spot" to visit throughout the semester. The likelihood of seeing displays decreases if their spot is on the top two floors or the side of the first floor without any exhibits. Additionally, there is no signage on the top four floors of the library notifying students of these displays.

Most students said they would like more displays in the library, especially identity-based ones. When asked if they would like any additions to the library, one student said, "Probably you know, expanding the art display." Another answered the same question with, "I love art, and I love dance. I don't know if there's a way to merge a library thing with some sort of visual performance aspect, but I think that would be really cool." This same student went on to describe what they saw in other libraries they visited in the past. The Teacher Development & Resources Library (TDRL), located on campus but separate from the main library, functions similarly to a school library to support the education program. The collection contains children's and young adult literature, prioritizing "materials which accurately represent the diverse identities and needs of the students of the Clark County School District" (UNLV University Libraries, n.d.). During the time of the interviews, their book display was "Women, Art, and Feminism" which included *Yayoi Kusama: From Here to Infinity* (Suzuki, 2017), *Frida Kahlo and Her Animalitos* (Brown, 2017), and The Crunk Feminist Collection (Cooper et al., 2017). Only one student used the TDRL, and because she saw her culture (and others) reflected in the displays, she had positive feelings towards that space. "When I go to the library at the Education Building, I do see different books just representing different people, Blacks, Latinos, Asians, you can just see it throughout the library. And I think in that way, yes, that's the most tangible thing. I can see, oh look, there I am." When asked if they would be interested in seeing more displays related to their identity, 12 participants agreed that they would enjoy seeing the display. Other ways to connect with students through displays include:

- Consider collaborating with faculty members to create displays related to their research, particularly with professors from interdisciplinary, gender, and ethnic studies.

- If the library does not have the space or capacity to support art or exhibits, library workers should consider other spaces on campus that could be used as display spaces.

- Investigate the library's digital space, either on a website or through social media. While these exhibits require time and labor, it does not require buying or shifting furniture in the library.

Desk interactions

Many interviewees were thankful when library staff treated them well, and it was clear they worried about being perceived negatively. Three participants specifically identified staff as "supportive," "helpful," and "positive," but followed the positive adjectives with "I was probably annoying," "they've never seemed like 'You're dumb, why are you asking,'" and "they definitely try to not make me feel stupid. Even if it's a dumb question that I'm asking." Unfortunately, many participants described being too intimidated to seek help from library staff. One student was a heavy user of school and public libraries when she was younger and specifically described how in those environments, she "was never scared to ask for help just because I had those good experiences." She even had an experience with UNLV library staff where they were helpful, but all those culminating positive experiences were not enough for her to feel like she could ask for help. She struggled to find enough information after her library instruction session, but she did not seek assistance from library staff because she did not "want to bother anybody" or "do something dumb or ask something stupid." Although another student was incredibly comfortable using the live chat online, she noted that her classmates were not. "I'll sit right here [with my classmate] and [tell her] you can converse with somebody and I'll be right here with you. And, she'll be like, okay, and, that will give her the confidence to do it herself." Encouraging desk interactions and questions can be accomplished through various techniques:

- Library staff who work desks should be trained to use positive language, re-affirm that it is an appropriate and smart question, and reassure students they are not bothering them.

- Library workers can try to boost student confidence to approach desks by describing typical desk questions during other interactions like outreach events, instruction sessions, or even in a display.

- Library staff could circulate the library with an "Ask Me" sign (especially since students are often told not to leave their belongings unattended in libraries).

- Libraries with live chat should regularly promote it since that can be a less intimidating form of communication.

Library Instruction and Resources

During most students' first year at UNLV, they will participate in a library instruction session through their composition class or first year seminar class. These are taught by instruction librarians who incorporate an area of information literacy, such as the ACRL Framework "Scholarship as Conversation" (ACRL, 2015), and then demonstrate UNLV's research tool "Quick Search." Almost all participants remembered these classes, one specifically said, "Maybe my English 102 class. Yes, we came for a little meeting, presentation with one of the librarians, she taught us how to research better." These sessions are where many students will learn about the function of the academic library and the research-based resources available to them. For many participants, these sessions were the only interactions they could remember having with a librarian throughout their academic careers. Although the liaison librarians teach upper division library instruction sessions, only one student remembered having an experience with a liaison librarian teaching their class.

While focusing on first year courses is an excellent strategy to introduce students to undergraduate research, it is also important to look for opportunities throughout a student's academic career. Transfer students, or students who did not need to take first year composition courses, did not have early librarian experiences and some did not feel they understood how to adequately use library resources. One participant, a transfer student from a PWI, said:

> I don't think I've ever properly used the resources here. I know they exist but it's finding the time to come and ask about them and dedicating however many hours to sitting here and learning how to use a library. I don't know, I feel like, as an academic, using a library is a skill that I do not have, and I cannot say that I have ever adequately learned how to use the library like that.

A few participants were engaging in advanced research, either through a class assignment or working directly with a faculty member.

However, only one student had a research consultation with a librarian. He was a research assistant sent to the library by his supervising faculty member. At the end of the consultation, the librarian pointed the student to research written by his supervisor. The student felt frustrated since he was unable to find new sources, and the librarian "made [him] go in a giant circle."

Research indicates that Latinx students use the academic library and library services less frequently than their white counterparts, and do not always understand the role of academic librarians (Solis & Dabbour, 2006; Whitmire, 2003). Participants were unaware of the role of liaison librarians or that there were specific librarians to support their major or college. To understand students' research practices, the researchers asked participants, "Where do you go for research help?" Nine students said they would talk to the professor who assigned the research and others mentioned other classmates, a major-specific tutoring center, or even an academic advisor. Almost all students said they would use the library, but they discussed the physical resources of the library such as study rooms and databases rather than utilizing the expertise of library staff. Only five students said that they would get help from a library worker with two mentioning circulation staff answering questions or providing directions, two mentioning librarians, and one discussing using online chat. Although 11 students referenced using some kind of electronic resource like a database, online article, or online book, four students did not. One senior said, "I haven't, me personally, used the databases here." A prospective law student said she was aware of subject-specific research databases such as LexisNexis; however, she had never used it and only heard it referenced in class. Subject-specific databases are a valuable tool for upper-level students, and necessary for graduate and professional students. This is especially important because 12 out of the 15 participants explained that they wanted to go to graduate school or professional school. Since research is a major component of higher-level degrees, interaction with librarians is essential. Possessing strong foundational knowledge of the library and its resources will help students become successful in their academic and professional careers. The following suggestions can help increase the use of library services:

- When doing library instruction sessions, librarians should explain their role in the library and consider describing other workers' roles.

- Throughout the semester, highlight different library workers, service points, and resources in library social media and communications.

- Create digital learning objects like infographics, videos, or tutorials that showcase subject-specific librarians and resources to share with different classes within that major.

- Regularly remind students (and remind faculty to remind students) that their college has a liaison librarian to assist them during their academic careers.

- For liaison and instruction librarians, seek out high impact research-based classes for instructional and collaborative opportunities.

Outreach

The UNLV library develops and hosts various outreach events that range from student mixers to Wikipedia edit-a-thons to stress relief activities. Barbara Blummer and Jeffrey M. Kenton's 2019 article states "outreach efforts provide an opportunity to include and educate library users, campus as well as community residents, on various subjects as well as demonstrates the library's value to the academy" (Blummer & Kenton, 2019, p. 180).

One of the most mentioned outreach events with the interview participants was Paws for a Study Break, which invites students to visit the library and spend time with a therapy dog from a local organization. Thirteen participants specifically recalled this outreach event and 9 actually participated. Out of all the co-curricular programming offered in the library, this event consistently has the highest level of participation. It coincides with midterms and finals, so students have a chance to unwind and relax during times of heightened stress. One student explained, "With the therapy dogs, it was perfect timing, because obviously finals, it was study week. It went perfect."

When asked what type of events they would like to see, several participants described wanting programming related to their interests or creative hobbies. In Steven D. Shapiro's 2016 article "Engaging a Wider Community: The Academic Library as a Center for Creativity, Discovery, and Collaboration," he questions why the academic library does not support students creative process by nurturing their "new ideas, multidisciplinary collaboration, discovery, and the entrepreneurial spirit" (p. 26). While instruction, preservation, and research support are the traditional responsibilities of the academic library, libraries should strive to support students' personal creative endeavors. One outreach event hosted by the library was "Virtual Reality Painting with Bob Ross" where students could use a virtual reality headset to create paintings with tips from Bob Ross videos. A participant said, "It was pretty good. I was kind of used to the VR and I like drawing." The same student described attending guitar lessons at the public library and said, "I would definitely come to guitar lessons. I've always wanted to learn guitar." He also noted that "there's a lot of people, especially here in the city, that want to be creative writers, but maybe they can't afford an MFA program." If the library is the heart of the campus, as it is so often claimed, then the library should support events that encourage creativity, passion, and connectedness.

The other type of outreach event requests was related to participants' identities, both their cultural identity and academic identity. Four out of 15 participants said they would be interested in attending an identity-based outreach event that could include a social mixer, food, and information sessions. A day before the interview, a student visited an Italian food event for her Italian Renaissance class and commented on the positive experience she had connecting with professors, students, and food. She described how she would enjoy a similar event for Latinx food. "I am sure that all over this campus, there are people from every Latin American country. Would you like to try food from Venezuela? I would love to do that. I would love to try food from Cuba or the Dominican Republic." The same participant also commented on the lack of support for non-traditional students on campus, and how an outreach event in the library catered to non-traditional students could greatly benefit the population's academic success. The Lied Library hosts Transfer Student Mixers where attendees can connect to each other, meet liaison librarians, and learn about campus resources such as the Alliance of Non-Traditional Students or the Office of International Programs, but does not have an event for other kinds of non-traditional students. Cultural and identity-based outreach was appreciated even by interview participants who were not able to attend. The library has two Wikipedia edit-a-thons each year that focus on increasing representation of marginalized groups such as LGBTQ+ people, Latinx people, and women and non-binary artists of color. One participant had never attended an edit-a-thon, but they appreciated these events. "You see stuff like that and it's affirming. Even if you can't go, it's like, wow, someone is doing that work and where can I Venmo?" Developing targeted outreach events that cater to students' identities, creative interests, and schedules could help invite Latinx students into library spaces and affirm them in the academic library. Outreach strategies can include:

- Utilize high participation events such as therapy dog visits to highlight less used services to a captive audience.

- Work with student organizations to brainstorm outreach events that are tailored to their interests.

- Experiment with events that are based on creative interests like crafting, writing, or playing music.

- Hand out bookmarks with liaison librarian's contact information while discussing Open Educational Resources (OER) at a welcome day booth.

- Share upcoming outreach events during campus and library tours.

Feelings about Libraries

All 15 participants had memories of their school and public libraries, and most of these memories were associated with positive feelings. The Pew Research Center's 2015 data showed that only about 72% of Latinx people used the public library (Brown & Hugo Lopez, 2015). Meanwhile, 87% or 13 interview participants visited public libraries in their childhood. Of the 13 public library users, 11 described going with a member of their family to either read and check out books or use the computers. The participants' parents placed a high value on reading and urged their children to check out books to read. A participant noted, "My dad was huge on that, he was like you have to read. I was reading a lot." Unfortunately, only five students had strong or favorable memories of public libraries during middle and high school. This decrease as they entered their adolescence years was attributed to having more freedom to pursue other interests rather than having a negative feeling towards libraries. One student said, "during high school I got way more into video games, so I stopped reading heavily."

The same trend of decreased usage was seen in school library use as participants moved from elementary school to secondary school. Typically, elementary school students have a specific time to visit the library as a class, but that kind of scheduled use was less common as students got older. Additionally, the positive feelings towards libraries in the participants' elementary libraries did not continue for their secondary school libraries. A participant reflected on his secondary school library and said it was, "not the best, I just did it. I'm like, all right cool, I'm just here to do this and that's it. It's not a place that made me feel like you can sit here for six hours." One student, who explained how his elementary school library made him feel special, said that the librarians in his high school library made him feel unwelcomed:

> In high school, the librarians, they were a mess, we wouldn't even want to be in there. They were so mean. Every time you'd go in there, we would have our little headphones in, and they'd literally rip it out of our ears, what are you doing in here? I was like, look, I'm not coming back. So, I just stopped going.

Luckily, the negative experiences in their high school library did not transfer to a negative opinion of the UNLV library, but this is not always the case. Academic librarians need to be aware that they are potentially having to prove themselves to Latinx students who have never been library users or who stopped using libraries because of negative experiences. A participant who transferred from a PWI, did not feel welcomed in their previous institution, including its library. Although the more diverse student population of UNLV generally made the student feel more comfortable in campus buildings, the feeling of alienation they experienced at the PWI continued at UNLV:

> I think it also has to do with going to [PWI] and not feeling welcome in that academic space has led to not feeling like I belong in any academic space. Even though I see people that look like me and way more diversity here, I just don't feel like academia is for me. So, when I go into the library, it's immediately intimidating, and I want to leave.

Conclusion

The intent of this research was to understand Latinx students' past perceptions of public and school libraries and present usage of academic libraries. Much of the existing research describes how Latinx students use libraries less than their peers without exploring contributing factors such as hours per week students need to work or negative experiences in libraries and on campus. Additionally, research often groups Latinx students into a monolith that ignores other cultural factors such as nationality, immigration history, and English language acquisition, as well as other intersecting identities such as being AfroLatinx, Indigenous, or LGBTQ. The researchers attempted to address these, but there is still so much left to analyze and explore.

All 15 students interviewed spent significant time in the physical space of the main UNLV library, but it is the hope of the researchers that Latinx students see the library as more than a conveniently located building with useful technology and furniture. Conducting the survey and interviews was the first step to connect students with library staff. Through the interviews, students learned about what exactly happens in a research consultation, which computers had creative software installed, and how to reserve study rooms. One student felt so comfortable with the researchers after her interview that whenever she had a library-related question, she directly emailed the interviewer. However, learning is not a one-sided interaction. The researchers learned about the importance of ongoing library instruction, new student organizations to connect with, and what kinds of outreach events Latinx students would be excited to attend.

The Latinx students who participated in this research felt that education was the way to achieve their aspirations, but even on the diverse campus of UNLV, they often felt alienated by higher education and pressured to assimilate. Almost one third of UNLV's students are Latinx, but the campus still looks much whiter than the predominantly Latinx communities that most of the interview participants were raised in. Library staff do not have the ability to change the demographics of the student body. They do, however, have the opportunity and responsibility to respectfully learn about, actively invite, and continually welcome and celebrate their Latinx students.

References

ACRL. (2015, February 9). *Framework for information literacy for higher education.* Association of College & Research Libraries (ACRL). https://www.ala.org/acrl/standards/ilframework

Adkins, D., & Hussey, L. (2006). The library in the lives of Latino college students. *The Library Quarterly, 76*(4), 456–480. https://doi.org/10.1086/513862

Blummer, B., & Kenton, J. M. (2019). Academic libraries' outreach efforts: Identifying themes in the literature. *Public Services Quarterly, 15*(3), 179–204. https://doi.org/10.1080/15228959.2019.1592058

Brown, H., & Hugo Lopez, M. (2015) *Hispanics and Public Library Use.* Pew Research Center. https://www.pewresearch.org/hispanic/2015/03/17/chapter-1-using-public-libraries/

Brown, M. (2017). *Frida Kahlo and her animalitos.* NorthSouth Books, Inc.

Chrousos, G. P., & Mentis, A.-F. A. (2020). Imposter syndrome threatens diversity. *Science, 367*(6479), 749-750. https://doi.org/10.1126/science.aba8039

Cooper, B. C., Morris, S. M., & Boylorn, R. M. (2017). *The crunk feminist collection.* The Feminist Press at CUNY.

Davis, L., & Fry, R. (2019). College faculty have become more racially and ethnically diverse, but remain far less so than students. *Pew Research Center.* Retrieved November 9, 2021, from https://www.pewresearch.org/fact-tank/2019/07/31/us-college-faculty-student-diversity/

Fullmer, N. S., & Fiedler, B. P. (2021, April). *Past Perceptions, Present Usage: Latinx Students and Academic Libraries* [Paper presentation]. *ACRL: Ascending into an Open Future,* Virtual. https://www.ala.org/acrl/sites/ala.org.acrl/files/content/conferences/confsandpreconfs/2021/PastPerceptionsPresentUsage.pdf

National Center for Education Statistics. (2019). *College student employment (The condition of education, 2020).* U.S. Department of Education. https://nces.ed.gov/programs/coe/pdf/coe_ssa.pdf

National Center for Education Statistics. (2019). *Postsecondary graduation rates.* U.S. Department of Education. https://nces.ed.gov/programs/raceindicators/indicator_red.asp

Saldaña, J. (2021). *The coding manual for qualitative researchers* (4th ed.). SAGE Publishing.

Santiago, D. A., Laurel, J., & Labandera, E. (n.d.). *Latinos in higher education: compilation of fast facts* (p. 31). Excelencia in Education. https://eric.ed.gov/?q=source%3A%22Excelencia+in+Education%22&id=ED595093

Shapiro, S. D. (2016). Engaging a wider community: The academic library as a center for creativity, discovery, and collaboration. *New Review of Academic Librarianship, 22*(1), 24–42. https://doi.org/10.1080/13614533.2015.1087412

Solis, J., & Dabbour, K. S. (2006). Latino students and libraries: A US federal grant project report. *New Library World, 107*(1/2), 48–56. https://doi.org/10.1108/03074800610639030

Suzuki, S. J. S. (2017). *Yayoi Kusama: From here to infinity.* Museum of Modern Art.

Sweeney, L., & Schonfeld, R. (2017). *Inclusion, diversity, and equity: Members of the Association of Research Libraries.* Ithaka S+R. https://doi.org/10.18665/sr.304524

UNLV University Libraries. (n.d.). *About UNLV university libraries.* Teacher Development & Resources Library. https://www.library.unlv.edu/tdrl/about

University of Nevada, Las Vegas. (2016, May 28). *Facts and stats.* About UNLV. https://www.unlv.edu/about/facts-stats

University of Nevada, Las Vegas. (2021, September 13) *U.S. News & World Report: UNLV again named nation's most diverse campus.* News Center. http://www.unlv.edu/news/release/us-news-world-report-unlv-again-named-nation-s-most-diverse-campus

U.S. News and World Report. (n.d.). *University of Nevada – Las Vegas student life.* Best Colleges U.S. News and World Report. https://www.usnews.com/best-colleges/unlv-2569/student-life

Whitmire, E. (2003). Cultural diversity and undergraduates' academic library use. *The Journal of Academic Librarianship, 29*(3), 148–161. https://doi.org/10.1016/S0099-1333(03)00019-3

Appendix A

Survey Questions

These five questions are an opportunity for us to get to know you as a person.

1. **Do you live on campus?**

- Yes
- No

2. **Are you currently employed?**

- Yes

  (if yes) During the semester, I work on average 1-10 hours per week

  (if yes) During the semester, I work on average 11-20 hours per week

  (if yes) During the semester, I work on average 21-30 hours per week

  (if yes) During the semester, I work on average 31-40 hours per week

  (if yes) During the semester, I work on average more than 40 hours per week

- No

3. **Are you a first-generation student? (You are a first-generation college student if neither of your parents have a college degree)**

- No I am not a first-generation student
- Yes I am a first-generation student

4. **We would like to have a representative sample that includes Latinx people from various parts of Latin America. Which region(s) are you and/or your family from? Select all that apply.**

- North America (Mexico)

- Central America (Belize, Costa Rica, El Salvador, Guatemala, Honduras, Nicaragua, Panama)

- South America (Argentina, Bolivia, Brazil, Chile, Colombia, Ecuador, Guyana, Paraguay, Peru, Suriname, Uruguay, Venezuela)

- Caribbean (Cuba, Dominican Republic, Haiti, Puerto Rico, etc.)
- Other (please specify below) [open comment box]

5. **We would like to have a representative sample that includes Latinx people with various backgrounds. At what point did you and/or your family come to live in the United States? If the answers are different for the different sides of your family, please select all that apply.**

- My grandparents, great grandparents, great-great grandparents, etc. came to the United States
- My parents came to the United States
- I came to the United States
  (if respondent came to the United States) At what age did you come to permanently live in the United States? [open comment box]

6. **We recognize that students might have different educational experiences in the United States depending on their language background. We would like to understand the relationship between English language background and library experiences. Is English your first language?**

- Yes, English is my first and only language
- Sort of—I also learned another language at the same time
- No, English is not my first language
  (if respondent did not learn English as their first language) At what age did you start learning English? [open comment box]
- My English language background is complicated (detail below) [open comment box]
  (if respondent identifies their English language background is complicated) At what age did you start learning English? [open comment box]

These four questions are to understand your library experiences.

1. **Before you started attending a college or university (whether UNLV or elsewhere), what kinds of libraries did you visit? Select all that apply.**

- Elementary school library (age 5-10)

- Middle school library (age 11-13)
- High school library (age 14-18)
- Public library (at any age)
- Academic library in a college or university (where you were not en-rolled as a student)
- None of the above

2. **What libraries have you visited in the past six months? Select all that apply.**

- Any college or university library NOT at UNLV
- Branch Library at UNLV (Architecture, Health Sciences, Law, Music, Teacher Development Resource)
- Lied Library at UNLV
- Public Library
- None of the above

3. **How frequently do you use UNLV Libraries? This includes Lied Library and/or any branch libraries (Architecture, Health Sciences, Law, Music, Teacher Development Resource Library)?**

- Daily
- Multiple times per week
- Once a week
- Once a month
- Once a semester
- Once a year
- Never

4. **What is the purpose of your visit(s) to the UNLV Libraries? This includes Lied Library and/or any branch libraries (Architecture, Health Sciences, Law, Music, Teacher Development Resource Library)? Select all that apply.**

- Borrowing items such as books, multimedia, technology
- Getting help doing research from library/university staff
- Socializing or hanging out with friends
- Special events
- Study space
- Tutoring
- Using technology (computers, printing, etc.)
- Other [open comment box]

These eight questions (and their follow ups) are an opportunity for us to understand your interactions with library staff.

1. **I feel confident that I know what a UNLV librarian does.**

- Strongly Disagree
- Disagree
- Agree

   (If respondent agrees) Can you describe what a UNLV librarian does? [open comment box]

- Strongly Agree

   (if respondent strongly agrees) Can you describe what a UNLV librarian does? [open comment box]

2. **Have you had any unscheduled interactions with library staff or librarians? This might be at the circulation desk, reference and information desk, online chat, or any interaction without a set starting and ending time.**

- No
- Yes

   (if respondent has had an unscheduled interaction) they are provided with a Likert scale for each of the following statements: Strongly Disagree, Disagree, Agree, Strongly Agree

   - In general, I feel like I can *find* library staff when I have questions or need help.
   - In general, I feel like I can *approach* library staff and ask questions.
   - In general, I feel like library staff answer my questions and/or direct me to another person for help.
   - In general, I feel like library staff treats me in a positive manner that shows they respect me as a student and a scholar.

- In general, I feel like library staff respect and understand my different identities (i.e., gender, gender expression, sexual orientation, race, ethnicity, languages spoken, disability, etc.)

- Thinking specifically about these unscheduled interactions with library staff or librarians, is there any other information you would like to share about your experiences with library staff? [open comment box]

3. **Have you had any scheduled interactions with library staff or librarians? This might be library instruction sessions with your whole class, a scheduled research consultation where you work 1-on-1 with a librarian, or any interaction that had a set starting and ending time.**

- No

- Yes

  (if respondent has had a scheduled interaction) they are provided with a Likert scale for each of the following statements: Strongly Disagree, Disagree, Agree, Strongly Agree

  - In general, I feel like I can *approach* library staff and ask questions.

  - In general, I feel like library staff answer my questions and/or direct me to another person for help.

  - In general, I feel like library staff treats me in a positive manner that shows they respect me as a student and a scholar.

  - In general, I feel like library staff respect and understand my different identities (i.e., gender, gender expression, sexual orientation, race, ethnicity, languages spoken, disability, etc.).

  - Thinking specifically about these scheduled interactions with library staff or librarians, is there any other information you would like to share about your experiences with library staff? [open comment box]

4. **For the following questions, your culture can refer to any of your different identities (i.e., gender, gender expression, sexual orientation, race, ethnicity, languages spoken, disability, religion, etc.) Students are provided with a Likert scale for each of the following statements: Strongly Disagree, Disagree, Agree, Strongly Agree**

- I see my culture reflected in the library's collections (books, articles, CDs, DVDs, etc.)

- I see my culture reflected in the library staff or librarians

- I see my culture reflected in the library's outreach and displays (social media, events, LibGuides, webpages, etc.)

- Thinking specifically about your culture being reflected in the library, is there any other information you would like to share? [open comment box]

5. **The following questions are about how you feel when you are in the UNLV Lied Library and/or branch libraries. Students are provided with a Likert scale for each of the following statements: Strongly Disagree, Disagree, Agree, Strongly Agree**

- I feel a general sense of belonging when I'm in the UNLV Lied Library and/or branch libraries.

- I feel welcomed as a student, scholar, and person when I'm in the UNLV Lied Library and/or branch libraries.

- I feel connected to the library's resources, spaces, and/or faculty and staff when I'm in the UNLV Lied Library and/or branch libraries.

6. **What are some positive things about UNLV Libraries? [open comment box]**

7. **What are some negative things about UNLV Libraries? [open comment box]**

8. **What changes or additions would you like to see in the UNLV Libraries spaces, services, collections, items, resources, etc.? [open comment box]**

Appendix B

Interview Questions

1. What is your major, what year are you in, and what are you planning on doing after college?

2. How many days are you on campus taking classes? Walk us through a typical day when you're on campus at UNLV.

3. Walk us through a typical day when you're not on campus at UNLV.

   • Potential follow up questions: Do you have any responsibilities outside of going to school like caring for family members or working or household responsibilities?

4. How do you think that your cultural background as a Latinx student influences your experiences here at UNLV?

5. When you have to do research for a class, where do you go to get help?

   • Potential follow up question: If you got stuck, what person or resource would you go to for help?

In the survey, we asked about your history using school libraries, public libraries, and potentially other college or university libraries.

1. **Thinking about the time from when you were born until you were 10 years old, which is usually 5th grade in the United States, what kinds of libraries did you use during that time?**

• Potential follow up questions: Who took you? What did you do in those libraries? How did those libraries make you feel?

• Potential follow up question: During this time, would you consider yourself a reader?

2. **Thinking about the time from when you were 11 years old to 18 years old, the middle school and high school years, what kinds of libraries did you visit during that time?**

- Potential follow up questions: Who took you? What did you do in those libraries? How did those libraries make you feel?

- Potential follow up question: During this time, would you consider yourself a reader?

3. **Are there any other libraries you visited before you came to UNLV? Can you talk to us about those?**

- Potential follow up questions: What did you do in those libraries? How did those libraries make you feel?

- Potential follow up question: During this time, would you consider yourself a reader?

4. **Besides the Libraries at UNLV, what other libraries are you still using?**

- Potential follow up question: What do you like about those libraries?

- Potential follow up questions: Do you consider yourself a reader now? What does being a reader mean to you?

5. **How did you become familiar with UNLV libraries? (potential suggestions: orientation, tours, classes, etc.)**

6. **Do you know that the library has outreach events like therapy dogs, voter education workshops, or tabling with library staff?**

- If yes: Have you participated in any of these outreach activities? Why or why not?

- If no: What kinds of outreach activities would interest you? What would influence whether or not you attended?

7. **What interactions have you had with UNLV library staff or librarians? Consider employees at the desks, in the classrooms, in the online chat, through email, etc? What were those interactions like?**

- Follow up question: What words would you use to describe the UNLV library staff or librarians?

8. Have you had any experiences in the UNLV libraries that stand out because they were positive or negative?

9. Do you feel safe when you're in the libraries? What contributes to that feeling?

10. Have you ever interacted with any librarians (anywhere) who were Latinx and/or spoke Spanish? Do you think there are or would be any benefits to working with a Latinx librarian and/or a librarian who spoke Spanish?

11. Do you feel like you see your culture (which you can identify however you want to) reflected in the materials that we have, the events that we have, the stuff that's on the wall, the displays that we have here in our library?

12. Have you ever considered becoming a librarian? Why or why not?

13. What changes or additions would you like to see in the UNLV Libraries spaces, services, resources, etc.?

14. Is there anything else you would like us to know about your experiences as a Latinx student at UNLV in general or in the library specifically?

Appendix C

Coding Frame

- Conflates library with campus or vice versa

- Course experiences

- Diversity at UNLV

- Educational Plan

- Fortunate

- Identity (national heritage, gender, socioeconomic status, LGBTQIA, non-traditional student, first-generation student, language, etc.)

- Latinx representation

    - Library thoughts

    - Non-library thoughts

- Library feelings

    - Comfortable/safe/cozy

    - Frustration/anger

    - Nervousness/anxiety/unsafe

    - Special/excited/fun/cool

    - Uncomfortable/dislike

- Library wishes

    - Identity

    - Non-identity

- Orientations and tours

- Perceptions of self/community

- Public library experiences

- Elementary
- Secondary
- Responsibilities
- School library experiences
  - Elementary
  - Secondary
- UNLV Libraries
  - Instruction sessions
  - Outreach and displays
  - Research resources
  - Space use
  - Special collections
  - Staff interactions
- Unspoken norms of academia

Coming Together as a Comunidad
Sharing Our Latinx Stories and Culture

Sally Najera Romero
Elizabeth V. Gomez-Hernandez
Alyssa V. Loera

Authors' Statement

As three Latina librarians, we write this chapter acknowledging that each of our identities, although similar in nature, are complex, intersectional, and unidentical. We are using this chapter as a space to challenge the traditional narrative of programming at academic libraries and focus on the importance of cultural programming. Our Spanish language use throughout the chapter is unapologetic and intentional in our attempt to resist the white-centered norms of writing styles but rather to connect on a deeper level with our gente. We came together for this chapter after identifying as the only Latina librarians in our academic library. We write to build comunidad and offer solidarity with other librarians of color seeking to share their cuentos and connect with the students of color on their campus.

Terminology

Throughout this chapter we use the term "Latinx" to be inclusive of those who identify as Latina, Latino, or Latinx. Although we agree that the term "Hispanic" and "Latina/o/x" are not interchangeable, we combine the terms throughout the chapter when referencing "Hispanic Heritage Month" in respect for preferences to those that associate with one term over the other.

Introduction

As diversity at universities increases at a rapid pace, the field of librarianship has struggled to keep up with professionals who reflect these changes. In a survey conducted by the American Library Association from 2009 to 2010, only 2.6% of "Higher Education Credentialed Librarians" identified as Latino. This is a 1% increase from the previous diversity count reported from the 2000 Census (American Library Association, 2012). More recently, according to the Department of Professional Employee's Library Professionals report (2020), Black, Indigenous, and librarians of color make up only a fraction of the profession, "just over 83% of librarians identified as white in 2020 while 9.5% of librarians identified as Black or African American, 9.9% as Hispanic or Latino (of any race), and 3.5% as Asian-American or Pacific Islander. Library technicians and assistants were slightly more diverse with 78.6% identifying as white in 2020."

Previous literature has established that students of color have varied experiences and perceptions with the library in an academic setting. Furthermore, studies show a demonstrated need for academic libraries and librarians to reach out and engage students of color. At Cal Poly Pomona (a California State University, and a Hispanic Serving Institution), the University Library and Cesar E. Chavez Center for Higher Education (CECCHE), a cultural center, came together to value the stories and culture of Latinx information professionals on campus, and to connect their stories, lived experiences, and culture to the broader community. Together, the organizations developed programming centered around Latinx culture.

During fall 2020 Latinx Heritage Month, a program featuring a panel of Latinx LIS workers was created. Developing the event and the panel led to an unmasking of vulnerabilities amongst our colleagues and connected LIS workers with the Latinx community. Because universities are also sites of oppression nested in the greater systems at work, coming together under the auspices of our lived experiences to talk about positionality, identity, family, and memory offered a way to connect more deeply with the surrounding campus community. Additionally, as a cultural touchpoint CECCHE and the Library offered a counterbalance to the ingrained perceived homogeny of higher education.

Academic Libraries and the Latinx Community

Literature about the interactions between the academic library and Latinx students is not comprehensive but has gradually increased in recent years. Whitmire's study on the academic library use amongst students of color in 2003 took a sampling of 9,327 students across 43 four-year colleges. The findings indicated that students of color used the library more than white students, however, retention rates for students of color were still lower than those of white students (Whitmire, 2003, p. 161). In a qualitative study, nine Latinx students were interviewed at a public university in the Midwest. Researchers found that Latinx students use the library and seek assistance from librarians less often than white students and other students of color (Long, 2011, p. 508). These findings establish what has long been known; there is a disconnect between academic libraries and Latinx students, furthermore, the research sheds some light on why this is happening.

Established research and studies shed light on Latinx students' perceptions of libraries and why they may not be utilizing academic libraries as a resource. A survey conducted at Portland State University examined the perception of the library to uncover if and why students of color view the library as a "welcoming space" (Elteto et al., 2008). The study found that confusion over the purpose of the library could be one hurdle that academic libraries face. Today, libraries of all types have evolved from a building that holds only physical resources, to one that contains physical items and access to online resources as well. In some cases, students may be unaware of the services that academic libraries and academic librarians can provide. In addition, Long (2011) found that Latinx students' low library usage numbers could be a result of confusion on the role of the academic library "because of the academic library's lack of familiar resources and expressions of cultural inclusion" (p. 510). A study conducted by Adkins and Hussey (2006), explored Latinx students' feelings of alienation, perceptions of, and the cultural purpose of academic libraries. They found that while most students did not feel directly alienated by the academic library, some were not comfortable with a "large, impersonal library" (p. 472). In addition, some students compared experiences they had with academic libraries to those they had in a public library. Students talked about how they viewed the public library as more of a social place, and where they can find cultural displays or materials in Spanish (Adkins & Hussey, 2006). On the other hand, students viewed the academic library as a place to focus on their studies and less likely to use for social or cultural pursuits (Adkins & Hussey, 2006). Montiel-Overall et al. (2016) uses a unique approach to discussing the needs of Latinx students in academic libraries. They incorporate published research with personal communications with Latinx librarians and their own perceptions of the library as they navigated through higher education. For many Latinx students, being in a college setting can be a lonely experience and being a first-generation college student meant that they felt that they had to "figure out a lot of things on their own" (Montivel-Overall et al., 2016, p. 128). A Latina library user described her reasons for not reaching out to a librarian because she was "afraid of what the librarian would think of her" and felt that the librarians at the public library were more approachable (Montivel-Overall et al., p. 128). Studies show that a lack of awareness of the resources that the academic library can provide, and what some students describe as a formal, or "impersonal" atmosphere in academic libraries can contribute to Latinx students' detachment from the library.

So, what can academic libraries do to improve Latinx students' perceptions of the academic library and meet their needs? In some of the literature, recommendations or best practices are offered as methods for improving Latinx students' perceptions and use of the academic library. In Montivel-Overall et al. (2016) some of the suggestions given to academic libraries are to "create a more personalized environment," "be visible," and "collaborate" (p. 143). Many Latinx students do not view the academic library as a place that provides cultural support, and the academic library is viewed as a place to complete assignments. Long (2011) suggests that "cultural traditions or celebrations could be showcased or performed at academic libraries, which increasingly dedicate space to student services and activities" (p. 510). Visibility is indeed a key area that academic libraries need to focus on, as collections increasingly shift online, students may not understand the need for assistance. Being collaborative and increasing visibility go hand in hand, as it creates more outlets for the library to be seen on campus or make students aware of the library as a space. Long (2011) suggests that libraries participate "with student organizations, student support services, and cultural houses for shared spaces dedicated for Latino student services" (p. 510). Bladek (2019) also lists several approaches that libraries can implement to enhance Latino students' experiences in the library. Among them are for academic libraries to develop cultural competence and remove barriers to library use (Bladek, 2017, p. 55-56). Montivel-Overall et al. (2016) suggests that libraries can work towards cultural competence by "creating space for study groups, social groups, and cultural groups" which in turn can provide "students with opportunities to develop personal connections with faculty, librarians, and other students" (p. 142). Studies also suggest that having librarians that are representative of the student body can make students more inclined to use library services. Elteto et al. (2008) wrote that "when an organization or institution is staffed in ways that are representative of their constituent populations, the odds are improved that better consideration and inclusive treatment of and service to all users will result" (p. 333). The literature offers many examples on how to outreach to Latinx students. Further exploration of the topic can benefit from discussion on outcomes and progress made once these methods are implemented.

Cal Poly Pomona & California State University

California State Polytechnic University, Pomona or Cal Poly Pomona (CPP) was founded in 1938 as a satellite campus for California Polytechnic University San Luis Obispo (Cal Poly San Luis Obispo). From Cal Poly Pomona's inception, its student body has been predominantly white. The campus admitted only males from 1938 until 1961 when it became co-ed. Gradually, the demographics of the student body began to shift and as of fall 2021, Cal Poly Pomona's enrollment totaled 26,973 undergraduate students and 2,130 graduate students for a total student body of 30,220. Moreover, the community also began to shift with Latinos/Hispanics making up 71.7% of the population in the city of Pomona, California, located in Los Angeles County (U.S. Census Bureau, 2022).

The university is a four-year institution and is part of the California State University (CSU) system, the largest system of senior higher education in the country, with 23 campuses, 485,550 undergraduates and graduate students (45% Hispanic), and 55,834 faculty and staff (California State University External Relations, 2021). Cal Poly Pomona is one of 21 campuses in the CSU system that meet Hispanic Serving Institution criteria.

The CSU system considers itself home to a diverse faculty and staff population across its 23 campuses. However, according to the 2021 Employees of the California State University report, in fall 2021, the CSU employment distribution by race/ethnicity was composed of 48.9% white, 20.9% Hispanic/Latinx, 16.0% Asian/Pacific Islander, 8.3%

American Indian, two or more races or individuals who did not indicate a race/ethnicity, and 5.8% African American/Black.

More specifically, within faculty distribution, 57.1% instructional faculty and 52.3% non-instructional faculty (coaches, counselors, and librarians) identified as white. Although CSU considers itself diverse, there is still the grueling obviousness that the Hispanic/Latinx student population (45%) within the CSU system does not match the lesser percentage of Hispanic/Latinx faculty.

CSU Libraries

Within the CSU non-instructional faculty, in fall 2021, librarians totaled 349 or 1.2% of the total faculty employee distribution (29,198).

Looking into the employee distribution of Hispanic/Latinx between instructional faculty and non-instructional faculty, Hispanic/Latinx faculty represent 12.7% and 16.0%, respectively, of all faculty. Similarly, Hispanic/Latinx CSU librarians only make up 13.2% of all faculty librarians within the CSU system and 0.16% of total CSU faculty. The Cal Poly Pomona University Library is currently made up of eleven librarians, 3.2% of CSU librarians. Within the 11 CPP librarians, three identify as Hispanic/Latinx, 0.86% of all CSU Librarians and 6.5% of Hispanic/Latinx CSU librarians. Through the need to create space for Hispanic/Latinx culture and experience where faculty representation is lacking, came a collaboration between the CPP University Library and its campus Cesar E. Chavez Center for Higher Education.

Cesar E. Chavez Center for Higher Education & University Library

The Cesar E. Chavez Center for Higher Education (CECCHE) was established in 1995 and focuses on "increasing the outreach, recruitment, retention, graduation, and cultural pride of Chicanxs/Latinxs at Cal Poly Pomona" (Cesar E. Chavez Center for Higher Education). The center offers a variety of services and events aimed toward Latinx students such as a mentorship program, Día de Los Muertos, and Raza Graduation. For the last five years, with the efforts of Latinx librarians, the University Library and CECCHE have been collaborating more and co-hosting events that provide a space for the Latinx community within both spaces.

Becoming collaborators with CECCHE was not a coincidence or luck. These thoughtful collaborations took time and intentionality. We have intentionally put ourselves out there and become more civically en-gaged with the people representing CECCHE, including forming great relations with the center's coordinator, and actively participating within the spaces and events hosted and aligned around CECCHE and Latinx identity and culture- spaces that we identify with. We partici-pated physically and virtually in back-to-school events, event plan-ning meetings, and any other meetings/get togethers where the li-brary could support the center in their mission to support Latinx students. In alignment with Dr. Nuñez-Alvarez' (2016) importance of collaboration, even with similar intersectional identities, our collab-orations required gaining the respect and trust of our partners in our humble attempt to find meaningful ways to connect with the Latino community in order to grow and become relevant within the universi-ty and library.

In fall 2020, in celebration of Hispanic/Latinx Heritage Month, and in col-laboration with CECCHE, we put together the first ever, virtual, program featuring a panel of Latinx Library and Information Science (LIS) work-ers- Meet the Latinx Librarians & Library Staff. Each year, Americans ob-serve National Hispanic Heritage Month from September 15 to October 15, by celebrating the historias, culturas, and contribuciones of Amer-ican citizens whose ancestors came from Spain, Mexico, the Caribbe-an, and Central and South America (National Hispanic Heritage Month).

Hispanic/Latinx Heritage Month – Meet the Latinx Librarians & Library Staff

> "Theory, then, is a set of knowledges. Some of these knowledg-es have been kept from us entry into some professions and aca-demia denied us. Because we are not allowed to enter discourse, because we are often disqualified and excluded from it, because what passes for theory these days is forbidden territory for us, it is vital that we occupy theorizing space, that we not allow white men and women solely to occupy it. By bringing in our own approaches and methodologies, we transform that theorizing space. (Anzaldúa, 1990, p. xxv)".

As we, the authors, have experienced traditional programming in ac-ademic libraries, much of it has felt uninviting and unrelated to our own cultural narratives and experiences. It wasn't until recently that we've given ourselves the opportunity and space to bring to life cultural programming in our work and step away from the white-centric approach to programming and storytelling. "Our understanding of knowledge (epistemology) is shaped by shared and collective experiences influenced by both the distribution and access to power" (Rodríguez, 2016, p. 138-139). Librarians of color and LIS workers of color have and continue to represent a small fraction of librarianship in academia (American Library Association, 2012). To provide space and community by celebrating historias and cultura, the Meet the Latinx Librarians & Library Staff panel event in honor of Hispanic/Latinx Heritage Month in fall 2020 at the University Library highlighted the lives, backgrounds, and cultural experiences of three Latina Librarians and two Latina/o Library Specialists and moved our cultural experiences from deficit connotation to Tara Yosso's (2005) concept of community of cultural wealth that often goes unacknowledged or unrecognized. Community cultural wealth recognizes that Hispanic/Latinx campus members have aspirational, social, navigational, linguistic resistant, and familial capital. Such capital highlights the multiple strengths communities of color bring with them from their homes and communities into the institution and library. By sharing our cultural capital with one another and other Latinx campus members, we identify and document cultural wealth to empower the Latinx community to utilize assets already rich in our comunidades.

Development and initiation of our cultural event led to an unmasking of vulnerabilities amongst each other as colleagues and gave space to connect our culture and roots with our Latinx campus community and each other. Because universities are also sites of oppression nested in the greater systems at work, coming together under the auspices of our lived experiences to talk about positionality, identity, family, and memory offered a way to connect more deeply with the surrounding campus community and held a space for intersectional conversation.

Planning

During the initial planning of the Hispanic/Latinx Heritage Month event at the University Library, we brainstormed about an event that would showcase a panel where LIS Latinx workers could share information about themselves regarding their culture, identity, and experiences in order to highlight the Latinx culture within our Library community. As three Latina librarians, we felt it necessary to give space for our LIS gente in our various internal units within the library and therefore sent an open email invitation to all LIS workers and targeted LIS workers who identify as Hispanic/Latina/o/x interested in being a part of this event. In our recruiting attempt, two LIS workers demonstrated interest in participating in the event. With a total of five panelists, we set off to schedule and plan the event.

With a little less than a month before the event, all five panelists met virtually to discuss how the event would be facilitated. After discussion, the panelists decided to create a PowerPoint presentation to go along with our verbal presentation that highlighted our unique family stories and significant traditions and cultural experiences. We panelists had a practice run with the CECCHE Coordinator, who in conjunction with a CECCHE student social justice leader would help facilitate and moderate the event.

In concurrence with our planning of the event, one of our librarians took the lead in coordinating the event with CECCHE. The librarian attended three virtual planning meetings hosted by CECCHE for all campus partners on the Hispanic/Latinx Heritage Month events. During the planning meetings, all campus partners brainstormed the best way to structure scheduled events for maximum participation and interest. These meetings included faculty, staff, student social justice leaders (culture center student employees), and student volunteers. The mixture of faculty, staff, and students from various campus departments allowed the opportunity to cross promote events. In addition to the general meetings, the lead librarian also met one-on-one with the CECCHE Coordinator to discuss how the event would be facilitated and presented. It was important for both collaborators, the University Library and CECCHE, to be aligned in goals, mission, and vision of the event. The collaboration and energy of support between the Latinx librarians and CECCHE was authentic and resulted in a fruitful and enriching experience.

Although the library promoted and marketed the event with internal efforts like displaying the event on the library's homepage and throughout the digital monitors in the building, having campus collaborators, especially under the guidance of CECCHE, allowed for a variety of attendees from the campus community and community at large. With the event under the purview of CECCHE's Latinx Heritage Month events, mass marketing (Figures 1 & 2), registration and details were handled by CECCHE staff.

As we prepared for the Latinx Heritage Month event, the three of us also put together a Latina/o/x Heritage Month research guide to

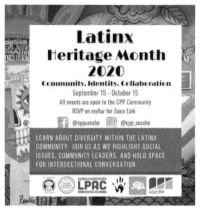

Figure 1 CECCHE Latinx Heritage Month 2020 Announcement

Figure 2 CECCHE Latinx Heritage Month List of Events

spotlight the celebration and highlight Latinx resources. Within the research guide, we included the Meet the Latinx Librarians & Staff webpage introducing the panelists. All this content lives within the overall Latina/o/x Studies research guide.

To solicit solidarity and inclusion throughout the month, a Latino/a/x Heritage Month virtual background (Figure 3) was created and shared with the library community to display as their own virtual backgrounds through the month celebration. The virtual background was also uploaded on the Latina/o/x Heritage Month webpage and available for download.

After reflection of our overall marketing efforts on Hispanic/Latinx Heritage Month and thinking on how to best represent and honor the month, we decided to intentionally create marketing material to include Spanish language words mixed in with English words, also known as Spanglish (Figure 4). "Spanglish is related to identity, in particular within the Mexican-American community- in its most basic function, language expresses identify, for identity is language" (Rothman & Rell, 2005, p. 525).

Sharing Our Stories

Our family stories are not common in the LIS field. Our stories are counter-storytelling— a method of telling a story that it not often told, often from those on the margins of society, and a tool for analyzing and challenging those in power and part of the dominant discourse

Figure 3 CPP Library Virtual Background   **Figure 4** CPP Library Latina/o/x Heritage Month Promotional Material

(Solórzano, 2001). Solórzano & Yosso (2001) addresses how through our counter-storytelling we can:

> "build community among those at the margins of society by putting a human and familiar face to educational theory and practice; and

> open new windows into the reality of those at the margins of society by showing the possibilities beyond the ones they live and demonstrating that they are not alone in their position." (p. 475)

Although all panelists, through the preparation of the event, spent time to get to know each other better and bond a little tighter, it wasn't until the sharing of our stories with each other and the campus community that united all of us more than we had ever expected. Whether we anticipated it or not, our storytelling offered a space for community healing through connectedness, collective memory and critical consciousness (Chioneso, 2020). As community healing we offered each other a space that has been historically oppressed to make statements, create shared identities, and uplift the importance of our lives.

The program agenda was designed to provide space and time for each panelist to share their story covering content they felt they were able and willing to share. In addition to each storytelling, we included information on the diversity and demographics of library professionals to showcase the disparity of people of color in the field. The outline and content of the agenda was formatted as followed:

Introduction to Latinx Heritage Month

- Land Acknowledgment

- Intentions for Program

- Department for Professional Employees. Library Professionals: Facts & Figures 2020

1. Over 83% of librarians were white, non-Hispanic; Technicians and assistants, 68.9% identified as white, non-Hispanic in 2019.

2. In 2019, just 5.3% of librarians identified as Black or African American, 7.1% as Hispanic or Latino, and 3.5% as Asian-American or Pacific Islander.

3. Women represented 71% of graduates in Master of Library Science (MLS) programs in 2017-2018. However, Black women only accounted for 7.4% of all MLS graduates, while Hispanic and Asian/Pacific Islander women made up 12.5% and 3.5% of the 2018 class, respectively.

- Panelist Storytelling

4. Latina Librarian

    - Hometown; 1st generation college graduate; Maya roots; educational journey; career journey; map of immigration of parents from Mexico to U.S.; Maya language (multilingualism); Maya geology; Maya cuisine

5. Latina Librarian

    - Hometown; 3rd generation Chicana; 1st generation college graduate; educational journey; map of parent's birth locations; family history/migrant farmworkers; language assimilation and racism.

6. Latina Librarian

    - 1st generation college graduate; educational journey; half Chicana/half German-British; parent's family history; geography.

7. Latino Library Specialist

    - 1st generation Chicano; hometown; family history/map of parent's hometown; 1st generation college graduate; educational journey; Mexicanos al Grito de Guerra; Chinelos de Morelos.

8. Latina Library Specialist

    - Family history; parent's birthplace and hometown (including map); 1st generation college graduate; not the typical Mexican family; graduate student at institution.

- Panelist Q&A
- Closing Remarks

In the brief synopsis of the programming content, it is distinct that although all the panelists seem to have recurring identities such as all are first generation college graduates and their ancestors originate from Mexico, our stories highlight differences in tradition and culture. Through our storytelling, we are offered the opportunity and space to share our family stories that explain folk customs which offers excellent means for breaking down barriers associated with race (Rollins, 1957).

Community Feedback

As the first ever Latinx LIS panel at the University Library, it was hard to gauge the type of feedback, if any, we were going to receive after the event. Fortunately, there was an overwhelming amount of support from our library and campus community. Immediately after the event, a member of our working group reached out with appreciation stating, "I just wanted to share gratitude! You all did amazing! We got really good questions from the attendees! Thank you for sharing more about who you are. I know I definitely feel connected!"

Attendees also shared their appreciation of our "braveness" for sharing our stories:

> This was a wonderful event, I enjoyed it soooo much. You each are so very brave and generous for sharing your story.

> I wanted to say thank you so much for putting forth and holding that awesome panel today! It was great to hear all of your backgrounds and stories and to get to know all of you even more. It's an honor and a pleasure to work with each one of you! Thanks for being brave, for being so willing to share with everyone, and for being inspirational too. I appreciate it a lot and I think everyone in attendance did as well! Thank you again.

A campus faculty member also reached out about how much they enjoyed the event, "I am really enjoying the wonderful presentation you and your colleagues are doing on the webinar!" It doesn't go unnoticed that our storytelling, and counter-storytelling left an impression on our library and campus community. Our lived experiences and knowledge exemplify our strength through storytelling, family histories, *cuentos, testimonios, and narratives (Solórzano et. al., 2002).*

Limitations

One of the limitations in our event recruiting efforts was targeting LIS workers who identify as Latina/o/x. With ambiguity, it was difficult to reach out with personalized invitations, and therefore lead us to send a general email invitation to all LIS workers—something we felt was not as personal.

Even with the enthusiasm of putting together our first ever Latinx LIS panelist programming, there was still worry from the panelists and the CECCHE coordinator that there might not be as much interest in our panel event. To our knowledge, this was the first time an event of this type would be held by the library. There was a bit of uncertainty if the campus community would participate in our attempt to connect with the Latinx community through this event. In addition, this event was to be held online amid the pandemic, when many participation numbers were low for online events. However, after honest discussion, we reflected that just sharing the space with the five panelists was enough for us. Attendance numbers were not our main priority for this event, instead having a space to call our own as Latina/o LIS workers was worth all the planning and preparation. The CECCHE coordinator agreed that it was worth moving forward with the event regardless of presumed attendance.

Continuing Efforts

In continuing our efforts to celebrate and honor Hispanic/Latinx Heritage Month the same five panelists reconvened to host an in-person pop-up event in fall 2021 (Figure 5). The pop-up event consisted of spending two hours inside the library highlighting a curated Latina/o/x collection along with passing out Latinx candy. It is important to note that fall 2021 was the first semester back to 30% capacity and in-person classes within the university. Our expectations of

Figure 5 CPP Library Latinx Heritage Month Promotional Material

participation were blown away by the 112 students that stopped by the pop-up station.

Our hope with bringing culture, tradition, and lived experiences to the forefront, is to open gateways for other library personnel to step forward and continue to tell their story. We cannot continue to allow formal structure and institutions to erase our heritage or the comunidad that could exist; instead, we must show our strength and knowledge from such lived experiences. Our goal through our cultural programming and continued efforts is to preserve the safe, welcoming space for our gente to be valued and heard.

Conclusion

In a field with roughly 7% librarians of color, our counter-storytelling cultural programming offered a trove of cultural wealth and, with or without realizing it, an opportunity for community healing. Only when our stories are shared, and our voices are heard will we truly free ourselves of the oppression of traditional storytelling.

When we began this process, individually and finally as a group, we did not know how much of our cultures were hidden to each other. In the workplace, talking about one's culture can sometimes feel taboo or alienating. For communities of color this can result in stifling one's experiences, especially in institutions constructed within predominantly white systems. By connecting to each other and engaging in projects that injected culturally competent teamwork, we were able to build confidence around who we are as people existing in our workplace setting.

Groups like CCECHE and the library have opportunities to provide programming that can act as counterbalances to the rules and structure ingrained in the academic experience. Where hierarchy and formality reign, culturally themed content led with authenticity can provide a means for students to see themselves reflected in a space that may otherwise be homogenous. The literature and our experiences demonstrate the desire for students to see themselves in their mentors, professors, and leaders. Relating to the university beyond purely academic interests, through informal learning like the ones we engaged in through this set of programming, is a supplemental means to increasing cultural inclusion. We as Latinx librarians have the cultural capital to share with each other and with our university peers, and the relief that comes from revealing one's own vulnerability surrounding their personal cultural history is immensely potent.

References

Adkins, D. & Hussey, L. (2006). The library in the lives of Latino college students. *The Library Quarterly (Chicago), 76*(4), 456–480. https://doi.org/10.1086/513862

Anzaldúa, G. (1990). Making face, making soul = haciendo caras: Creative and critical perspectives by feminists of color. Aunt Lute Books.

American Library Association. (2012). *Diversity counts 2012 tables.* ALA.org. Retrieved February 7, 2022, from https://www.ala.org/aboutala/sites/ala.org.aboutala/files/content/diversity/diversitycounts/diversitycountstables2012.pdf

Bladek, M. (2019). Latino students and the academic library: A primer for action. *The Journal of Academic Librarianship, 45*(1), 50–57. https://doi.org/10.1016/j.acalib.2018.12.001

César E. Chávez Center for Higher Education, Cal Poly Pomona. Retrieved from February 23, 2022, from https://www.cpp.edu/oslcc/cesar-e-chavez-center-for-higher-education/index.shtml.

California State University. (2022, March). *2021: The employees of the California State University.* https://www.calstate.edu/csu-system/faculty-staff/employee-profile/Documents/Fall2021CSUProfiles.pdf

California State University External Relations. (2021, May). *California State University's Hispanic-Serving institutions.* https://www.calstate.edu/impact-of-the-csu/diversity/Documents/HSI-fact-sheet.pdf

Cal Poly Pomona Office of Institutional Research, Planning, and Analytics. (2022, February). *Cal Poly Pomona fall 2021 fast facts.* https://www.cpp.edu/data/documents/cpp-facts/fall_2021_fast_facts.pdf

Chioneso, N. A., Hunter, C. D., Gobin, R. L., McNeil Smith, S., Mendenhall, R., & Neville, H. A. (2020). Community healing and resistance through storytelling: A framework to address racial trauma in Africana communities. *Journal of Black Psychology, 46*(2-3), 95-121. https://doi.org/10.1177/0095798420929468

Collins, T. W., Grineski, S. E., Shenberger, J., Morales, X., Morera, O. F., & Echegoyen, L. E. (2017). Undergraduate research participation is associated with improved student outcomes at a Hispanic-serving institution. *Journal of College Student Development 58*(4), 583-600. doi:10.1353/csd.2017.0044

Elteto, S., Jackson, R. M., & Lim, A. (2008). Is the library a "welcoming space"?: An urban academic library and diverse student experiences. *Portal (Baltimore, Md.), 8*(3), 325–337. https://doi.org/10.1353/pla.0.0008

Department for Professional Employees. (2021, June 10). *Library professionals: facts & figures, 2021 act sheet.* https://www.dpeaflcio.org/factsheets/library-professionals-facts-and-figures

Gulati, A. (2010). Diversity in librarianship: The United States perspective. *IFLA Journal, 36*(4), 288–293. https://doi.org/10.1177/0340035210388244

Long, D. (2011). Latino students' perceptions of the academic library. *The Journal of Academic Librarianship, 37*(6), 504–511. https://doi.org/10.1016/j.acalib.2011.07.007

Montiel-Overall, P., Nuñez, A. V., & Reyes-Escudero, V. (2016). Latinos in libraries, museums, and archives: cultural competence in action!: An asset-based approach. Rowman & Littlefield.

Nuñez-Alvarez, A., Clark-Ibáñez, M., Ardón, A. M., Ramos, A. L., & Pellicia, M. R. (2018). Cultivando respeto (cultivating respect): Engaging the Latino community. *Metropolitan Universities, 29*(2), 118-134.

Rodríguez, C., Martinez, M. A., & Valle, F. (2016). Latino educational leadership across the pipeline: For Latino communities and Latina/o leaders. *Journal of Hispanic Higher Education, 15*(2), 136-153. https://doi.org/10.1177/1538192715612914

Rollins, C. (1957). StoryTelling-Its value and importance. *Elementary English, 34*(3), 164-166. https://www.jstor.org/stable/41384579

Rothman, J., & Rell, A. B. (2005). A linguistic analysis of Spanglish: Relating language to identity. *Linguistics and the Human Sciences, 1*(3), 515-536. https://doi.org/10.1558/lhs.2005.1.3.515

National Hispanic Heritage Month. (n.d.). About National Hispanic Heritage Month. https://www.hispanicheritagemonth.gov/about/

Smallwood, C., and Becnel, K. (Eds.). (2013). Library services for multicultural patrons: Strategies to encourage library use. The Scarecrow Press.

Solórzano, D. G., & Yosso, T. J. (2002). Critical race methodology: Counter-storytelling as an analytical framework for education research. *Qualitative inquiry, 8*(1), 23-44. https://doi.org/10.1177/107780040200800103

Solórzano, D. G., & Yosso, T. J. (2001). Critical race and LatCrit theory and method: Counter-storytelling. *International journal of qualitative studies in education, 14*(4), 471-495. https://doi.org/10.1080/09518390110063365

U.S. Census Bureau. *U.S. Census Bureau quickfacts: Pomona City, California.* United States. Retrieved February 23, 2022, from https://www.census.gov/quickfacts/pomonacitycalifornia

U.S. Department of Education. *Hispanic Serving Institutions (HSIs).* Retrieved February 23, 2022, from https://sites.ed.gov/hispanic-initiative/hispanic-serving-institutions-hsis/

Whitmire, E. (2003). Cultural diversity and undergraduates' academic library use. *The Journal of Academic Librarianship, 29*(3), 148–161. https://doi.org/10.1016/S0099-1333(03)00019-3

Yosso, T. J. (2005). Whose culture has capital? A critical race theory discussion of community cultural wealth. *Race, Ethnicity and Education, 8*(1), 69–91. https://doi.org/10.1080/1361332052000341006

Applied Care Work and Authenticity in Undergraduate Instruction and Outreach

Lisa Cruces
Jess Williams

Across higher education, COVID-19 exacerbated existing financial strains for colleges and universities, shrinking budgets and declining enrollment, even more so for Hispanic students. An report published by in March 2022 by The Hispanic Association of Colleges and Universities (HACU) and Excelencia in Education (Excelencia), the severity of the decline in HSI's (New Data, 2022). Hispanic-Serving Institutions, HSI, are defined in federal legislation as a school with 25% or more undergraduate Hispanic students with full-time equivalent (FTE) enrollment. For the first time in twenty years, the total number of colleges and universities with HSI designation decreased, from 569 to 559 (New Data Shows, 2022). The pandemic created new anxieties and barriers to obtaining a degree for Hispanic students in various unique and individual ways, from navigating new remote learning models to becoming caregivers for family members (Ibarra, 2021). Statistics from the National Student Clearing House show the steepest decline in relative enrollment at 4-year institutions in those 24 years of age and older (Sedmak, 2022).

More than any other ethnic group, Hispanics experienced the most significant decreases in first-time registration, persistence (i.e., continued enrollment), and completion rates. In early 2020 at the start of the global pandemic, the University Libraries at Texas State University, like its peers, rallied to respond to the digital divide accelerated by the shift to remote learning. The Libraries' Information and Under-graduate Services department (IUS) recognized the need to respond to students' well-being, mental health, and sense of uncertainty more fully and authentically. The pandemic became part of everyday life, and so did worry, anxiety, and depression in young people. An article in the Journal of Medical Internet Research identifies COVID-19-related symptoms in college students as including ear infections, frustration, boredom, financial loss, and stigma (Son, 2020).

This chapter discusses how care work in tandem with authenticity in-creases the sense of belonging in undergraduates and, in turn, the likelihood of resilience–as individuals and as scholars. Given the un-precedented challenges created by COVID-19 and Texas State Universi-ty's student body, predominantly first-generation and most likely His-panic, IUS prioritized collaborative outreach. Recognizing care work in capitalist systems, i.e., higher education, can be better defined, as-sessed, and rewarded (Donabedian, 1988). In turn, workers like librari-ans are motivated to be their whole authentic selves and equally em-powered and affirmed to exercise boundaries. Care is labor.

Care Work, Authenticity, Relational Cultural Theory

Though care work and authenticity intersect in the literature, each concept contains its branches of knowledge. The healthcare field and feminist care ethics, and society's changing perception of gender roles have set the foundation for this conversation. In contrast, pop-schol-ar Brené Brown and changes in management philosophy, especially since the beginning of the COVID-19 pandemic, have ushered words like "authenticity" and "vulnerability" into the common U.S. vernacu-lar. Therefore, the concepts presented herein are not exhaustive but instead focus on articulating the values we have attempted to live out through our work as academic librarians.

Recognizing and Valuing Care Work

Defining care work is slippery and ambiguous to many and thus chal-lenging to discuss and measure. For example, the 2008 work by Eichler describes some of these difficulties:

> When we looked at the data collected through the questionnaires, we encountered four levels of difficulty: first, the meaning of the

term care work is ambiguous for people. Second, we needed to find an unambiguous way to deal with the ambiguity. Third, the relevant scholarly literature on the topic is also ambiguous. Fourth, there was no clear distinction between the way, respondents saw house-work and care work. (p. 12)

For clarity and consistency, this discussion applies The Blackwell Encyclopedia of Sociology's definition of care work: "Care Work refers to the work of caring for others, including unpaid care for family members and friends, as well as paid care. Care Work entails taking care of children, the elderly, the sick, and the disabled and doing domestic work such as cleaning and cooking. As reproductive labor, care work is necessary for human well-being and the continuation of every society" (Malhotra and Misra, 2012, p. 1).

England states, "Care work is done in the home and markets for pay" and provides several frameworks for conceptualizing care work (England, 2005, p. 1). Sometimes overlapping, England's frameworks help better understand care work's devaluation in a capitalist society:

Five theoretical frameworks have been developed to conceptualize care work; the frameworks sometimes offer competing answers to the same questions, and other times address distinct questions. The "devaluation" perspective argues that care work is badly rewarded because care is associated with women, and often women of color. The "public good" framework points out that care work provides benefits far beyond those to the direct recipient and suggests that the low pay of care work is a special case of the failure of markets to reward public goods. The "prisoner of love" framework argues that the intrinsic caring motives of care workers allow employers to get away with paying care workers less more easily. Instead of seeing the emotional satisfactions of giving care as its own reward, the "commodification of emotion" framework focuses on emotional harm to workers when they have to sell services that use an intimate part of themselves. The "love and money" framework argues against dichotomous views in which markets are seen as antithetical to true care. (England, 2005, p. 381)

Occupations in nursing, social work, and senior services are defined and easily recognizable practitioners of care work. "In most capitalist societies, care work, such as social services, cleaning, cooking, elderly care, and child-rearing, are still mostly unpaid or low-paid tasks and are mainly carried out by women in private households. The extent of its (de)commodification and (de)familiarization, however, varies" (Müller, 2019, p. 1).

Care Work in Higher Education

Unpaid care work in higher education is manifested in a variety of granular ways, some visible and others less so. Beyond the librarian's service duties, care work takes the form of more authentic and individualized mentoring, academic advising, or an informal conversation between librarian and student to establish rapport before an instruction session.

The current state of care, both paid and unpaid, is devastatingly visible. Caregivers and recipients of care in nursing, K-12 education, and family systems are fatigued. Ongoing research shows that COVID-19 is increasing post-traumatic stress disorder rates for caregivers and recipients of care work (Bethel, 2020). Setting aside but keenly aware of the care work exchanged in community building, domestic life, and similar interpersonal relationships, this chapter focuses on care work in higher education and its impact on outcomes for undergraduates and for practitioners, i.e., librarians.

Librarianship is a female-dominated profession like nursing and teaching, but unlike them, current performance evaluations and merit-based compensation tend to ignore the value of care work to organizational success. Vocational awe, as defined by Fobazi Ettarh (Vocational Awe and Librarianship, 2018), is "the set of ideas, values, and assumptions librarians have about themselves and the profession that result in notions that libraries as institutions are inherently good, sacred notions, and therefore beyond critique." This concept of vocational awe along with the stereotyping of undergraduate librarians as youthful, bubbly, and benevolent also reinforces the exploitive economics of care work. Veronica Arellano-Douglas, a prolific scholar and leader in critical librarianship and emotional labor, articulates the intertangled nature of care work in the workplace and the capitalist definition of value.

Her quote will resonate with many:

> I don't see myself as selfless or giving to a fault. I do the work of helping and teaching in libraries because I gain satisfaction from this work. I enjoy facilitating learning in and out of the classroom

because I want to help people recognize the critical thinkers and researchers inside themselves. I feel like in doing this, I am doing some good in the world. I am helping to build an educated, critical populace. In helping to empower others I am also empowering myself.

BUT (of course, there is a "but"), I want to be valued for this work. I want to be paid adequately. I want to feel as though the relationships I engage in through my work are reciprocal and genuine, not exploitative. This is a job I enjoy, but it is still my job. I offer my care and good work at this job, and I expect care in return. (Douglas, 2018)

Authenticity

In the *Handbook of Positive Psychology* (2005), Susan Harter begins the chapter on authenticity by acknowledging:

There is no single, coherent body of literature in authentic-self behavior, no bedrock of knowledge. Rather, there are unconnected islands that address different aspects of authenticity in a rather piecemeal fashion, including historical analyses, clinical treatments, social-psychological perspectives, and developmental formations. (p. 382)

Harter goes on to suggest that thinking about authenticity is best done by considering its opposite: "false-self behavior" which can include hiding one's true thoughts and feelings, having multiple selves for different environments or circumstances, or—in a phrase frequently used by Holden Caulfield— "being phony" (2005, p. 382). Our definition of authenticity is a combination of two other definitions in the library science literature (Arellano-Douglas, et al., 2019; Klipfel, 2014); authenticity is a person's ongoing ability to represent their true self more fully in daily life.

For the sake of this discussion, we will focus on authenticity within education, and more narrowly, within higher education and academic library services. Kreber and a team of all-female authors surveyed the authenticity literature broadly, exploring the identity and spirituality aspects of authenticity, moral education, the ethic of care, and how these ideas apply to the student-teacher relationship. They conclude,

Authenticity in teaching involves features such as being genuine, becoming more self-aware, being defined by oneself rather than by others' expectations, bringing parts of oneself into interactions with students, and critically reflecting on self, others, relationships and context, and so forth." (2007, p. 41)

Kevin Michael Klipfel found that librarians using autonomy-supportive pedagogy in the classroom increased motivation and student learning. Students were taught to select research topics that were authentic (that is, representative of one's true self and interests) by a librarian modeling this process through narration. In this case, the librarian's authenticity creates space for students to be authentic as well. In contrast, students in the control group chose topics they deemed best for the assignment (Klipfel, 2014). Klipfel expands the discussion to reference work in a later article and notes that "increasing the level of authenticity a student feels in a particular task should increase the motivation of the student because it makes the activity more meaningful. This increased engagement, in turn, should increase how much students learn" (2015, p. 23). Klipfel goes on to discuss the work of David Maxfield, who was one of the first librarians to publish on the emotional labor of reference work in 1954. Maxfield's paper, Counselor Librarianship, advocates for library workers to meet students where they are; noting that the process involves "acceptance, understanding, communication, and collaboration" (1954, p. 11 & 15).

Sixty-seven years after Maxfield, in an article entitled Teaching to Transgress During COVID-19 and Beyond for Racial Justice and Decolonization, Phelps-Ward, McCloud, and Phelps (2021) discuss authenticity within the context of the COVID-19 pandemic and systemic American racism: "Through self-actualization, educators can create spaces for learning outside of the typical classroom confines (e.g., the cafeteria or the quad), engage in vulnerability through confessional narratives that situate and make relevant academic discussions, demonstrate how students can listen and hear each other, value the diversity of students' expressions, and encourage excitement in the learning process" (p. 198). The library is also one of these "spaces for learning outside the typical classroom" and library professionals have the opportunity to bring their authentic selves into the space, to inspire individual learning and collective change.

Praxis: Combining Care Work & Authenticity

It is impossible to separate the practice of reflection in the work of instruction and outreach. Even in the absence of formal assessments, undergraduate librarians will think back to sessions and events and ask the same kinds of questions: did that learning activity work? How did the students feel? Did they learn? Will they return? Will that seed I tried to plant grow? Going beyond ourselves and our institutions gives this exercise power, so we embrace the definition of praxis as the "process of applying theory through practice to develop more informed theory and practice, specifically as it relates to social change" (Doherty, 2005, p. 1). Ironically, taking the praxis of care work and authenticity beyond our own spheres requires closely examining ourselves as educators, as knowledge workers, and as humans.

One way to examine ourselves is through the concept of burnout. Burnout among academic instruction librarians is well documented; Maxfield was observing the "wear and tear" that this type of care work takes on librarians back in 1954. Performing emotional labor is difficult to quantify and exhausting. Ashforth and Humphrey defined emotional labor as "the act of displaying appropriate emotions, with the goal to engage in a form of impression management for the organization" (Ashforth, 1993, p. 90). Despite this, as librarians who care deeply for students, the temptation remains to take on responsibility for them, to become empaths, to sacrifice self for the sake of the student. But doing so often elevates the librarian to a position of power or authority, as someone who knows better. In 1978, Paulo Freire argued that "authentic help means that all who are involved help each other mutually, growing together in the common effort to understand the reality which they seek to transform. Only through such praxis— in which those who help and those who are being helped help each other simultaneously—can the act of helping become free from the distortion in which the helper dominates the helped" (Freire & Hunter, 2016, p. 3). Freire's work preceded Relational Cultural Theory as it currently exists, but the value of mutuality is shared in both cases. Combining authenticity with care work gives the librarian permission to also care for themselves, to expand the reflection process to include their own wellness and state of being. It gives permission for the librarian to be cared for, and it gives freedom to set boundaries and to be honest about capacity. Put another way, Noddings (2013) says, "an ethic of caring is a tough ethic. It does not separate self and other in caring, although, of course, it identifies the special contribution of the one caring and the cared-for in caring. [..] It has no problem in advocating a deep and steady caring for self. [...] If caring is to be maintained, clearly, the one-caring must be maintained. She must be strong, courageous, and capable of joy" (p. 93).

COVID-19 caused a worldwide pause. In this pause, people began re-flecting on their lives and relationships to work and to self. Phelps-Ward (2021) describes how "the pandemic not only launched me into thinking more critically about making spaces for students to pres-ent themselves as more whole (people with emotions and worries) within the classroom space, teaching to transgress has also led me to emphasize that same value for self-care and self-love for my-self" (p. 202). Here Phelps-Ward (1994) echoes bell hook's charge that "teachers must be actively committed to a process of self-ac-tualization that promotes their own wellbeing if they are to teach in a manner that empowers students" (p. 15). Librarians can better support students and still receive the joy that accompanies care work while resisting vocational awe with self-care and authenticity (Ettarh, 2018).

The Alkek Library at Texas State University

One hundred and four years after Maria Elena Zamora O'Shea, the first Hispanic college student in Texas enrolled at Texas State University, the U.S. Department of Education designated it a Hispanic-Serving In-stitution (Office of Institutional Research, 2022). Minority enrollment has steadily increased in recent years, with Hispanic enrollment mak-ing up nearly 40% of total enrollment and overall minority enrollment over 50%. The ratio of female to male students at Texas State has increased slowly but steadily. Approximately 60% of fall 2020's en-rollment was female. The demographics for full-time staff are pretty similar, with more female than male workers and a slim margin be-tween non-Hispanic and Hispanic employment overall. As of fall 2021, total enrollment at the university was 38,077 (Texas State Institution-al Research, 2021).

The University Libraries is made of two physical libraries at each cam-pus: one in San Marcos, Texas and the other, the Round Rock Campus Library, one hour away in Round Rock. Alkek Library opened in 1990 and is located at the University's central campus in San Marcos. The Round Rock Campus was founded in 1996 to increase access to Texas State by providing scheduling and geographic flexibility for first-time college and non-traditional students in the greater-Austin metropo-lis. As of 2019, the total staff count for the entire library system is ap-proximately 120. In fall 2020, the University Libraries joined the Asso-ciation of Research Libraries (ARL).

Information and Undergraduate Services (IUS), the equivalent of most public service units in academic libraries, is part of the Research and Learning Services at Alkek.

Applying Care Work and Authenticity to Undergraduate Services

For students who feel like outliers on campus, finding a place where they feel safe is the first step in belonging. Only once they feel safe can they begin to live authentically, or represent their true self more fully in daily life. In our efforts to facilitate belonging for our Hispanic students, we focused our efforts on first year students and first-generation college students, of which the majority are Hispanic. Various applications are discussed here, though they focus on instruction, outreach, programming, and getting outside of the library to collaborate with student support staff across campus.

I. Undergraduate Instruction

Library instruction is traditionally well-suited for building students' confidence–the librarian exists outside of the typical class structure and does not assign grades; they are explicitly not faculty. Making the decision to intentionally apply care ethics to the classroom allowed us to situate ourselves beside students and support their autonomy through our pedagogy. Diffusing authenticity and power with (not power over) shifts the librarian's labor to prioritize care work first, and content later. The classroom becomes a no-judgment zone, where failure is embraced and students hear, without us saying, we get it. Instruction sessions like these often result in the librarian translating jargon-heavy research assignments, situating information literacy concepts into digestible, everyday analogies, and soothing stressed-out students who stay after class.

But traditional library instruction is increasingly unsustainable and questionably effective, as the literature on burnout for teaching librarians has documented for decades (Maxfield, 1954; Affleck, 1996; Sheesley, 2001; Badia, 2018). Intentionally applying care ethics becomes both important and urgent when instructions methods need to be reexamined and expectations for virtual delivery modalities increased due to the COVID-19 pandemic. Though the following examples attempt to make the shift towards sustainability, we recognize them as products of an iterative design process that is still very much in progress.

First Year Research Program (FYR Program)

Like Morin (2021), we believe that first-year instruction sessions are particularly in need of applied care ethics. But acknowledging the reality of burnout, we sought to create an information literacy model that is sustainable for teaching librarians—one without high-volume, repetitive one-shot sessions. Undergraduate librarians in partnership with English department chairs, teaching assistants, and adjuncts reimagined the existing information literacy model for English 1320. English 1320 is a required course for Texas State students. The FYR Program prioritizes sustainability both for instructors (instruction librarians and English 1320 faculty) and the organization. Lastly, and most importantly, a hybrid model creates flexibility and agility for the future—a future with or without a global pandemic.

The two parts of the FYR Program are the FYR Foundations Canvas Course and the FYR Workshops; the image below includes the characteristics of each. The Workshops operate in a pseudo-flipped classroom model that allows students to learn information literacy concepts at their own pace and then apply what they have learned to their individual research needs in a librarian-supported environment. Both are structured to allow for quantitative and qualitative assessment, and students who complete the Canvas Foundations course receive a certificate upon completion.

1: Foundations Canvas Course

- Introduces writing students to information literacy and core research skills.
- 45 minutes; 9 modules.
- Students complete the course independently.
- Includes a downloadable certificate of completion (PDF) for proof of completion.

2: Optional Research Workshops

- Students register for an in-person or Zoom workshop or drop in and work on their research topics.
- Most importantly, attendees have immediate access to librarian expertise, research coaching, and demonstrations of research exercises, tips, and tricks at point-of-need.
- Proof of attendance can be integrated into your Canvas course.*

Figure 1

The First Year Research Foundations Canvas (FYR-Canvas) course has allowed us to scale information literacy instruction for COVID-19 times and after, ensuring that more students are equipped with the skills to find, evaluate, and apply information literacy more fully to their everyday needs. The benefits are personal and academic. At the same time, the First Year Research Workshops (FYR-Workshops) have created student-centered library instruction; students access research help in real-time of need. Librarians meet each student where they are in the research process instead of assuming their knowledge level. The workshops have become beautiful examples of the care work and authenticity praxis. Students feel safe enough to be vulnerable, the librarian takes power with posture, and reflective learning happens at individual and collective levels.

University Seminar Instruction & Tours

Participation by librarians as instructors of US 1100, a required course for incoming students designed to help their transition to college and the university community, provides insight into incoming student needs. The IUS unit provides library instruction sessions orienting students to the library and a primer on research services available.

Like most forms of instruction since the COVID-19 pandemic, the library now provides a hybrid option for university seminar students. Instructors may choose to embed a seminar-focused LibGuide into their Canvas course, schedule an instructional face-to-face tour at the library, or both. Library instruction is scaffolded to build on knowledge from Bobcat Preview orientation, a program that complements new student orientation by providing knowledge about campus resources. The number of in-person tour requests in fall 2021 increased by 213% compared to fall 2019. In-person sessions provide the opportunity for the library staff leading them to lean into their authentic personalities and make connections with individual students, hopefully lowering levels of library anxiety while doing so.

In fall 2021, two librarians applied to teach multiple sections of the university seminar in addition to their formal library positions. Texas State compensates existing employees through a teaching overload. The librarians had two objectives—to increase US 1100 instructor awareness of IUS as a resource for student success and deepen their understanding of students' and instructors' diverse needs and circumstances.

The data collected from teaching this course will directly inform future instruction, outreach, and programming that the IUS department develops.

II. Student Engagement

Outreach and engagement activities have long been a part of librarianship, but how those activities (and terms) have been defined has become murkier in the digital age (Schlak, 2018). The field's struggle to define this work also means that measuring success for these activities is often inconsistent with organizational goals. For example, though there is a high value placed on relationship building with faculty and students, the most common metric used to communicate success is the number of people who show up to programming events.

First Gen #StudyWithMe

The transition to remote learning caused by the COVID-19 pandemic in the spring of 2020 was abrupt, and first-generation students faced unique challenges. During the summer, Texas State University colleagues surveyed first-generation students about their experience during this transition. Using a culturally responsive evaluation framework, the survey revealed that 57% of respondents' living situation had changed and that 62% reported their psychological well-being became much worse or worse than before the pandemic. 51% of the responding students were Hispanic. The qualitative data revealed that first-generation students lacked opportunities to meet new people, find a community, and access needed technology (Black et al, 2020). A second COVID-19 impact survey was distributed in fall 2020, and the results were presented to the campus-wide First Gen Proud committee in January 2021.

Inspired by these survey results and the popular #StudyWithMe YouTube trend in which creators live stream themselves studying, often with ambient music and timed segments—the library began hosting weekly First Gen Proud #StudyWithUs events. Events were posted on the library calendar:

Various librarians and library staff attended, and the sessions were intentionally informal. Though folks were encouraged to drop-in and sign-out at any time, most students arrived at the beginning of the session. After introductions and time for casual conversation, a library

First Gen Proud #StudyWithUs Wednesday, March 10, 2021 8 - 10 PM

Missing meeting your study group? This semester, Alkek Library invites you to join other First Gen Proud students and library staff for live #studywithme sessions on Zoom. We'll use a Pomodoro timer and ambient music to guide our time, alternating between periods of focused work and breaks for socializing. You'll share your goals, talk about your semester, and get stuff done.

We hope these sessions provide accountability, fun, and encouragement. Pets, mugs of tea, and sweat pants are all welcomed.

Every Wednesday Evening: bit.ly...

Location	Online via Zoom
Campus Location	Alkek Library
Room	Zoom
Audience	Undergraduate Students
Event Type	Online Event, Student Activity
Cost	Free
Sponsor	Alkek Library

Figure 2

staff member would start a Pomodoro timer, beginning intervals of 25 minutes of work followed by 10 minutes of a break. Library staff were almost always working from home and would state their goals and focus on their work alongside the students. During breaks, people got to know one another, talked about their current struggles, and occasionally received research help. Conversation about heavy topics, debates about the best sparkling water, and laughter were heard equally during these times. At the end of the session, everyone in attendance would report back to the group about what they had accomplished that evening. The setting and time of day created an atmosphere of safety, allowing all participants to be themselves and to feel seen and supported. More than any other event, these sessions became venues for a reciprocity of care.

The event was promoted on both the library and First Gen Proud social media channels, in a monthly First Gen Proud newsletter, and through the First Gen student organization. Students from both campuses attended, many of whom had never visited the library physically yet. Though attendance varied week to week, there were a handful of students who showed up every week. These students became library advocates, and two now serve on the Library Advisory Board.

Students were asked to complete a six-question survey at the end of each session (see Appendix 1). Notably, when asked why they decided

Figure 3

to attend, students most frequently selected the following options: "I had a hard time focusing lately and thought this would help," "I wanted to study with other people," and "I needed accountability for completing a project/task or studying for an exam," Zero students selected "I needed help from a librarian."

At the end of the semester, the event was combined with the long-standing tradition of Long Night Against Procrastination and participants were eligible to win prizes. Long Night Against Procrastination is a student support event that lasts late into the night. Many academic libraries across the world host such events that typically take place in-person with support from librarians and writing tutors and provide snacks and coffee. This was Alkek Library's first-time hosting on Zoom.

Annual Team Goal: Student Employee Experience

In addition to outreach and instruction, the information & undergraduate services department (IUS) is responsible for the main floor reference desk, one of the four service points in Alkek Library. This includes staffing the desk for 111 hours a week, or every hour that the library is open. Student library assistants are vital to this service. Though it varies from semester to semester, on average 50% of the students in the department are Hispanic.

Student library assistants in this department tend to be curious, affable, and motivated. Though library budget constraints have kept hourly wages lower than the department would like, it is common knowledge that the position allows students to do homework while on the desk. While this is indeed a perk, IUS staff members decided to be more intentional about adding value to the student work experience. To do so, they adopted a shared annual performance goal; each team member leading one area, and everyone contributing to each area:

I. Hiring & Onboarding

In hopes of removing bias and increasing transparency, Alkek Library is in the process of standardizing current hiring and onboarding practices. Library administration has recommitted to fostering a staff reflective of the student body and greater campus community. This area was led by the student employee supervisor who formalized job descriptions, expanded the number of job boards the position is posted on, and helped move portions of the onboarding training to the campus learning management system, Canvas. Because there is some research to suggest that students who work 10-19 hours per week are more academically successful, the supervisor strategically schedules between five and 20 hours per week, considering off-campus jobs as well (Dundes & Marx, 2006).

II. Documentation, Decision Tree, & Desk Procedures

Between the fall 2019 and spring 2020 semesters, two external factors caused major change to the reference desk: a renovation and relocation of the desk and a split from a desk shared with circulation and the COVID-19 pandemic. These shifts in the work environment meant that the team needed to reevaluate where documentation was kept for policies, procedures, and shared knowledge that student assistants commonly needed. Creating documentation and standardizing procedures isn't flashy, but it creates the necessary framework for student assistants and their success.

III. Continued Education & Training

Formalized and consistent training for student employees is a priority. Previously, students received the bulk of training upon hire and on the job. IUS staff is in the process of designing events and training pertaining to information literacy, advanced search skills, citation management, and similar topics relevant to their academic studies.

IV. Professional Development

Student staff can attend events such as a LinkedIn workshop that allows student employees to build their profile in a non-judgmental space, begin networking with their coworkers, and receive endorsements from their supervisors and other library staff. Part of the spring 2022 pilot was to gauge student confidence with their on-the-job skills development and to benchmark the needs of the average student worker while also creating space for students to communicate their needs and individual context. LinkedIn workshops are closed and tailored to the average student worker's existing skills and developing expertise.

Workshops also encourage students to communicate their needs and particular context such as their academic major, cultural sensitivities, and career aspirations and fears. Students and librarians exchange care by sharing a safe space for vulnerability and resilience. The following statement from a workshop attendee who also happens to be Hispanic and the first person in her family to attend college indicates measurable and actionable benefits.

The instructor was very knowledgeable and was able to answer every question I had. I think it was nice that it was geared for all majors, and there we went over certain ways how to improve word choice on my resume. Also, being informed about things that I didn't think were as important to include on my resume or LinkedIn account are actually important and can stand out to employers. I think the workshop was great and a lot of people can benefit from the information that was shared. It was a great opportunity!

V. Implementing Iowa GROW Framework

The University of Iowa launched Iowa Guided Reflection on Work (GROW) in 2009, and has since shared the framework with other colleges and universities. The framework helps student employees connect their academic studies with their on-campus work, a high-impact practice that furthers student success (Iowa GROW, n.d.). This team piloted the GROW intervention with student assistants. They focused on gathering data through a student employee survey and training student supervisors. Though the initial survey indicated that student assistants at the library were already having open and candid conversations with their supervisors and other staff, additional informal input from supervisors suggests the language provided by the Iowa GROW training better equipped them to initiate reflective conversations about the work being done in the department.

Bobcat Preview

In addition to new student orientation, incoming students also participate in Bobcat Preview the week preceding the start of classes. The goal of this complimentary orientation is to build community among students and connect them to campus resources. Though the program underwent changes due to the pandemic, in the current iteration, students participate in a hybrid environment, completing six modules on Canvas and then attending face-to-face events throughout the week.

The IUS department created a library module for the online component and in fall 2021 hosted a community event. Students received a "passport" that they could take around to key service points of the library, learn what resources they have to offer, and receive a personalized stamp on their passport. Students who completed all six pages of their passports received a sticker as a prize. The event was titled "Alkek Crossing: New Possibilities," a play on Animal Crossing: New Horizons, a popular Nintendo video game containing cute animals and relaxing gameplay that became popular during the COVID-19 pandemic. The act of play is an essential part of the human experience and library staff hoped that using a game-based event structure would invite students to engage the fun part of themselves in the library's space. Similarly, staff wished to communicate that we cared about all aspects of students and their experience, not just the academic part. Over 200 students attended the event, and all post-event participants surveyed expressed increased confidence in using library space and scholarly resources.

III. Collaborative Outreach with First Gen Proud Committee

Actively participating in the campus wide First Gen Proud Committee has opened the door for numerous outreach collaborations. The university, adopting the terminology from an amendment to the Higher Education Act of 1965, defines a first-generation college student as "someone whose parents/guardians did not complete a four-year college degree or a student raised by a single parent/guardian who did not complete a four-year college degree" (Congressional Research Service, 2021). The mission of the Committee is to "to support our first-gen population by welcoming and celebrating their successes. We focus on cultivating students' strengths and accomplishments while providing individual mentorship and other forms of institutional resources— from college to commencement to career" (Mission and Vision, 2021). The head of information & undergraduate services is a member of the First Gen Proud Committee and serves as chair of the Resources Subcommittee, a group dedicated to connecting students to academic, social, wellness, and career resources on campus. Through this involvement, the library has been able to increase outreach to and interactions with first-generation Hispanic students.

The First Gen Proud Committee also represents a safe place for staff members who serve on it. For many, it is one of the few places on campus that feel comfortable being vulnerable and authentic. Most committee members are first-generation college students themselves, and their dedication to ensuring that the next generation of first-gen students succeed drives them to perform care work on a regular basis. They provide emotional support, advocate on behalf of students, conduct research aimed at improving the first-gen student experience, practice reflective pedagogy, examine their own biases, and, unfortunately, are at a higher risk for burnout. The collaborations with the First Gen Proud Committee and the library are a result of their shared commitment to authenticity and care work.

New Student Orientation Presentations

During a two-day orientation to the university, newly admitted students and their families have the option to attend a variety of information sessions. One such session, "Navigating Texas State as a First Gen Student," was presented by volunteer members of the First Gen Proud Committee. The undergraduate librarians presented several sessions, discussing what it means to be first-gen and how to navigate a degree plan and campus resources. Like other events, the new student orientation presentations provided library exposure and representation; unlike other events, this one gave the librarians the opportunity to spend time with parents and families. The librarians were able to show up authentically and share parts of their personal journeys and speak directly to family members about how they could best support their first-gen students.

First Gen Welcome

First Gen Welcome is an event that takes place during the second phase of Bobcat Preview. At this event, first-generation college students are invited to a short presentation that concludes with a t-shirt giveaway, snacks, and informal conversation and networking. The presentation goes over what to expect as a first-gen student at the university, and the time for conversation provides the opportunity to discuss both the strengths and challenges of this identity. For example, in fall 2021, a librarian attending the event talked with a group of students about breakaway guilt, anxiety, finding community and meeting friends during COVID-19, and work ethic. This last point led to a discussion about finding employment on campus and, as a result, one of the students was hired by the library the following week.

First Gen Welcome is an event planned, organized, and executed by the First Gen Proud Committee. It is an example of the value of collaboration and simply showing up. Providing library representation demonstrated to the students that they were cared for; it also gave the librarian insight into the needs and perspectives of students.

Relational Committee Connections

Beyond participation in events and committee work, perhaps the most valuable result of librarian membership on the First Gen Proud Committee is the connections made with other staff members and their work on various initiatives around campus. So far, librarians have been invited to give presentations, help identify open educational resources (OER) for courses, meet with student organizations, and teach sections of university seminar. Many more future collaborative endeavors are in progress. Selected relational connections include:

- Project Maestros, a teacher preparation program for transfer students
- HSI STEM Impact, a program that strengthens the STEM success pipeline through technology assistance and undergraduate research
- Generación STEM, a grant-funded program focusing on improving HLI student success by creating institutionalized pathways and providing academic, social, and career preparation support
- TRIO Programs, including Student Support Services, Talent Search, and Upward Bound

- Office of Institutional Inclusive Excellence–Student Initiatives, leading campus in creating equitable opportunities and services for underrepresented students

- FLIP at Texas State, a student organization "providing community and support for all First-Gen, Low Income (FLI) students" at the university (txstate.edu)

Building connections across campus through the First Gen Proud Committee not only created opportunities for librarians to better serve and understand students but also provided companionship and community for the librarians as individuals.

Relational Cultural Theory

While we consciously applied care ethics and authenticity to our work, it should be noted that we discovered Relational Cultural Theory during the composition of this chapter and could have also approached this work through its lens. Relational Cultural Theory (RCT) is a feminist model of human development first developed at the Stone Center at Wellesley College; over time, the theory grew and was revised to "pay attention to how systems of oppression impact our everyday lives and relationships" (Arellano-Douglas et al, 2019) It is within this framework that we can recognize that libraries were built on the structures of white supremacy and misogyny, that it is a privilege to be authentic in this space. Lalitha Nataraj summarizes this reality, "Those of us with marginalized identities do not always feel safe enough to deploy our most authentic representations, particularly when such representations do not align with institutional norms and practices" (Arellano-Douglas et al, 2019). Because the "literature on authenticity is largely white," (Kreber, 2007) and largely male when narrowing the scope to academic libraries, and because the literature on care work spans so many disciplines and vocations, the principles embraced in RCT provide a holistic approach to working with students in the academic library.

In their 2019 ACRL presentation titled "The soft stuff is the real stuff: Reframing librarianship through a relational-cultural lens," Arellano-Douglas, Chiu, Gadsby, Kumbier, and Nataraj (2019) describe many of these principles and how they work to practice them as academic librarians. The authors presented mutuality, empathy, vulnerability, openness, power with, and valuing conflict as the core of the practice. In their discussion of vulnerability, they use the word vulnerability interchangeably with the word authenticity, which inspired our definition of authenticity.

Another important tenant of Relational Cultural Theory is the assertion "that people grow through and towards connection with others" (Bruce, 2020). In the case of the academic library, both librarian and student are demonstrating intersubjective mutuality, as opposed to remaining in the traditional roles of carer and cared for, teacher and student. Intersubjective mutuality, which Arellano-Douglas (2018) discusses in detail in the context of a reference interaction, provides a powerful interpersonal model for library practitioners to remove power structures from our pedagogies, to be responsive in our service. This concept pays homage to bell hooks (1994), who said "To teach in a manner that respects and cares for the souls of our students is essential if we are to provide the necessary conditions where learning can most deeply and intimately be. [...] Such teachers approach students with the will and desire to respond to our unique beings, even if the situation does not allow the full emergence of a relationship based on mutual recognition. Yet the possibility of such recognition is always present" (p.13). One of the most powerful components of RCT is the way it combines care ethics, authenticity, self-care, and sustainability for the practitioner.

Conclusion

We know that students at HSIs need care and authenticity now more than ever. We also understand that the work is happening from our efforts and colleagues worldwide. We don't know how to be genuinely recognized and compensated for this care work. Future work includes improving assessment to understand better and replicate the impact of authenticity and care work on student success. There is still not enough qualitative and quantitative data from student users for us to make meaningful conclusions, but instruments such as exit interviews, satisfaction surveys, and analysis of workshop participation and academic outcomes.

As enrollment, staffing, and energy levels decrease, we will work to scale our efforts even within the reality of this scarcity. May we all receive care as we give it, grow in our ability to represent our true selves more fully in daily life, and celebrate the joy created in our work with students.

_____

References

Affleck, M. A. (1996). Burnout among bibliographic instruction librarians. *Library & Information Science Research*, 18(2), 165–183. https://doi.org/10.1016/S0740-8188(96)90018-3

Arellano Douglas, V. (2019). *The soft stuff is the real stuff: Reframing librarianship through a relational-cultural lens.* Retrieved September 21, 2021, from https://docs.google.com/presentation/d/1PeYoD_jwGiiG9c2EpmxGs3r9rHxj3pvlJ3HC1-BPqwA

Arellano Douglas, V. (2018, July 23). *My service is sot selfless.* Libraries + Inquiry. https://veronicaaarellanodouglas.com/tag/vocational-awe/

Arellano-Douglas, V. (2017). From Interpersonal to Intersubjective: Relational theory and mutuality in reference. In K. Adler, I. Beilin, & E. Tewell (Eds.), *Reference Librarianship and Justice: History, Practice and Praxis*. Litwin Books, LLC.

Ashforth, B. E., & Humphrey, R. H. (1993). Emotional labor in service roles: The influence of identity. *The Academy of Management Review, 18*(1), 88–115. https://doi.org/10.2307/258824

Badia, G. (2018). Forty ways to survive IL instruction overload; or, how to avoid teacher burnout. *College and Undergraduate Libraries, 25*(1), 65–71. https://doi.org/10.1080/10691316.2017.1364077

Bethel, C., Reed, P. G., Brewer, B. B., & Rainbow, J. G. (2022). Selecting a theoretical framework to guide research on the COVID-19 pandemic impacts on nursing care delivery and the critical care work system (using Reed's Intermodern approach to theory critique). *Applied Nursing Research*, 63, 151513. https://doi.org/10.1016/j.apnr.2021.151513

Black, V. G., Martinez-Ramos, G. P., & Gonzales, S. T. (2020). Assessing the needs and experiences of First-generation students' transition to remote learning due to COVID-19 pandemic at a Hispanic Serving Institution. *HETS Online Journal*, 34–59. Congressional Research Service. (2021). *The Higher Education Act (HEA): A Primer* (No. R43351). https://crsreports.congress.gov

Division of Student Life. (n.d.). Iowa GROW. Retrieved February 9, 2022, from https://studentlife.uiowa.edu/initiatives/iowa-grow%C2%AE/

Doherty, J. J. (2005). Towards Self-reflection in librarianship: What is praxis? *Progressive Librarian*, (26), 11.

Donabedian A. (1988). The quality of care. How can it be assessed?. *JAMA, 260*(12), 1743–1748. https://doi.org/10.1001/jama.260.12.1743

Dundes, L., & Marx, J. (2006). Balancing work and academics in college: Why do students working 10 to 19 hours per week excel? *Journal of College Student Retention: Research, Theory & Practice, 8*(1), 107–120.

Eichler, M. (2008). Integrating carework and housework into household work. *Journal of the Association for Research on Mothering, 10*(1), 9–19.

Ettarh, F. (2018, January 10). *Vocational awe and librarianship: The lies we tell ourselves*. In the Library with a Lead Pipe. Retrieved April 26, 2022, from https://www.inthelibrarywiththeleadpipe.org/2018/vocational-awe/

England, P. (2005). Emerging theories in care work. *Annual Review of Sociology*, 31, 381–399. https://doi.org/10.1146/annurev.soc.31.041304.122317

Freire, P., & Hunter, C. St. J. (2016). *Pedagogy in process: the letters to Guinea-Bissau*. Bloomsbury Academic, an imprint of Bloomsbury Publishing Plc.

Harter, S. (2005). Authenticity. In C. R. Snyder & S. J. Lopez (Eds.), *Handbook of positive psychology*. Oxford University Press.

Ibarra, N. (2021, October 23). Hispanic college enrollment: Years of progress stunted by the pandemic. *Brown Political Review*. https://brownpolitical-review.org/2021/10/hispanic-college-enrollment-years-of-progress-stunted-by-the-pandemic/

Jeung, D. Y., Kim, C., & Chang, S. J. (2018). Emotional labor and burnout: A review of the literature. *Yonsei Medical Journal, 59*(2), 187–193. https://doi.org/10.3349/ymj.2018.59.2.187

Klipfel, K. M. (2014). Authentic engagement: Assessing the effects of authenticity on student engagement and information literacy in academic library instruction. *Reference Services Review, 42*(2), 229–245.

Klipfel, K. M. (2015). Authenticity and learning: Implications for reference librarianship and information literacy instruction. *College & Research Libraries, 76*(1), 19–30. https://doi.org/10.5860/crl.76.1.19

Kreber, C., Klampfleitner, M., McCune, V., Bayne, S., & Knottenbelt, M. (2007). What do you mean by "Authentic"? A comparative review of the literature on conceptions of authenticity in teaching. *Adult Education Quarterly, 58*(1), 22–43. https://doi.org/10.1177/0741713607305939

Malhotra, R. S., & Misra, J. (2015). Carework. In *The Blackwell Encyclopedia of Sociology*. Editors?John Wiley & Sons, Ltd. https://doi.org/10.1002/9781405165518.wbeosc008.pub2

Maxfield, D. K. (1954). Counselor librarianship: a new departure. University of Illinois Graduate School of Library Science Occasional Papers, 38, 1–39.

Mission and Vision. (2021, October 19). First gen proud committee. http://www.ucollege.txstate.edu/first-gen-proud/about/mission.html

Morin, L. (2021). The First-year library instruction One-shot: A place for caring. *Communications in Information Literacy, 15*(1). https://doi.org/10.15760/comminfolit.2021.15.1.5

Müller, B. (2019). The careless society—Dependency and care work in capitalist societies. *Frontiers in Sociology*, 3. https://www.frontiersin.org/article/10.3389/fsoc.2018.00044

New data shows decrease in the number of Hispanic-serving institutions for the first time in 20 Years, but significant increase in emerging HSIs. (2022, March 17). Hispanic Association of Colleges and Universities. https://www.hacu.net/NewsBot.asp?MODE=VIEW&ID=3656

Noddings, N. (2013). *Caring: a relational approach to ethics & moral education* (Second edition, updated). University of California Press. Office of Institutional Research. (2020, February 24). Enrollment Reports. http://www.emm.txstate.edu/resources/enrollment-reports.html

Phelps-Ward, R., McCloud, L., & Phelps, E. (2021). Teaching to transgress during COVID-19 and beyond for racial justice and decolonization. *Journal of the Professoriate, 12*(1), 195–216.

Schlak, T. (2018). Academic libraries and engagement: A critical contextualization of the library discourse on engagement. *The Journal of Academic Librarianship, 44*(1), 133–139. https://doi.org/10.1016/j.acalib.2017.09.005

Schlak, T. (2020). Libraries and leaders as creators of suthentic community: Shifting our story from isolation to ownership. *Journal of Library Administration, 60*(6), 645.

Sedmak, T. (2022). *Fall 2021 undergraduate enrollment declines 465,300 students compared to fall 2020*. National Student Clearinghouse. https://www.studentclearinghouse.org/blog/fall-2021-undergraduate-enrollment-declines-465300-students-compared-to-fall-2020/.

Sheesley, D. F. (2001). Burnout and the academic teaching librarian: an examination of the problem and suggested solutions. *The Journal of Academic Librarianship, 27*(6), 447–451. https://doi.org/10.1016/S0099-1333(01)00264-6

Son, C., Hegde, S., Smith, A., Wang, X., & Sasangohar, F. (2020). Effects of COVID-19 on college students' mental health in the United States: Interview survey study. *Journal of Medical Internet Research, 22*(9), e21279. https://doi.org/10.2196/21279

Texas State Institutional Research. (2021, March 4). *Undergraduate persistence rate*. http://www.ir.txstate.edu/student/Restricted-Student-Reports/Undergraduate-Persistence-Rate.html

Texas State university to become 125th member of arl. (n.d.). Association of Research Libraries. Retrieved April 13, 2022, from https://www.arl.org/news/texas-state-university-to-become-125th-member-of-arl/

Texas State University. (2022, April 13). Texas State University. http://www.txstate.edu/

Todorinova, L. (2018). A Mixed-Method study of undergraduate and first year librarian positions in academic libraries in the United States. *The Journal of Academic Librarianship, 44*(2), 207–215. https://doi.org/10.1016/j.acalib.2018.02.005

Wilkison, G. (1965). *President Johnson at Southwest Texas College*. Texas archive of the moving image. https://texasarchive.org/2008_00022

Wood, A. M., Linley, P. A., Maltby, J., Baliousis, M., & Joseph, S. (2008). Authenticity Scale: The authentic personality: A theoretical and empirical conceptualization and the development of the Authenticity Scale. *Journal of Counseling Psychology, 55*(3), 385–399.

Appendix 1:

Study With Us Event Feedback

1. How was your overall experience at the event?

2. Why did you decide to attend? Select all that apply!

    *   I needed accountability for completing a project/task or studying for an exam.
    *   I needed help from a librarian.
    *   I wanted to study with other people.
    *   I wanted to win that Air Fryer, obvi!
    *   I had a hard time focusing lately and thought this would help.
    *   Online classes leave me feeling lonely! I wanted to connect with others,
    *   I wanted to learn study and productivity tips
    *   Other: _____

3. What could have been better? What was missing?

4. How did you hear about the event?

5. What kind of events would you like to attend in the future? Check all that apply.

- Study with me
- Guide Pomodoro sessions
- Study with animals (with a live stream of pandas or some such wonderful creature)
- Time management workshop
- Study skills workshop
- Planner/Organizing workshop
- Crafting or Maker sessions
- Yoga, meditation, or stress relief sessions
- Budgeting, meal planning, goal setting, life-related workshops
- Other: _____

6. What kinds of support–either in-person or at a distance–can the library provide that would be helpful for you?

7. One last question: What do you think about the library's response to COVID-19? What can we do to improve?

Section 2
Decolonizing Information Literacy

"Estamos para Servirte"
Enhancing and Delivering Online Services to Hispanic and Latinx Community College Students

Elizabeth Teoli-Thomason
Alejandra Méndez Irizarry

Introduction

The Massachusetts Association of Community Colleges represents all 15 state-funded community colleges in the Commonwealth (About MACC, n.d.). This includes the first Hispanic Serving Institution (HSI) in New England, Northern Essex Community College (NECC), which has campuses in Haverhill and Lawrence. Nestled in the woods of northeastern Massachusetts on a parcel of land encompassing 110 acres, sits NECC's Haverhill campus. This campus is home to the majority of the administrative team, the Centers for Business & Accounting, Liberal Arts, Professional Studies, and Professional Development, as well as all of the athletic teams and a large number of Canada geese and wild turkeys. Its sister campus is the opposite. It is situated in "The Immigrant City" of Lawrence, MA (*About the City*, n.d.), slightly askew from downtown. While both campuses serve NECC students, the Lawrence campus is home to several unique and highly sought-after programs such as Nursing, Radiologic Technology, and a highly competitive English as a Second Language program. This urban campus consists of four stand-alone buildings. Each building has its pros (the Revolving Test Kitchen is a beautiful collaboration with the city) and cons (buildings are spread out across multiple city blocks making communication and collaboration difficult at times). The Revolving Test Kitchen is a commercial kitchen and food business incubator located in the heart of downtown Lawrence and operated by the Foundation Kitchen with the help of the Lawrence Partnership. It has been in existence since late 2016 and supports the culinary arts program at NECC as well as the Lawrence community food businesses (Greenslade, 2021). The uniqueness of these campus-specific programs draws students into the bustle of downtown Lawrence.

Currently, the "NECC student population is 42% Hispanic – most of whom are from the Dominican Republic and Puerto Rico" (NECC, n.d.c). Not only are a number of these students new to the area, but many of them are new to the role that libraries play in higher education and are unaware of the services afforded to them. NECC's goals include graduating and transferring its students to four-year universities as well as offering valuable certificate programs and various career-related credentials. It is the responsibility of professional support staff members, such as tutors, academic coaches, and librarians, to help prepare them for entry into the larger academic field. It can be challenging for each of these groups, but especially so for librarians as they regularly encounter students who are unfamiliar with normal library practices, such as the ability to physically take books out of the library or get research assistance from a professionally trained librarian.

Community colleges are (typically) affordable places where students can enter into several two-year programs. Some of the benefits of going to community colleges are that students can gain transfer credit to a 4-year institution, learn a vocation, or begin a career in many "cutting-edge fields such as biomedical technology, biotechnology, robotics, laser optics, internet and computer technologies, and geographic information systems" (EducationUSA, n.d.). Community colleges such as NECC offer opportunities in other fields with extremely optimistic growth projections such as nursing, dental assisting, and radiologic technology (U.S. Bureau of Labor Statistics, 2021), as well as culinary arts and others. These programs traditionally have lower costs than their 4-year counterparts; they also boast smaller class sizes and increased support services — all of which are "highly beneficial for international students as they adjust to the pace of U.S. academic life and practice their English-language skills" (EducationUSA, n.d.). Regardless of the success rate of these programs among Hispanic students, there is still a noticeable gap in degrees awarded between students who self-identify as "Hispanic or Latino" and "Not Hispanic or Latino" at

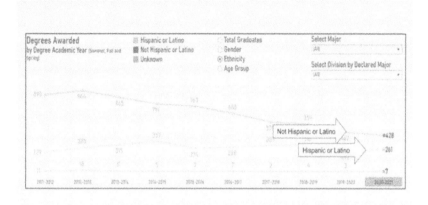

Figure 1 Successful Course Completion Rates: Degrees Awarded (by ethnicity)

Note The data shows the difference in the number of degrees awarded by ethnicity with AY
2020–2021 singled out (NECC, 2021b). The line on the top reflects the non-Hispanic or
Latinx students, while the line at the bottom of the figure represents the Hispanic or
Latinx students.

NECC (see Figure 1). A similar trend can be seen with course completion
rates. For the purpose of this chapter, the authors will define student
success as the completion of a program or course, retention, and degrees awarded (New England Commission of Higher Education [NECHE],
2021). The authors recognize that this definition of student success is
rooted in settler-colonial practices that do not reflect the catalytic
power of education (Patel, 2021). However, NECC uses the aforementioned standardized indicators as evidence of student success.

Community colleges are also where "each student brings their own
unique story…resulting in robust class discussion, an emphasis on cultural awareness, and a rich learning experience" (Contrada, 2019, p. 13).
Many community college librarians echo this sentiment, describing it
as a passion (Leeder, 2013). For a refreshing bit of reading, see the survey responses under Research Question Three in Chapter Four: Findings of Cunningham's dissertation (2012).

> A librarian at an isolated community college has noted that the col-
> lege's focus on "meeting the needs of students, especially basic
> skills students" means that professors can understand the impor-
> tance of the library's "role in students' success [by] providing bridge
> services for academic success, not just [being] the steward of ma-
> terials. (pp. 148-49)

Community college librarians often see their libraries as the bridge between public libraries and 4-year academic libraries, therefore they choose to spend their careers helping a group of traditionally older, lower-income students of color—and find it to be gratifying (Leeder, 2013).

As collections within our institutions are traditionally tied to "active course offerings, as opposed to a split focus on course offerings and graduate student and faculty research areas" (Leeder, 2013, p. 194), they are often significantly smaller than that of 4-year schools. This also demands that community college librarians "gain exposure to a wide variety of fields to address a spectrum of reference queries" (Leeder, 2013, p. 195), not unlike that of a public librarian. Cunningham's 2012 study showed what the authors of this article have experienced first-hand, that their students were more willing to interact with them and seemed to truly "want support from librarians" (p. 149). The willingness to assist and the dedication to support our students is strong, and it is focused on helping students succeed and overcome library anxiety as well as digital barriers (Leeder, 2013).

Library Services

The Elephant in the Room: Serving Hispanic Students During a Global Pandemic

Before the spring of 2020, NECC's two libraries offered 60+ hours a week of in-person services and were staffed with five full-time librarians and three part-time evening librarians. Duties included staffing reference desks, monitoring virtual chat forums, teaching information literacy courses, meeting with students face-to-face, sitting on college governance committees, and participating in professional development activities. The team of reference librarians frequently reviewed the library's holdings for collection development purposes and found time to participate in several community activities. The COVID-19 pandemic caused dramatic changes to library services, staff, and buildings, and like many offices within the College, the library ceased all its in-person services.

The librarians took a number of steps to ensure that NECC's students would not be left behind during these chaotic times: increasing online offerings both within the collection and via virtual services, offering assistance in a number of modalities that may not have been previously available, extending lending periods for necessary materials such as laptops and calculators, and instituting a remote printing service. Most individuals that visited the libraries on both campuses did so to print their Blackboard course content, readings, instructions, and grades. Most students printing at the Lawrence campus library expressed that they did not have reliable internet access at their homes, which, as Contrada (2019) states, is often "the difference between passing and failing" (p. 14). The library's academic technology assistants created a remote printing service that would still afford students an opportunity to learn in their chosen manner. As the setup of the Lawrence campus library is significantly different than that of the Haverhill campus, the team was able to provide dedicated lockers (Figure 2) for students to pick up their printouts whenever the main building was open.

This was especially important as the library was operating on a limited, appointment-only schedule during this time; librarians and academic technologists would only go to the library when a student booked an appointment to check out materials or use the computers. The remote printing services were heavily promoted via the library's

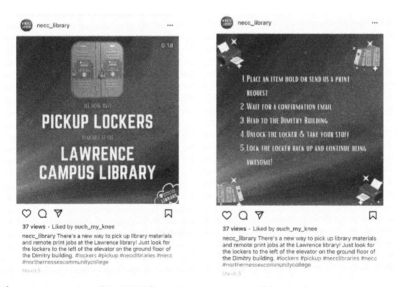

Figure 2 Screenshot of the NECC Library Instagram Post on Pickup Lockers

Note Screenshot of the NECC Library Instagram profile promoting the pickup lockers at the Lawrence Campus Library. The post includes instructions on both the promotion, location within the building, and how to access materials placed inside the lockers.

social media channels (Northern Essex Community College Library, 2021, March 5). During the spring 2021 semester, the libraries had a total of 90 bookings for printing and pickups from 48 unique users. Unfortunately, due to extenuating circumstances, this service had to be put on hold in Haverhill. However, the Lawrence Campus was able to continue the after-hours pickup library service due to the pick-up lockers mentioned above.

Sirviéndole a la comunidad (Serving the Community): How the Instruction and Research Team Seeks to Meet the Needs of its Community

The NECC student body identifies itself as 42% Hispanic, with many being non-English speakers (NECC, n.d.c). Most of this Hispanic population are from the Dominican Republic and Puerto Rico, two Caribbean countries whose native language is Spanish. Many students from these countries are not proficient in English and take English as a Second Language (ESL) courses. Usually, ESL courses are a requirement for students with a low score on their reading comprehension and/or WritePlacer ESL Placement Test (NECC, n.d.a.). ESL courses ensure students succeed in every step of their college journey and their overall professional journey in New England and beyond. Because of the need to communicate clearly with all students, the library undertook the large task of translating its main subject guides, videos, and signage into Spanish. The entirety of this work has been completed by Alejandra Méndez, NECC Haverhill's Assistant Librarian at the time. Méndez is a Hispanic Caribbean librarian who migrated to Massachusetts in early 2020. It is crucial for librarians to bond with the student population. When Méndez began her journey as a librarian at NECC, she noticed that many students came to her struggling to communicate. It was then that she saw that many students needed someone who spoke their language. Méndez undertook the translation of some of the content curated and created by the library. She also offered individualized information literacy (IL) sessions in Spanish to aid the students in better understanding how to navigate the library website and take advantage of the various services that the library has to offer. Many of the virtual sessions that were conducted in Spanish were offered on an individual basis. Méndez personally asked students if they would prefer to speak in Spanish or have the session in English. In the spring of 2021, there were a total of 15 students who engaged in Spanish IL sessions. However, this type of offering has been limited and has not been formally offered as an option to NECC students. For Méndez, it is essential for students to find someone who shares their culture, race, and language, especially when far from their home country. As a result of these translations and exchanges, Liz Teoli-Thomason, at that time the Research and Instruction Librarian in Lawrence, began to work closely with Méndez on creating and curating bilingual content for the college community. Together they created a series of videos on the online research management software, NoodleTools (more details below), citation help, and other subjects. All of these videos are available in both English and Spanish. They follow the principles of Universal Design for Learning (Eagleton, 2021), allowing for the information within them to reach a wider audience.

At this point, it is difficult to foresee if the influx of online courses will linger after the COVID-19 pandemic draws to a close. Higher education websites have published opinions that virtual learning is here to stay (Darby, 2020). Yet, faculty, staff, and students have expressed their desire to return to in-person modes of teaching and learning (Elshami et al., 2021; Zhou, 2020). For low-income Hispanic students, it has been challenging to adapt to online environments due to the barrier of accessing a secure and reliable internet connection (Brown et al., 2016; Huerta et al., 2019). Access to educational materials such as textbooks has also been challenging; many students find digital reading tiresome and prefer paper over a screen (Brandle et al., 2019; Jhangiani et al., 2018). Students have reached out to the reference librarians requesting printed versions of e-textbooks or help printing sections of their e-textbooks to study and complete their assignments. In some cases, this is aggravated because some of the students are ESL learners, who are still acclimating to the nuances of the English language, and the learning management system (Blackboard) used by the college.

Faculty and instructors who teach IL intensive courses, defined by NECC as courses where "students will learn to identify their information needs and use appropriate resources to find and communicate this information" (NECC, n.d.b), are required to schedule a research instruction session with the library, as well as require their students to meet individually with a reference librarian to complete a research checkpoint. The research checkpoint is an IL service designed by the librarians to aid students in achieving academic success. It requires students to meet one-on-one with a librarian about their specific assignment. In this appointment, librarians offer students individualized information literacy instruction, source review, citation review, and help with course-specific formatting styles. In addition, the librarians provide vital services and suggest references that can aid the student in completing their coursework. The librarians recognize the difficulty that some students may have in attending an in-person appointment, so they offer these checkpoint services via various modalities, including, Zoom, virtual chat, and email. In all instances, the students share the specifications of their assignment and their initial research before the scheduled appointment.

One of the recurring issues that many IL instruction librarians face is that one-hour sessions are not enough (Contrada, 2019; Oakleaf et al., 2012; Wengler & Wolff-Eisenberg, 2020). As Oakleaf et al. (2012) boldly note in their article, "[n]o one knows better than librarians the limitations of this format, yet [they remain] central to our teaching efforts" (p.6). Difficulties with retention of information for one-shot instruction sessions are even more prevalent in community colleges, where students have different learning styles and often an "insufficient grasp of English and Western academic norms [that makes] it extremely difficult for them to follow and participate in discussions of nuanced topics such as source evaluation and academic integrity" (Hodge, 2020, p. 82). They also tend to lack digital literacy skills (Contrada, 2019; Quiñonez & Olivas, 2020). Therefore, we must have one-on-one meetings with them to assist them with their research and assignments.

The librarians seek suggestions on how to improve their approach, teaching, and services while actively aiding students. It is essential to receive this feedback and consider their requests, as it allows us to cater our approaches to their specific needs and situations. An example of this has been the library's migration from LibCal to Navigate for appointment management. The library had been using one of Springshare's tools, LibCal, to manage student appointments. When using this tool students would often be confused or would have a difficult time finding how to schedule an appointment with a librarian as it was different from all other such tools used by the college. The difficulty was the result of students having slow internet service, or because they were dependent on mobile technology. It should be mentioned that various services (i.e., web pages at NECC) do not have a mobile view, thus making the user experience (UX) navigation difficult for students, because of visibility, navigation, and language barriers for those who do not have English proficiency. Over the course of the previous academic year, the College adopted EAB's Student Success Management System, Navigate, to manage the majority of student

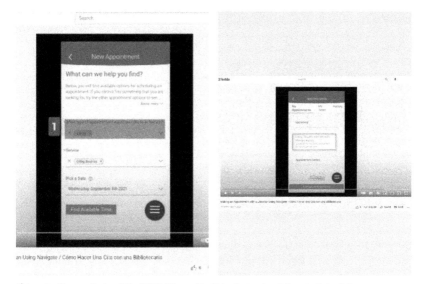

Figure 3 Screenshots of the NECC Library YouTube Page about How to Schedule
Appointments through Navigate.

Note The video provides a step-by-step visual guide on how to schedule an appointment
through the Navigate platform. The image on the left displays the initial step to
schedule an appointment with a member of the library staff. The image on the right
shows the confirmation of the type of appointment that the patron has scheduled
(Northern Essex Community Library, 2021e).

services. Understandably, students became more acquainted with using Navigate, making the usage of other tools (such as LibCal) more confusing. In the fall of 2021, the reference team unanimously agreed to migrate their appointment system to the Navigate platform to ensure that students are able to reach them when they need to schedule an appointment (in-person or virtual) for their information literacy and research needs (see Figure 3). The reference team heavily promoted this change via their social media channels and through personal communication with different committees and departments (NECC Library, 2021e).

Students are not the only ones who benefit from these one-on-one sessions. Librarians also gain insight about possible workshops, sessions, and materials, sometimes intentionally, most often not. During the spring 2021 semester, Teoli-Thomason was invited into a student Zoom session between three classmates that required assistance with NoodleTools, an online citation management system subscribed to by the NECC libraries. After walking the students through the different steps of creating citations within the platform, one of the students

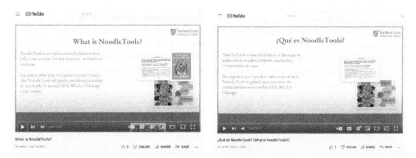

Figure 4   Screenshots of the NECC Library YouTube Page "What NoodleTools Is?"

Note   The videos are a brief introduction on what NoodleTools is and how to use it. The left image displays the English version of the video, while the right image shows the Spanish version (Northern Essex Community College Library, 2021c; 2021d).

asked, "Okay, you keep saying NoodleTools this and NoodleTools that. But, Miss, please, I don't understand what a NoodleTool is and why I should use it." Teoli-Thomason had been so busy teaching the resources that she had not taken the time to explain what they were. The students' questions and reactions prompted her to create a brief (78 seconds) introductory video telling people about NoodleTools and why they would want to use it.

This video (as seen in Figure 4) now begins the playlist of NoodleTools tutorials. Each video on this list addresses students' academic and linguistic needs in an easy-to-digest format and length. Brief videos (< 2 minutes in length) are easily consumable, are accessible via mobile devices, and are available to be shared through social media channels and Blackboard to reach wider audiences.

Embedding Services in Learning Management Systems

The librarians also work closely with faculty and instructors to address the needs of their students. As the use of Blackboard increases at the college, instructors seek various ways for students to access course content, readings, and supplementary materials. Instructors frequently contact the librarians to secure access to specific databases, subject guides, and library tools and resources. Thus, the librarians have implemented Learning Tools Interoperability (LTI) in Blackboard. LTI allows faculty to embed course specific LibGuides directly into their LMS course shells. During the spring 2021 semester, Méndez and another professional library staff member created the "How to

Embed Library Resources in Blackboard" subject guide to aid instructors. Having key library resources directly inside course shells simplifies how students can access these vital services. Providing direct links is essential, as many students access their courses through mobile devices, which leads to increased difficulty navigating and accessing websites when using college services. Similar to what was previously mentioned, mobile navigation proved to be tedious and difficult for students because the web pages do not have a mobile view. Other aspects that trump over UX are spotty service and language barriers, in the case of ESL students. As a result of this, providing hyperlinks that provide direct access to the library via their Blackboard course will save students time, bandwidth, and will point them in the right direction. This is especially important as many ESL learners struggle to understand some of the information provided to them by their instructors. With the increased shift to online course offerings at NECC, Teoli-Thomason and Méndez have observed that many students use their mobile devices to connect through video calls (i.e., Zoom). However, at times, the connection tends to be interrupted because of bandwidth issues or lack of privacy on the student's end. What would usually be set to be a 30-minute meeting, extends to 40 or 60-minute interactions. The reference and instruction team understands that this is an issue that students face, so we have tried to expand how students can reach us. We have also opted to help students locate research resources because of their limitations to accessing a reliable internet connection. Among the options that we have provided students, we have used email communication and SMS communication. This way, students can answer at their own pace and through a more reliable form of communication. Yet, these solutions are not without fault. Communication through SMS services can be challenging.

When designing and selecting library services for the College, it is vital to consider how these will benefit everyone, most importantly, the students. It is crucial to understand that although these resources and materials are helpful and enrich their academic and learning goals, the students will need assistance understanding how to use them. Through our reference and academic technology interactions with students, we have noticed that many students require support with Blackboard and other academic online tools that the college has been increasingly reliant upon or implemented over the last two years. The librarians and academic technologists have provided students with individual digital literacy lessons to teach them how to navigate Blackboard, MS Office

Suite, Google Suite, and the college's Student Success Management System (Navigate). Teaching students how to use the college's virtual tools and the technology required to complete coursework helps minimize the anxiety that some of the Hispanic and other BIPOC students experience (Contrada, 2019).

LibGuides to the Rescue?

LibGuides editing is no small task, and overall, "guide maintenance may be [seen as] a mundane task to perform" (Ornat et al., 2021, p. 14). However mundane librarians may feel the task is, it is imperative that students have access to accurate and up-to-date information. It can take hours to go through a single guide or months to go through all current guides that a college has to offer. Larger institutions often have librarians dedicated to online content, such as LibGuides. Community colleges operate under much smaller budgets and therefore do not have the benefit of a dedicated individual to do all LibGuides maintenance. This is where the concept of the "Reference 'and' Librarian" (Contrada, 2019, p. 13) comes into play. At NECC, each librarian is responsible for several LibGuides. However, a central librarian monitors the "Link Checker" page weekly, if not daily. The librarian checks for an updated page link and replaces the outdated one. This is why librarians and other guide curators are strongly encouraged to use asset functionality instead of simply hyperlinked text. Springshare's link crawlers cannot check the validity of the hyperlinked text, but they will catch any broken linked asset. Guide creators are urged to reuse assets to ensure ease of editing whenever possible. This is especially important for assets that are peppered heavily through a multitude of guides, as the mapping saves countless hours of page clicks, and it ensures that this information will be accurate across all guides.

Another task that Teoli-Thomason and Méndez recently embarked upon was integrating Spanish translations of heavily used guides into their English counterparts. These translations are part of an inclusion initiative for students who are not English proficient and require library assistance.

The first LibGuides translations were done during the spring semester of 2020. Méndez chose two LibGuides to translate first: "When You Can't Come to the Library [Cuando no puedes visitar la biblioteca presencialmente]" and "Using the Library [Uso de la biblioteca]." These two guides were selected because of the urgency during the early days of

ID	Type	Original Guide Title	Spanish Translation	Updated	Impact
1128263	Writing, Communication & Literature	Citation Guide	Guía de formato de citas	2021-10-04	20 hits
1198877	Writing, Communication & Literature	How to Format Your Research Paper	Cómo formatear un ensayo de investigación	2021-12-2	37 hits
1022375	General College & Library Guides	When You Can't Come to the Library	Cuando no puedes visitar la biblioteca presencialmente	2021-09-15	28 hits
1128029	Writing, Communication & Literature	Evaluating Websites and Other Sources	Evaluando portales web y otras fuentes	2021-03-03	57 hits
1129522	General College & Library Guides	Using the Library	Uso de la biblioteca	2021-03-22	57 hits

Table 1 LibGuides translated to Spanish at Northern Essex Community College

Note List of the translated guides to Spanish, and the number of times these have been consulted. Most guides were translated during the 2020-2021 academic year, except for "When You Can't Come to the Library [Cuando no puedes visitar la biblioteca presencialmente]", which was translated in the spring of 2020. The table shows the number of hits from spring 2020 to fall 2021.

the COVID-19 pandemic, as well as the various weather-related closures that the College typically experiences during the spring semester. These appear within the list of LibGuides linked on the library's main page, in the library's FAQ page, and on the library's dedicated Services During Coronavirus page. The subsequent guides that were identified as essential and pertinent to translate were those related to citation styles and evaluating resources.

Although the librarians understand that LibGuides are not the only answer, they recognize the importance of providing critical static resources for students when in-person services are minimal, or students may be suffering from cases of library anxiety (Leeder, 2012). This has led the librarians to explore other ways in which they can provide critical services at point-of-need, even if librarians are not available in person.

Meeting the Academic Components of the College

The Core Academic Skills: Information Literacy

In the fall of 2014, NECC implemented its "Core Academic Skills" program, which requires students to "take at least one course that's intensive in each of Northern Essex's six core academic skills in order to be eligible to graduate" (NECC, n.d.b). These competencies (global awareness, information literacy, public presentation, quantitative reasoning, science and technology, and written communication) "reflect those skills which faculty and staff determined are essential to ensure students' adequate preparation for further academic pursuits and careers" (Northern Essex Community College Library, 2021).

As of the fall 2021 semester, there are 21 active Information Literacy Intensive courses for a total of 51 sections. Of these sections 14 are in-person (eight in Haverhill and six in Lawrence), and 15 are online asynchronous courses. Implementing the Information Literacy Core Academic Skill has ensured that faculty and instructors teach students necessary research and information literacy skills, in concert with the research librarians. During one-shot sessions, librarians teach students about online searching, source evaluation, subject databases available through the library, the NoodleTools citation manager, research guides, and other helpful resources that the library has curated. Once the session concludes, the students are required to meet with the librarian of their choosing and have a one-on-one appointment to locate sources, refresh content, review their citations, or get feedback about their research.

Some of the most active courses that have collaborated with the library have been World Civilization, Advanced Radiology, Marine Biology, Human Services Seminar, Criminal Justice Capstone, and Practical Logic. Most of these courses have been taught online since fall 2020, except those with a laboratory component. Therefore, all IL instruction has been done remotely, and the one-on-one appointments have also been conducted virtually.

For Teoli-Thomason and Méndez, implementing critical information literacy and critical digital andragogy lenses to their instruction has been essential, as nearly one-third of all NECC students are over the age of 25 (NECC, n.d.e.). For the academic year 2020-2021, there were 1,416 students who self-identified as being over age 25, with the median age being 26-36. Additionally, there were 3,299 who self-identified as being under age 25 with the median age being 18-25 (NECC, n.d.e.).

By using a critical digital andragogy lens, various instructors have centered research assignments on topics relevant to students' experiences and their community. Therefore, it is crucial to provide students with culturally relevant tools that support their learning process. In various instances, many of these research projects have empowered students to think critically about the existing power structures in the information they are reviewing, their communities, and in some cases, their work (Waddell & Clariza, 2018). While conducting one-on-one sessions, Méndez and Teoli-Thomason have been engaging students through research assignments. One such way that the authors have implemented these critical lenses into their instruction is by pre-researching the specific topics that the students themselves are researching. This allows them the opportunity for a deeper discussion of the purposes and intentions of the sources they are using. Many of the students that Méndez met with are from Hispanic and Afro-Caribbean backgrounds. Therefore, it was necessary to find culturally relevant resources such as research guides in Spanish, community centers in the city of Lawrence (most relevant for Human Services Seminar students), and concrete examples of what an academic research paper of BIPOC issues looked like. Other culturally relevant resources are those within the College that offer services that address the needs of Latinx, Hispanic, and BIPOC students.

The accuracy of sources is also a significant access issue affecting ESL students more than others (Patterson, 2011). There are elements of language, culture, and assimilation that come into play (Solis & Espinoza, 2021) increasing the potential for confusion. Some students are not familiar with the anglophone jargon of the discipline that they are studying, as well as the types of misinformation that are common in the U.S. It is the job of the IL librarian to show students how to find "access to the kinds of research skills, concepts, practices, and dispositions essential for success in higher education" (Patterson, 2011).

Information Literacy intensive courses represent an emerging requirement trend in community colleges in the U.S. (Arnold, 2010). This goes in hand with the American Association of Community Colleges (National Council of Learning Resources, 2017) statement about information literacy, the Middle States Commission of Higher Education Standards (2015), and the New England Commission of Higher Education Standards (2021) for accreditations. One example is standard 4, Academic Program, of NECHE (2021):

> Graduates successfully completing an undergraduate program demonstrate competence in written and oral communication in English; the ability for scientific and quantitative reasoning, for critical analysis and logical thinking; and the capability for continuing

learning, including the skills of information literacy. They also demonstrate knowledge and understanding of scientific, historical, and social phenomena, and a knowledge and appreciation of the aesthetic and ethical dimensions of humankind. (p. 9)

It should also be pointed out that various professional associations and their respective accreditation certificates require students to have IL-related courses. These courses are structured around the six frames identified by the Association of College & Research Libraries (ACRL) in the Framework for Information Literacy for Higher Education (2016). The "cluster of interconnected core concepts" (ACRL, 2016, p. 7) that the frames are based upon are parallel to the core skills mentioned from the accrediting associations. Each of these concepts are taught by the Reference Team to NECC students with an emphasis on the novice-learner lens.

For some ESL students, their IL skills are linked to language acquisition and proficiency. There have been instances when students have struggled with IL-intensive courses because of the language barrier (Bordonaro, 2020). For these students, LIS terminology, Blackboard, and citation rules and formats can be challenging to understand, especially since most of these do not have a Spanish translation. As students familiarize themselves with the tools provided by the College and the Library, their skills evolve and improve. This is usually observed when students enroll in research-intensive seminars at the end of their studies.

Some of the courses at the College incorporate Latinx and Hispanic literature and U.S.-based Latinx and Hispanic authors and scholars. To support the curriculum created by the faculty, the library has created subject and research guides that use themes from Latinx countries. This is most noticeable within the English Composition II course guide. This guide showcases topics on the history of the Dominican Republic and is especially relevant as "60% of the students studying at NECC's Lawrence Campus are Hispanic, largely with roots in the Dominican Republic" (NECC Newsroom, 2016, par. 3). The ENG 102 course has designated Julia Álvarez's novel *In the Time of the Butterflies* as required reading. Within the discussion of this novel, the instructors have created assignments related to the history of the Dominican Republic during the rule of Rafael Leónidas Trujillo Molina. Teoli-Thomason and Méndez understand the importance of showing meaningful connections between research and reality to their students, and it allows them to find more cultural affinity with the Latinx and Hispanic students.

For those of us who are from outside of a community, it can be a rather intimidating task to learn about the cultures, the ideals, the barriers, and the histories of the community they reside or work within. Although it is daunting, it is necessary to meet students where they are so that you, as the librarian, can understand what the students are learning, how they are learning, and how to help them succeed. The library has created subject guides dedicated to various geographic regions. This is part of a larger program, One Geographic Region (OGR), that was established at NECC in the 2015-2016 academic year as a way for the college to come together with the intention being "to promote learning across disciplines and borders" (NECC Newsroom, 2016). When the focus of OGR turned to the Caribbean, Teoli-Thomason offered to create library materials revolving around the texts being focused on in various classes (*The Farming of Bones*, *In the Time of the Butterflies*). Being that she was new to the area and very new to the Caribbean and Hispanic cultures, this was a way for her to learn, understand, and ensure that she would be able to make more meaningful connections with her students from the region. Although Méndez grew up in the Caribbean, she was also new to the Merrimack Valley of Massachusetts, where the college is located. She had to learn about the Hispanic/Latinx experience in the area while navigating her own experience. Learning about students' experiences while studying at the College has been one of the main interests of Méndez. She continuously tries to make students feel welcome by speaking Spanish or letting them know they can talk to her in Spanish.

The College's Equity Agenda

While the Library has made various efforts to bring culturally appropriate lessons and resources to students, the College has also acknowledged its diverse community. This has been through multiple sectors of the College, including but not limited to the creation of the Center for Equity and Social Justice (CESJ) in 2020. CESJ's mission is as follows:

> [A]ctively engaging with campus and community partners to identify opportunities for the college to create or contribute to new services and partnerships, or enhance existing ones, that will benefit our students through strengthening their communities, ensuring equity, and addressing social justice needs. (Glenn & Custodia-Lora, 2020)

This has allowed and supported some of the library's efforts to expand its collection, research guides, and services. Although the Center for Equity and Social Justice is in its early stages, Méndez and a fellow Lawrence campus librarian have met with the Lawrence Campus Vice-President to find ways that the library can partner with the Center. Within the initial efforts, the Library and the CESJ have started a digital repository using LibGuides. Méndez has also discussed potential ways to target grant and funding opportunities to incorporate resources that address BIPOC, LGBTTQIA+, diverse functionality, and social justice topics. As of this writing, the library has collaborated and promoted resources that support the CESJ activities (e.g., workshops and guest speakers for Student Life activities).

Along with collection development and the curation of materials, Teoli-Thomason began working on a collection audit at the Lawrence campus library. The audit focused primarily on the fiction and juvenile literature sections and was done to identify the number of BIPOC and LGBTTQIA+ authors the library had. Additionally, Teoli-Thomason used this audit to develop a plan for a more extensive diversity audit of the full collection. Most professional literature and courses available on collection diversity audits focus on children's and young adult literature in public libraries. This information does not always transfer across library types quickly, as Teoli-Thomason noted in her 2020 Massachusetts Commonwealth Consortium of Libraries in Public Higher Education Institutions (MCCLPHEI) presentation on course offerings through *Library Journal*.

All selected resources and materials are assessed for academic, linguistic, and cultural pertinence to the students. In the case of books and databases, the reference librarians identify how these can enrich students' research assignments while targeting potential interests. Each of these materials reflects the themes and topics that students have researched or mentioned as interests. The reference and instruction librarians have incorporated questions within their appointment scheduler that ask students to state the topic they're interested in. This has allowed for data collection showing the most requested topics. The two primary overarching themes of these responses were ways to provide aid to local communities and how to increase the overall quality of life. Within these two themes, race, language, environmental change, and migration have been present. Most of these topics have emerged in the Human Services Seminar (HUS), English Composition (ENG), and Early Childhood Education (ECE) courses. The librarians had a total of 86 appointments during the spring semester of 2021. Méndez alone had 28 students with topics regarding Latinx quality of life and Black Lives Matter.

Topics such as Latinx issues and Black Lives Matter movement have become prominent research subjects for students. As part of the library's efforts to meet the needs of its students, resources and collections have been curated to meet these demands. Additionally, Méndez has been invested in working with the Fenway Library Organization's IDEA (Inclusion, Diversity, Equity, and Accessibility) Committee. Yet, while working to meet social and cultural needs, Méndez and Teoli-Thomason ask themselves: how do we meet cultural competence without falling victim to a trend within academia or tokenizing BIPOC staff members? The increasing demands for diversity and equity in Higher Education have led to the incorporation of services that address these issues. NECC has increased its efforts to expand its offerings regarding student, and faculty/staff services, namely creating the Center for Equity and Social Justice (CESJ) which officially addresses race, ethnicity, sexuality, accessibility, and disabilities in the NECC community. Prior to the inauguration of the CESJ, faculty often addressed these topics in their courses with their students. Some activities and initiatives have centered these topics through projects that have been created in the Center for Professional Development's Leadership Academy, a program for college faculty and staff to develop strategic projects that identify and address needs within the college community.

The library's strategic plan also states the need to increase accessibility, culturally relevant resources, and community engagement to ensure student success. One of the goals that ensure this is within the Equitable Spaces and Services priority. Within this priority, the NECC Library (n.d.) establishes the following goals:

> The Lawrence campus library will be planned and developed as an excellent and inspirational learning space for improved student learning.

> The library will evaluate the accessibility of online and physical resources in an effort to improve the research experience for all users (par. 2).

As mentioned earlier in the chapter, the Lawrence campus library is significantly smaller than its Haverhill counterpart and it serves a greater percentage of Hispanic students. Because of the disadvantages in space, the Lawrence campus library has sought ways to ensure that it provides the same quality of services as Haverhill.

Another theme when it comes to equity in spaces and services is the goal to continually improve access to both physical and online resources. Online accessibility has been an ongoing project for the library, with a primary project being providing dual language (English and Spanish) guides, videos, and tutorials. In the Lawrence campus library, the librarians have actively purchased dual-language books for students. Yet, accessibility is not limited to English and Spanish resources. The library has also sought ways to meet the demands of its visually impaired and deaf or hard of hearing population. One such way that the library did so is by doing an accessibility audit for all LibGuides assets to ensure that all images were tagged with alt-text and that all resources were accessible by screen-reading technologies.

Along with the Library's strategic plan, the College's strategic plan addresses the diverse student population and the importance of meeting their needs. The Integrated Student Experience goal states that the College seeks to "Increas[e] the student sense of belonging and participation in the campus community" (Northern Essex Community College, n.d.d.). It is important to emphasize that a "sense of belonging" is a common theme in the literature related to the BIPOC experience in academia (García, 2019; hooks, 1994; Osei-Kofi, 2014). Hispanic and Latinx students struggle with the sense of belonging in academia and colleges due to the minoritization of their identities and culture, as well as systemic inequalities. Therefore, creating spaces and fostering inclusivity and a sense of belonging in the campus community is one of the many steps that can ensure equity within the College.

Since spring 2021, the College has been working through various committees to create a new version of its strategic plan. In the internal communications, the College administration and stakeholders have recognized the importance of addressing the needs of Latinx/Hispanic students, ESL students, and Latinx/Hispanic faculty and staff.

Social justice librarian and professor Dr. Nicole A. Cooke starts her book *Information Services to Diverse Populations* (2017), stating, "Diversity is ever-present and increasing in our society, and libraries should be able to meet their communities where they are, instead of offering a prepared slate of services and resources deemed suitable for them" (p. 1).

Conclusion

In 1880, the chief librarian at Harvard University, Justin Winsor, published the following statement:

> [W]e have not discovered what the full functions of a college library
> should be; we have not reached its ripest effects; we have not orga-
> nized that instruction which teaches how to work its collections as
> a placer of treasures. (p. 7)

Bringing accessible education to underrepresented groups is at the
heart of community college missions and bringing accessibility to resources is at the heart of our library's mission. Northern Essex Community College, especially its Lawrence Campus, has been a place where
Hispanic students have found an opportunity to pursue a degree or
begin their academic careers. The libraries' services to students aim
to be accessible, pertinent, just, and constructive to their education
and daily lives. Teoli-Thomason and Méndez recognize that their efforts are just the beginning. To them, the library should be a place
where Hispanic students find comfort and nurturing on their path to
higher education. Although we are unable to identify the exact number of Hispanic and Latinx students that are struggling from the issues discussed within this chapter, one must pause and reflect on the
difference in the number of Hispanic or Latinx graduates and that of
other ethnicities, primarily white. In the 2020-2021 Academic Year (see
Figure 1), there were 186 fewer degrees granted to Hispanic or Latinx
students than to non-Hispanic or Latinx students (NECC, 2021b). The
authors acknowledge that there are systemic barriers that impact and
widen degrees conferred. However, the authors' goal, along with the
library staff at NECC, has been to provide a space where Hispanic and
Latinx students can find support. The NECC Library strongly holds the
college's equity imperative, as well as its mission as a Hispanic Serving Institution. Through this mission, the library strives to challenge
the inequities that Hispanic, Latinx, and other BIPOC students face
in U.S. institutions of higher education. It should be mentioned that
through efforts to uphold equity goals, NECC has been able to recruit
two Afro-Latina vice-presidents, various Hispanic and BIPOC administrators, and faculty members. The College is hopeful that these initiatives will close the gap among its Hispanic students. Yet, more needs
to be done, the college is still facing achievement gaps, and continues
to identify its Hispanic population as "at risk." The ratio between Hispanic faculty and Hispanic students is disproportionately lower than

that of white faculty and white students, a trend that is not unique to NECC (Davis & Fry, 2019; NECC, 2021c; Vargas et al., 2020). As the enrollment of NECC's Hispanic student body has grown to almost 50%, this continues to be a cause of concern for the authors. The literature on the topic has shown time and again that BIPOC students feel more welcomed and a stronger sense of belonging if they have BIPOC faculty and staff members around them. As a result of the various DEI initiatives that have been undertaken in academia, the employee demographics are starting to reflect that of the student population (Patel, 2021). For some, this is the beginning of an equitable education, one that will be just for our Hispanic and Latinx students in the U.S. Yet, as women and BIPOC persons in higher education, we must ask ourselves if this is enough?

References

About MACC. (n.d.) Massachusetts Association of Community Colleges. https://masscc.org/about-macc/

About the city. (n.d.) City of Lawrence, Massachusetts. https://www.cityoflawrence.com/501/About-the-City

Arnold, J. (2010). The community college conundrum: Workforce issues in community college libraries. *Library Trends, 59*(1-2), 220-236.

Association of College & Research Libraries. (2016). Framework for information literacy for higher education. https://www.ala.org/acrl/standards/ilframework

Bordonaro. (2020). Overcoming language barriers for non-native speakers of English: Learner autonomy in academic libraries. In N-Y. Tran & S. Higgins (Eds.), *Supporting today's students in the library: strategies for retaining and graduating international, transfer, first-generation, and re-entry students* (pp. 23-37). Association of College and Research Libraries.

Brandle, S., Katz, S., Hays, A., Beth, A., Cooney, C., DiSanto, J., Miles, L., & Morrison, A. (2019). But what do the students think: Results of the CUNY cross-campus zero-textbook cost student survey. *Open Praxis, 11*(1), 85-101. https://www.learntechlib.org/p/208070/

Brown, A., López, G., & Lopez, M.H. (2016, July 20). Digital divide narrows for Latinos as more Spanish speakers and immigrants go online. *Pew Research Center*. https://www.pewresearch.org/hispanic/2016/07/20/digital-divide-narrows-for-latinos-as-more-spanish-speakers-and-immigrants-go-online/

Contrada, C. (2019).Reference and information literacy in the community college library. *Reference & User Services Quarterly, 58*(4),12-16. doi: http://dx.doi.org/10.5860/rusq.59.1.7220

Cooke, N.A. (2016). *Information services to diverse populations: Developing culturally competent library professionals.* Libraries Unlimited.

Cunningham, A. D. (2012). Paradoxes and play: An emergent theory of how community college librarians sustain library instruction programs (Publication No. 3529069) [Doctoral dissertation, California State University–Fullerton]. https://www.proquest.com/docview/1056978551/fulltextPDF/74398FB453AF41A6PQ/1?accountid=37958

Darby, F. (2020, July 16). Sorry not sorry: Online teaching is here to stay. *The Chronicle of Higher Education.* https://www-chronicle-com.ezproxyness.helmlib.org/article/sorry-not-sorry-online-teaching-is-here-to-stay

Davis, L., & Fry, R. (2019, July 31). College faculty have become racially and ethnically diverse, but remain far less so than students. *Pew Research Center.* https://www.pewresearch.org/fact-tank/2019/07/31/us-college-faculty-student-diversity/

Eagleton, M. (2021). Universal Design for Learning (UDL). *Salem Press Encyclopedia.*

EducationUSA. (n.d.) *Community College.* U.S. Department of State. https://educationusa.state.gov/your-5-steps-us-study/research-your-options/community-college

Elshami, W., Taha, M.H., Abuzaid, M., Saravanan, C., Kawas, S.A., & Abdalla, M.E. (2021). Satisfaction with online learning in the new normal: Perspective of students and faculty at medical and health sciences colleges. *Medical Education Online, 26*(1). https://doi.org/10.1080/10872981.2021.1920090

García, G.A. (2019). *Becoming Hispanic-Serving Institutions: Opportunities for colleges and universities.* John Hopkins University Press.

Glenn, L. (2020, March 20). Coronavirus, community colleges, and the equity gap. *Running the Campus.* https://president.necc.mass.edu/coronavirus-community-colleges-and-the-equity-gap/

Glenn, L.A., & Custodia-Lora, N. (2020, September 12). College has a new vision for supporting students, community. *The Eagle-Tribune.* https://www.eagletribune.com/opinion/column-college-has-new-vision-for-supporting-students-community/article_02f0648c-8797-545c-8c6f-c031e58d07e6.html

Greenslade, E. (2021, September 15). Revolving Test Kitchen reopens with new focus. *NECC Newsroom.* https://www.necc.mass.edu/newsroom/2021/09/15/revolving-test-kitchen-reopens-with-new-focus/

Hodge, M. (2020). Online learning through LibGuides for English language learners: A case study and best practices. In N-Y. Tran & S. Higgins (Eds.), *Supporting today's students in the library: Strategies for retaining and graduating international, transfer, first-generation, and re-entry students* (pp. 78-89). Association of College and Research Libraries.

hooks, b. (1994). *Teaching to transgress.* Routledge.

Huerta, J., Winkel, M., & Eisenman, R. (2019). Access to the internet by Hispanic college students: Some findings from a college with a high rate of student poverty. *Journal of Information Ethics, 28*(2), 66-86.

Jhangiani, R. S., Dastur, F. N., Le Grand, R., & Penner, K. (2018). As good or better than commercial textbooks: Students' perceptions and outcomes from using open digital and open print textbooks. *The Canadian Journal for the Scholarship of Teaching and Learning, 9*(1). https://doi.org/10.5206/cjsotl-rcacea.2018.1.5

Leeder, K. (2012). Open access: The community college reconsidered. *Journal of Library Administration, 52*(2-3), 189-198. https://doi.org/10.1080/01930826.2013.853502

Middle States Commission of Higher Education. (2015). *Standards for accreditation and requirements of affiliation.* https://www.msche.org/standards/

National Council of Learning Resources. (2017). *AACC position statement on information literacy.* http://nclr-aacc.org/on-information-literacy/

New England Commission of Higher Education. (2021). *Standards for accreditation.* https://www.neche.org/resources/standards-for-accreditation

Northern Essex Community College. (n.d.a). *Academic ESL–Preparing for classes in English.* https://www.necc.mass.edu/learn/innovative-programs/academic-preparation/preparing-classes-english-esl/

Northern Essex Community College. (n.d.b). *Core academic skills.* https://www.necc.mass.edu/succeed/academic-support-services/academic-advising/core-academic-skills/

Northern Essex Community College. (n.d.c). *NECC is a Hispanic Serving Institution.* https://www.necc.mass.edu/discover/serving-the-hispanic-community/

Northern Essex Community College. (n.d.d.). *Strategic plan 2020: Integrated student experience.* https://www.necc.mass.edu/discover/strategic-plan-2020-goal-integrated-student-experience/

Northern Essex Community College. (n.d.e.). *Student success data–Enrollment age group by term* [Dataset]. https://www.necc.mass.edu/discover/consumer-information/student-success-data/

Northern Essex Community College. (2021a). *All majors by term–Fall 2021* [Dataset]. https://tableaupub.mass.edu/t/NECCDecisionSupport/views/MajorsbyTerm/MajorsbyTerm?%3Aembed_code_version=3&%3Aembed=y&%3AloadOrderID=2&%3Adisplay_spinner=no&%3AshowAppBanner=false&%3Adisplay_count=n&%3AshowVizHome=n&%3Aorigin=viz_share_link

Northern Essex Community College. (2021b). *Successful course completion rates: Degrees awarded (by ethnicity)–Academic year 2020–2021* [Dataset]. https://tableaupub.mass.edu/t/NECCDecisionSupport/views/DegreesAwarded/DegreesAwarded?:embed_code_version=3&:embed=y&:loadOrderID=2&:display_spinner=no&:showAppBanner=false&:display_count=n&:showVizHome=n&:origin=viz_share_link

Northern Essex Community College. (2021c, February 10). *NECHE accreditation Self-Study.* https://www.necc.mass.edu/resources/neche_self-study_2.21.2021.pdf

Northern Essex Community College Library. (n.d.). *NECC library strategic plan 2018–2021.* https://www.necc.mass.edu/library/library-information/library-strategic-plan/

Northern Essex Community College Library [@necc_library]. (2021, March 5b). *There's a new way to pick up library materials and remote print jobs at the Lawrence library! Just look for* [Video]. Instagram. https://www.instagram.com/p/CMDGputnbfp/?utm_source=ig_web_copy_link

Northern Essex Community College Library. (2021, June 16c). *What is NoodleTools?* [Video]. YouTube. https://www.youtube.com/watch?v=fFLXJZ36QC0

Northern Essex Community College Library. (2021, June 17d). *¿Qué es NoodleTools? (What is NoodleTools?)* [Video]. YouTube. https://www.youtube.com/watch?v=WeBigli18Zk&t=0s

Northern Essex Community College Library. (2021, September 1e). *Making an appointment with a librarian using Navigate. Cómo hacer una Cita con una bibliotecaria.* [Video]. YouTube https://www.youtube.com/watch?v=ESwBHlAsaXM

Northern Essex Community College Newsroom. (2016, January 21). *NECC builds partnership with colleges in the Dominican Republic.* Northern Essex Community College. https://www.necc.mass.edu/newsroom/2016/01/21/necc-builds-partnerships-with-colleges-in-the-dominican-republic/

Oakleaf, M., Hoover, S., Woodard, B., Corbin, J., Hensley, R., Wakimoto, D., Hollister, C. V., Gilchrist, D., Millet, M., & Iannuzzi, P. (2012). Notes from the field: 10 short lessons on one-shot instruction. *Communications in Information Literacy, 6*(1), 5-23. https://doi.org/10.15760/comminfolit.2012.6.1.114

Ornat, N., Auten, B., Manceaux, R., & Tingelstad, C. (2021). Ain't no party like a LibGuides party: 'cause a LibGuides party is mandatory. *College & Research Libraries News, 82*(1), 14-17. https://doi.org/10.5860/crln.82.1.14

Osei-Kofi, N. (2014). Race in (out)side the classroom: On pedagogy and the politics of collegiality. En G. Yancy, & M.G. Davidson (Eds.), *Exploring Race in Predominantly White Classrooms: Scholars of Color Reflect* (pp. 162-172). Routledge.

Patel, L. (2021). *No Study without Struggle: Confronting settler colonialism in higher education.* Beacon.

Patterson, D. J. (2011). *Becoming researchers: Community college ESL students, information literacy, and the library* (Publication No. 3499041) [Doctoral dissertation, University of California–Berkeley]. https://www.proquest.com/docview/928947886?pq-origsite=gscholar&fromopenview=true

Quiñonez, T. L., & Olivas, A. P. (2020). Validation theory and culturally relevant curriculum in the information literacy classroom. *Urban Library Journal, 26*(1).

Solis, D., & Espinoza, J. (2021). Entre mundos y fronteras: An exploration of linguistic visibility and value in libraries. In A. Ndumu (Ed.), *Borders and Belonging: Critical Examinations of Library Approaches Toward Immigrants*, (pp. 139-167). Library Juice Press.

Teoli, E. (2020, January). *Refocusing public library-centric courses for use in an academic library setting* [Google Slides]. Massachusetts Commonwealth Consortium of Libraries in Public Higher Education Institutions. http://bit.ly/TeoliMCCLPHEI

U.S. Bureau of Labor Statistics. (2021, September 8). *Healthcare occupations.* Occupational Outlook Handbook. *United States Department of Labor.* https://www.bls.gov/ooh/healthcare/home.htm

Vargas, N., Villa-Palomino, J., & Davis, E. (2020). Latinx faculty representation and resource allocation at Hispanic Serving Institutions. *Race Ethnicity and Education, 23*(1), 39-54. https://doi.org/10.1080/13613324.2019.1679749

Waddell, M. & Clariza, E. (2018). Critical digital pedagogy and cultural sensitivity in the library classroom: Infographics and digital storytelling. *College & Research Libraries News, 79*(5), 228-232. https://doi.org/10.5860/crln.79.5.228

Wengler, S., & Wolff-Eisenberg, C. (2020). Community college librarians and the ACRL "Framework": Findings from a national study. *College & Research Libraries, 81*(1), 66–95. https://doi.org/10.5860/crl.81.1.66

Winsor, J. (1880). College libraries as aids to instruction: Volumes 880-883. *Circulars of Information.*

Zhou, N. (2020, December 1). Up to 50% of university students unhappy with online learning, regulator finds. *The Guardian.* https://www.theguardian.com/australia-news/2020/dec/02/up-to-50-of-university-students-unhappy-with-online-learning-regulator-finds

The NVC Zine Library
Teaching with Zines

Rosemarie Rodriguez

Acknowledgements

I would like to thank my colleagues and Northwest Vista Library Director, Norma Vélez-Vendrell for their support, trust, and willingness to try something new. As well as their help with this article.

Introduction

My name is Rosemarie Rodriguez, and I am an early career, academic librarian at Northwest Vista College (NVC), which is part of the Alamo Colleges District. NVC is a 2-year community college located on the far Northwest side of San Antonio, Texas. In 2019 the Alamo College board unanimously approved AlamoPROMISE which ensures affordability and accessibility for seniors graduating from Bexar County high schools. Students receive free tuition to Alamo Colleges (Donaldson, 2019). Participating high schools were chosen because of their high concentration of economically disadvantaged students and their low rates of college enrollment. Statistics show 63% of the San Antonio community is of Latino or Hispanic origin. For the fall semester of the program's second year, the five Alamo colleges admitted 2,423 students, with 87% of them Hispanic and 6% African American (D'Orio). "This promise investment is going to yield benefits for the community for many generations to come," according to Rosye Cloud, executive vice president of the College Promise Campaign. More than half of Latino college students attend community colleges. They were 27%, about 3.2 million, of the 11.8 million students of all backgrounds en-rolled in community colleges nationally in 2019, according to the Amer-ican Association of Community Colleges (Gamboa, 2021).

Due to the AlamoPROMISE, we have received an influx of first-gener-ation (first-gen) students, many of whom are not college ready. More than 40% of students entering a Texas public institution do not meet state college readiness standards. Among those who are not college ready in math, reading, or writing, only 40–60% meet readiness stan-dards within two years, and only about 25–40% go on to complete a college level course (Toner, 2020). This new generation of students also has a different approach to learning that institutions must accommo-date. Generation Z students have high expectations of their colleges. They want everything to be accessible and tailored personally to them. They learn best through interaction with one another and their teach-ers. In order to meet them where they're at and assist them, the North-west Vista College Library has integrated zines as a solution.

First time AlamoPROMISE college students are required to write a research paper and include scholarly or peer-reviewed sources. For many students this is their first time, or they might be a bit rusty with writing a research paper and the last thing they want to do is read a peer-reviewed article filled with a bunch of jargon and academic lan-guage they don't understand. I believe it's important to introduce stu-dents to what bell hooks has said about education, that "education is the practice of freedom" (bell hooks, 1994). According to bell hooks, university education can only become this type of energetic practice if students and educators experiment and take risks in the classroom. We don't want to scare them away from reading and writing. As an academic librarian my goal is to introduce research to students at a steady pace and through a lot of practice. Returning students, first-gen, and especially veterans have a distinct, and sometimes difficult transition into college. What do first generation college students en-counter when coming inside the gates of higher education? Having a writing assignment that requires only peer-reviewed articles. This ap-proach might not be the best introduction. So, what can colleges do to engage and empower them? We have found out that incorporating zines into the classroom can help repurpose the learning space. Our goal is to continue to incorporate information literacy zines into li-brary instruction but also introduce them to AlamoPROMISE students. Instructors will see that students will see zines as a tangible finished product that engages participatory learning, places a positive impact on self-confidence, validating personal experiences, and the development of critical thinking skills (Creasap, 2014).

What are Zines?

Some might be wondering, what's a zine? The description I like to use when introducing zines to students is that zines are a blend of a traditional research paper and a collage or a mini paper booklet with an origami type fold (Creasap, 2014). In the 1930s zines were known as fan magazine or fanzine for short. They were an outlet for science fiction fandoms. Today, zines can be defined in many ways. They are inexpensive and an organic way for people to feel empowered by self-publishing their work. They allow communities to share knowledge and personal stories. Zines are a way to document everyday life, record history for future readers, and explore authorship. In academia, zines are specifically used for research and learning on topics that wouldn't normally be found in the library collection.

Why do students have an immediate connection with them? I believe it's because they see a finished product that they can touch. They have something tangible that they can walk out of the classroom holding. The significant part is that *they created it*. They can see what their dedication and learning have produced. They can see that they are makers and creators. They get a taste of publication and a self-confidence booster. Their viewpoints matter and their experiences are meaningful, and they can see that with zines. Zines are small but filled with a lot of meaning. They provide a space for thoughts and feelings for people that need to speak out about their experiences. They especially offer fellowship and inclusion to those that are going through the same experiences. Using zines in the classroom entails research, synthesizing information, using critical information literacy skills, and practicing creativity.

Zines have also been a success because they are inclusive, have a personal approach, and are an easy-to-understand document that abandons hard to understand jargon. Have you done research on a topic and wondered, "Why hasn't anyone published anything on the topic I'm looking for?" Well, with zines *you* can. For instance, a student was looking for information on how to care for your body after an abortion. We don't have a published book in our collection on that topic, but we have a zine, and it provides a perspective that puts treatment in the hands of the people experiencing it.

Information Literacy Mini Zine Series at Northwest Vista College

A student can only have one first day. If the start is horrifying, it can easily affect the entire experience. The library I work at is especially mindful of this. We have come up with solutions to adapt to our students' needs. We have developed new programs like the Pop-up Library, which is similar to a paleta cart bicycle where we venture out and take the library to the students. We have also offered new services such as the Information Literacy Mini Zine Series. The Information Literacy Mini Zine Series is used as a supplement in our Information Literacy classes. The Information Literacy Mini Zine series was the start of something magical. It was different, and students were really engaged. I would ask the class if they wanted a zine on Boolean operators and all hands would be raised in the air. Usually when I mentioned Boolean operators during information literacy classes, the students' attention would go out the window, but the Information Literacy Mini Zine Series has been a success because it involves hands on engagement, active learning, and creativity. For instance, I presented Boolean operators for information literacy instruction using emojis and language that students could relate to. I created the Information Literacy Mini Zine Series to help students overcome their fears of research and to bring excitement to the library one-shot. I started at Northwest Vista College as a young librarian with little teaching experience and I was scared of the classroom. The last thing I wanted was for students to fall asleep during my library one-shot. I have discovered that zines are a powerful teaching and learning tool in academia. All I had to do was make a change and try something new. The other zines in the series are *What's a Peer-Reviewed Journal?*; *Imagine, Explore, Create: Welcome to Northwest Vista College–a Guide for New Students; How to Evaluate Sources Using the CRAAP Test;* and a zine on Noodletools, a citation software. Survey results show that the series has had a positive impact on students' learning (see Appendix A). For our students to be successful we need to meet the students where they are at. We found that integrating zines into the classroom was a good starting place. Imagine taking a few pages of 8.5 x 11 computer paper and folding them in half. Now, imagine this paper "booklet" being filled with content you wrote based on research and personal stories, and memories you lived through. Opinions and facts are free to be shared. Topics range from music related writing, gardening tips, political ideology, an archive of photographs from your iPhone, and personal narratives on practically anything. Imagine holding this creation in your hand and then deciding to leave a copy at your local coffee shop. Next, someone comes along and picks it up. They're intrigued and they start to read it from beginning to end. They either keep it or leave it for the next person. You are sharing knowledge and your truth with the world. All we really have is our own story and truth. Take what you need and share the rest with others. So, what does this all mean? It means you are an author, and your work is published for all to read. Who says that authors can only be published in a big publishing press? You have the power to change a person's life through your writing and storytelling.

The Making of the NVC Zine Library

In 2019 I received an NVC Foundation Innovation grant to start the NVC Zine Library at the Northwest Vista College Library. My colleague, Veronica Buendia, and library director, Norma Vélez-Vendrell, joined me in the planning meetings and showed continuous support on this new idea. Every planning meeting we had was documented and saved. We did our research and took a trip to Austin, Texas to visit the Austin Public Library Zine Collection and the Perry-Castañeda Library at the University of Texas at Austin. We even reached out to fellow zine librarians to get an idea on how to organize and catalog zines. (A big thank you goes out to zine librarian, Jenna Freedman of Barnard Zine Library.) After several planning meetings we decided to catalog our collection as well as make it circulate. The cataloging was spearheaded by Veronica. This project would not have run as smoothly as it did without her knowledge and experience. The NVC Zine collection is small but growing, with currently a little over 120 zines. See Figure 6.1. The collection is housed in its own space where students can lounge while studying or reading a zine. See Figure 6.2. We also have zine making kits for check out with supplies for getting started. We encourage students to create zines to be cataloged and used as a resource. To date we have had seven instructors from various disciplines offer a zine assignment or as an option to create a zine as a final project. I am very grateful for the NVC faculty who have been open minded towards the idea of using zines in the classroom and willing to try something new.

Zines have especially helped us create new collaborations between faculty as well as deeper connections with our students. Each semester we have at least one new instructor reach out expressing interest in having the library conduct a Zine Making Workshop for their classes.

Figure 1

Figure 2

It's always a pleasure to teach students about the history of zines and introduce them to this art form.

My Personal History with Zines

I was first introduced to zines in the Fall of 2018 while enrolled in an ALA eLearning course called *Introduction to Critical Information Literacy: Promoting Social Justice through Librarianship*. Zines were presented as a do-it-yourself form of publication. I thought this was an amazing concept that I immediately wanted to share with every student on campus. Little did I know that Northwest Vista would be the first community college in Texas to have a circulating zine collection.

Since 2019 I have facilitated over a dozen zine making workshops, collaborated with instructors on zine assignments, and have taught students about the history of zines and the importance they hold in academia, especially in the classroom. I have also delved into my own zine making. As a person in recovery, I feel like I have a lot to share to the world about what life was like, what happened, and what life is like now. It's not easy being vulnerable, but zines make it less hard. This year for Women's History month I presented a talk on *Zines as Feminist Resistance* at the University of Texas at San Antonio (UTSA). I expressed to students that zines are a gift for marginalized communities, especially people of color, the LGBTQA+ community, and veterans. It's a platform and space for people to express their feelings, opinions, research, and stories on paper for all to read. Zines are something this world needs more of because we especially need more love, support, and valuable information to be shared.

In 2021, I presented *Literary Art of Zine Making* to UTSA's Mexican American Studies Latina/o/x Cultural Expressions Dual Credit class held at Fox Tech High School in San Antonio, Texas and the response was intimate. Students were engaged and very curious. This was their first time learning about zines, and most of them decided to change their final project to a zine. These students are all first-generation college students. Based on feedback (Appendix B), the presentations I have taught have really helped the students understand how important zines are for healing, documenting, and expressing themselves.

I like to ask students what happens after they dedicate hours to research and writing. The responses I get are either a blank face or "nothing." My response is, "I'm guessing that research paper now lives on your desktop or USB drive forever or until it is deleted?" I ask students why not take that information and synthesize it into a zine for others to read? Being able to see their face light up and their eyes widen is priceless. I love seeing their reactions and expressions of excitement, fear, confusion, curiosity, and empowerment.

I always tell students, "There's really no wrong way to make a zine." I remember making my first zine. I was scared and overwhelmed with anxiety. I stared at the blank paper and thought, "How can I do this?" As an undergrad I didn't have anyone tell me, "You can do this!" As an academic librarian I feel my purpose is to help others, teach, and to encourage them along the way. My role is to help students become better researchers and to find their curiosity and passion. When I'm teaching an information literacy class the first thing I do is encourage students to face their fears and just dive in. This is exactly what I do when I present zines to students. The first thing I do is explain how to fold and make a zine. Zines contain content but also can contain images from Community Commons or Canva, illustrations made by hand, newspaper or magazine clippings, or portions of saved ephemera from your life. Zines are often made using the cut and paste method or collage method. They vary in size. They are usually black and white but can be printed in color on any type of paper you'd like. The best thing about zines is the frugality of it all. Zines are fairly inexpensive and can be made and distributed en masse using a copy machine.

Students who are trying to see where they fit in can see themselves in the library zine collection. Students are encouraged to make zines and donate to the collection so other students learn from their experiences and can cite their work. We have had a couple of students donate their zines to the library and they are currently in the process of being cataloged.

Conclusion and Future Plans

Last year my coworker and I received an NVC Innovation Grant to create the Vista Veterans Library. Our campus serves a student veteran population of 15 % and it's a group that the library is wanting to nurture. One of my future plans is to offer a zine writing club for students, but I would specifically like to start with student veterans. Participants will write about what it was like before the military, what it was like during the military, and what it's like currently or after the military. This will give our student veterans an opportunity to write about their experiences. I truly believe there's something spiritual about the writing process and getting stories out on paper for others to read. Everyone has their own truth and each one of us has a significant story to tell. It's important for me to express that we want students to know that they have a choice. They are free to share or not to share with the world. Whether they would rather keep it bottled up inside that's their choice, but we want them to know that we have created a safe space for them to be vulnerable and grow if they choose that path. This is what libraries are about, creating a sacred space for continuous learning and growing.

You might be wondering, "How do I help students discover zines?" I suggest advocating for zines. Don't be afraid of to try something different! Bring zines into new spaces on campus. I always try to tie zines into an event that is being offered on campus. Apply for grants, create a Zine LibGuide, and offer zine-making workshops each semester. That's exactly what I did, and I will continue to do in order to help students flourish. Make more zines!

References

About alamoPROMISE. (n.d.). AlamoPROMISE. https://www.alamo.edu/promise/

Alamo colleges launches 2-year free-tuition program. (n.d.). Spectrum News 1. Retrieved October 2, 2019, from https://spectrumlocalnews.com/tx/san-antonio/news/2019/10/02/alamo-colleges-launches-2-year-free-tuition-program

Camille, P. (2020, September 30). *Alamo colleges delays expanding eligibility for PROMISE scholarship amid pandemic.* Texas Public Radio. https://www.tpr.org/education/2020-09-30/alamo-colleges-delays-expanding-eligibility-for-promise-scholarship-amid-pandemic

Creasap. (2014). Zine-Making as feminist pedagogy. *Feminist Teacher, 24*(3), 155. https://doi.org/10.5406/femteacher.24.3.0155

Donaldson, E. (2019, July 15). *Alamo promise set to recruit from 25 local high schools this fall.* San Antonio Report. https://sanantonioreport.org/alamo-promise-set-to-recruit-from-25-local-high-schools-this-fall/

D'Orio, W. (n.d.). *This Texas community college group is offering free tuition – and much more.* The Hechinger Report. Retrieved January 18, 2022, from https://www.alamo.edu/pac/news-events/news/2022/january/this-texas-community-college-group-is-offering-free-tuition—and-much-more/

Gamboa, S. (2021, October 20). *Without free community college, can it still be a game changer for Latino students?* NBC News. https://www.nbcnews.com/news/latino/free-community-college-can-still-game-changer-latino-students-rcna3122

Rodriguez, R. (2022). *Zines at NVC.* LibGuide: Northwest Vista College Library. https://nvcguides.libguides.com/NVCzines

Toner, M. (2020, Winter). *Precision education: As ACCT chair, Dawn Erlandson wants to ensure that community college leaders meet the needs of every student — both in and out of the classroom.* Trustee Quarterly: The Voice of Community College Leaders, 19-21. https://www.acct.org/files/Trustee%20Quarterly%20Winter%202020.pdf

Appendix A

Examples of Survey Results

Course: English 2327-006

1. **What are your thoughts on having to create a zine as part of an assignment for a grade?**

   - I enjoyed it. Good idea.

   - I liked having to try to be more creative.

   - I think it was an amazing idea, introducing a creative outlet to students who are accustomed to a more rigid atmosphere.

   - It was a fun little project that was nice to present.

   - I really needed this, it helped me to relax and have fun.

2. **Do you personally think there are benefits to using zines in the classroom?**

   - Yes. Fun, engaging, and creative. Also makes you think deeply about the subject.

   - I think it is a good way to show students how to publish something on your own.

   - Yes, it's a very creative way to present an idea.

Course: SDEV

1. **What are your thoughts on having zines used as instructional materials?**

   - Rose showed us samples of different kinds of zines. Some reminded me of little graphic novels that I love. This is a fun take on research.

   - Zines on Career Choice was a great way to explore a day in the life of a professional photographer.

- Using zines for instructional materials is a fun creative project. It made me look a little deeper about my career choice.

- I liked this assignment about my career.

- I think that zines are extremely helpful and easy to understand.

- I think any kind of brochure or pamphlet will serve the same purpose. Anything similar would be good.

- I believe it is extremely beneficial to have learned about zines so that I know about citation of sources in peer reviews.

- The zine is a helpful way to explore a topic.

- It is very helpful.

- They are really helpful.

- The zines were nice. They're very quick and straight to the point.

- I think it's a fun and engaging way to inform people as long as it is cited.

2. **What are your thoughts on having to create a zine as part of an assignment for a grade?**

- I liked working on the zine booklet. I did my research on what my career was going to provide for me and why I was interested in that particular career.

- I was afraid of making a mistake on my zine at first, but I started to really enjoy this process.

- I enjoyed Rose's presentation on the history of zines from a cultural view.

- I think it is a creative way to learn a little more about your career.

- It was a fun take on research.

- It was an easy and fun way to learn new things.

- It was fun and informative.

- I do not have any thoughts on zines as being a part of assignment grades, but other than that, they are very useful.

- I feel that we should get familiar with the zine book and have the opportunity to work on some.

- I like it, it is so creative.

- It's honestly pretty fun to see how many different ones you can make.

- It was fun. I like creative art assignments.

3. **After learning about zines, do you personally think there are benefits to using zines in the classroom?**

   - One benefit about a zine, I think, is to motivate us. Especially on the topic of career choice.

   - There is focus on information and design.

   - Yes, this was a great project and we had clear expectations on how to complete them.

   - Yes, it is a fun project and you can also be creative making a zine.

   - Working together and seeing what each other came up with.

   - Yes, it's an easy way to read important information.

   - Yes because any interactive activity like this makes for a good classroom experience.

   - Yes because they are incredibly useful for citing sources on articles and peer reviews.

   - It gives a lot of information.

   - Yes, it helps you take or acquire notes in a real organized way.

   - Yes, it is a way of getting your point across quick and easy without having to go through a whole book.

Additional responses:

- The zine materials in the library should have more stuff like decorative tape.

Appendix B

Dual Credit Survey Results

My favorite part of the workshop was...

10 responses

- Making the zine

- Looking at the different types of zines

- How we are making a Zine

- When we became hands on and created our own

- Creating my own

- The history and all the personal stories and connections!

- I enjoyed when we got to see actual zines

- When we physically were able to look at the zines

- I liked when she talked about her friend that passed, cause I've been experiencing the same thing for the past few months.

- Making a zine

Inclusive and Culture-Enhancing Programming in the Academic Library
The Día de los Muertos Celebration in Context

Stephanie B. Fletcher
Beronica Avila
Jill Bambenek
Molly Mansfield

Introduction

Dominican University is a private, Roman Catholic-affiliated university located in suburban River Forest, Illinois. The university's mission, rooted in its relationship-centered Sinsinawa Dominican identity, is to prepare students to pursue truth, give compassionate service, and participate in the creation of a more just and humane world. A significant percentage of the student population is self-identified Hispanic, totaling 63.4% of undergraduate and 24.2% of graduate students in Fall 2021 (Dominican University, 2021). Dominican has been recognized as a Hispanic Serving Institution (HSI) since 2011 and is actively expanding its services and educational opportunities for Latine students through a Title V grant that supports career development services, financial literacy, student support services, and advising. The socio-economic effects of COVID-19 on the Dominican community, many of whom are students who commute from traditionally underserved Black and Brown neighborhoods in nearby Chicago, further activated the necessity of creative and reactive support services across the university, including within Dominican's Rebecca Crown Library.

The purpose of this chapter is to provide a model for Latine-enhancing programming in academic libraries of HSIs. It describes Dominican University's 2020 Día de los Muertos program, co-organized by Rebecca Crown Library and University Ministry; enumerates and analyzes the elements of the program; and demonstrates how the production team enhanced, expanded, and improved aspects of the program for the 2021 celebration. This chapter places the components of the Día de los Muertos program within the context of ongoing library and university-wide diversity, pedagogical, curricular, and Latine-serving initiatives. We demonstrate that the Día de los Muertos event at Dominican University is representative of the robust, collaborative, and inclusive programming essential to academic libraries at HSIs, which in turn amplifies and enhances the voices of their students.

Literature Review

A growing body of literature exists on HSIs and the university services that support students at these institutions, such as student affairs offices, faculty or academic senates, a curriculum that centers on justice and equity, and financial aid support. Topics include assessing HSIs; academic success, student retention, and graduation rates of Hispanic students; pedagogy at HSIs; and the organizational identity, culture, and racialization of HSIs (Garcia, 2019; Contreras & Contreras, 2015). In her book *Becoming Hispanic-Serving Institutions: Opportunities for Colleges and Universities*, Garcia (2019) emphasizes that two ways, among others, to better serve Latine students are to provide programs and curricula that are grounded in justice and equity, and to preserve the Spanish language by maintaining and enhancing cultural and linguistic customs. This chapter explores these two points within the context of the Día de los Muertos celebration.

Literature on the ability of academic libraries to serve underrepresented groups and diverse populations complements the work of Garcia and others, although few studies specifically consider library programming designed especially for Latine students at HSIs (Walter, 2005). The literature does explore topics like library instruction, the use of library materials, library space, and other factors that correlate with student success. However, library materials, space, and instruction are not the only services that academic libraries offer in their efforts to support Hispanic students. As Murray (2015) states, high-impact practices – engaging practices that require considerable time and energy from students – are exceptionally suited to take place in the academic library. High-impact practices include first-year experiences, undergraduate research, collaborative projects, learning communities, and common intellectual experiences, as set forth by the American Association of Colleges & Universities (Murray, 2015).

Some authors report successful library programs and displays, especially when the library partnered with other entities on campus. One academic library program that built community around a library display project is the University of the Pacific's Diversity Book Display Initiative, which was a partnership with that university's Multicultural Affairs office. An outcome of this program was that students from across diverse cultures saw library staff and faculty as allies in the creation of a campus environment that fostered inclusivity and social justice (Maloney, 2012). In another example, Walter (2005) states that a collaboration between the University Libraries and the Multicultural Student Center at Washington State University had the potential to positively impact information access and use among students of color. Finally, Dabbour and Ballard (2011) at California State University, Northridge analyzed Latine use of library and information literacy results, concluding that the library may need to redesign outreach, pedagogy, and assessment methodologies to improve information literacy among their Latine student population. Together, these sources demonstrate that academic libraries must understand the information, academic, and social needs of Latine students and build relationships with them that encourage library use and trust.

Partnering with student services beyond the library – such as writing centers, career centers, or multicultural centers – enables libraries and their partners to move toward the shared goal of a campus environment that supports diversity. In her article on libraries and minority student services, Love (2007) encourages academic librarians to identify and secure partnerships, then take steps to ensure these partnerships are lasting, effective, and willing to assess and improve their services. Benefits include increased library use by minority students; the creation of trusted and allied partnerships across campus; and a demonstration of the library's commitment to diversity initiatives. In their subsequent article, Love and Edwards (2009) discuss in greater detail how to identify, cultivate, and sustain a successful relationship between an academic library and a student services collaborator. In the case of the Rebecca Crown Library, University Ministry had sponsored a Día de los Muertos program in previous years, so librarians recognized the opportunity to partner with University Ministry, expand the program, add information literacy elements, and center it within the library space. The library assessed the impact of the program and then enhanced it in 2021, building a stronger relationship with University Ministry and capitalizing on the departments' shared outreach efforts.

Finally, academic libraries at HSIs must personalize their services in response to the ways Latine students utilize the library and contribute to the overall community of the university. "Focusing on and highlighting the positive contributions Latinos make to the college community," writes Bladek, promotes cultural diversity, respect for other cultures, and recognition that our differences foster creative and innovative thinking (Bladek, 2019, p. 23). Thus, academic libraries are called to recognize and promote these diverse communities, which in turn leads to creation and innovation.

Rebecca Crown Library as a Culture-Enhancing Space

The motto of Dominican University, as a Sinsinawa Dominican-sponsored institution, is to prepare students to pursue truth, give compassionate service, and participate in the creation of a more just and humane world. Rebecca Crown Library's collections, hiring practices, spaces, and programming support Dominican students in these pursuits by building an inclusive community and collections. Social justice became a rally cry on campus in 2020, as it did across America, and the library supports these social justice efforts by partnering with the Title V office to develop equitable open-access teaching materials; collecting in the areas of social justice, antiracism, inclusive pedagogy, and diversity studies; and sponsoring events, displays, and programming that explore racialization, LGBTQ lives, Latine and indigenous cultures, racism, and anti-racism. We provide a space where all students can access library resources and study space, and we want students to feel accepted and welcome. We help meet the university-wide goals of truth, service, and social justice by developing in-person programming, digital collections and research guides, and annual programs and events inclusive of cultures, spiritualities, and ethnicities that challenge white norms and traditions.

At Rebecca Crown Library, staff and faculty build community and diversity in several ways. One example is a renewed effort to collect Spanish-language books, graphic novels, and films in disk and streaming format. Supervisors hire bilingual student workers, when possible, and encourage them to communicate with library patrons in whichever language is appropriate. We are expanding our print and digital collections on the topics of social justice and equity, and we use these resources to support library programming as well as instruction and learning across the university curriculum. Library instruction staff and faculty make efforts to build more equitable and inclusive lessons and learning spaces, both in-person and online.

Recent renovations at Rebecca Crown Library redefined the space and reaffirmed our role as a campus hub for research, study, and collaborative learning. The library building itself is a mid-century structure connected on all four levels to historic Lewis Memorial Hall, home to Rosary College of Arts and Sciences and many of Dominican's student services, such as the admissions office; the offices of financial aid, the registrar, and student accounts; and the Support Center for technology and ID card services. In spring and summer 2020, an extensive remodel of the building created the Learning Commons, a space on the main floor that offers centralized student support services (see Figure 1). The Learning Commons includes the circulation and reference desks; the library-staffed WeatherTech Innovation Lab (WIL); an accessible library instruction classroom; the Academic Success Center,

Figure 1   The Learning Commons on the main floor of Rebecca Crown Library at Dominican University.

which houses testing spaces, tutoring support, and Accessibility and Disability Services; and the Student Success and Engagement (SSE) offices. This new physical layout, encircling the library's central staircase on its bright, busy main level, enables students to locate a variety of services in one space. The Learning Commons design visually and spatially integrates the library with other university departments that advance student success.

When library staff and faculty returned to the renovated space in August 2020, they faced a new challenge: How to best utilize the newly remodeled and reconfigured space to welcome the university's diverse student population and use that space for creative and inclusive instruction, displays, library services, and programming? Garcia (2017) writes that one way to serve Latine students at HSIs is for faculty, staff, and administrators to serve as institutional agents who actively work to disrupt barriers to success for Latine students and who thereby help create a Latine-serving culture on campus. Another way to achieve a supportive campus culture is to involve students' families and communities (Montiel-Overall, et al., 2016). As such, library faculty and staff determined that one focus of the new space, and especially the innovation lab, must be culturally accessible programming that fosters a sense of community and familiarity – especially during the socially isolating months of late 2020. Therefore, the centerpiece of the library's fall programming was the Día de los Muertos event held in the WIL during the first week of November 2020.

Further, Garcia (2019) writes that "providing an experience that is racially and culturally enhancing for minoritized students is a form of serving them" (p. 49). She continues that traditionally white institutions should "provide spaces that not only recognize minoritized students' ways of knowing and being, but enhance their sense of belonging, engagement, racial and ethnic identity, and personal knowledge of self" (Garcia, 2019, p. 49). The Día de los Muertos program in 2020, and then again in 2021, encouraged civic engagement and exemplified the diverse programmatic offerings that Garcia states are essential to Latine-enhancing HSIs. In both years, the Día de los Muertos programs included Spanish-language music and recitations, drop-in activities like decorating sugar skulls, and the creation of ofrendas for the campus community to display pictures of their loved ones who had passed away in the last year. These elements helped amplify Latine culture on campus while making the new Learning Commons a center of inclusive activity and a model for Latine-enhancing campus programming.

Library Programming at Rebecca Crown Library

The development and subsequent success of the Día de los Muertos program has its roots in earlier, inclusive library programming efforts. Library staff and faculty have long recognized the value of diverse programming initiatives to decrease cultural isolation on campus and to promote a sense of belonging for every student who walks through our doors. A highlight of the Rebecca Crown Library's early programming efforts over the last ten years was the After-Hours Open Microphone series, located in the Cyber Café on the lower level of the library. The event was well attended and eventually grew into a music showcase, in collaboration with the Campus Activities Board. Survey results collected after each event indicated that students were excited about using the library space in a new way, after regular library hours. In these years, the library was also approached by various student-led groups willing to sponsor and participate in the Open Microphone event. The library, in turn, began to build relationships with student organizations across campus.

Inspired by the success of the Open Microphone event, library employees continued to create programming and monthly book displays. This initial group was specifically interested in enhancing the library's services through programming, but lacked an official outreach and social media team, as well as the dedicated time and funding required to create and execute these events on a regular basis. Nevertheless, there were some successes that grew out of this initial programming group: a popular original-scripted annual Murder Mystery event, created in 2016, with student actors as characters; and an increase in library participation in university events, such as the annual Campus Haunted Tour.

The Media Center in the Rebecca Crown Library – the precursor to the innovation lab – was pivotal in early programming efforts. It developed a reputation as a safe space on campus and was a location for inclusive, innovative, and creative thinking. Two popular and ongoing library programs grew out of this supportive climate: Letters to the Sisters, an annual holiday event established by a student employee in 2016 with the goal of creating and delivering messages of cheer to the Sinsinawa Dominican Sisters; and an annual miniature golf event, introduced in 2017, with a course in the library itself, constructed entirely from repurposed items, 3D-printed objects, and withdrawn books.

The library's efforts to increase diversity in hiring practices also resulted in more diverse library programming, as student employees representing distinct cultures and ethnicities became more involved in the creation and planning of events and displays. For example, student employees participated in creating a diverse cast of characters for the original Murder Mystery script, and another student employee curated a prominent Latine Heritage Month display that highlighted her heritage. This student-centered approach continues with the Día de los Muertos program.

Rebecca Crown Library hired an Outreach Librarian in 2017 and library programming efforts grew more robust. At this time, library services began to focus more acutely on first-generation college students and HSI initiatives. In collaboration with campus partners including Career and Financial Aid Services, the library developed a Game of Life event to teach financial literacy skills and prepare students for life after graduation. In a similar pedagogical effort, an Escape Room Welcome Weekend event for students and their families called on students to use library skills to escape a study room and complete a library scavenger hunt.

The Outreach Librarian position was vacated in 2018 and remains unfilled due to budgetary constraints. As a result, outreach services at Rebecca Crown Library lacked designated leadership until the first Learning Commons Librarian was hired in July 2020. While there are still budgetary restraints that keep the library from hiring more faculty and staff, there is greater success in outreach with the new Learning Commons Librarian and the collaboration across departments.

Pedagogical Goals in the Library

In addition to programming, outreach, and hiring practices, library instruction also contributes to an inclusive and Latine-enhancing environment at Rebecca Crown Library. Library instruction, or information literacy instruction, even plays a role in programming, as it brings the librarians into the classroom or invites the students to come to the library for instruction. Inviting students for an instruction session in the library's classroom, which mirrors the way they are accustomed to learning, gives them a chance to experience the library and learn about its space and programs. When students see themselves reflected in the library space and the instruction itself – through visual cues, content, or programming – they feel more welcomed and comfortable in the space. Instruction librarians also take this opportunity to highlight library programs and events taking place right outside the library classroom.

At Dominican, first-time, first-year students in 2021 were 68.6% Hispanic and 68% commuter students (Dominican University, 2021). Therefore, the library instruction program focuses heavily on working with first-year students and coordinates instruction for core courses such as English 102, which has an information literacy requirement that a librarian always designs, teaches, and grades. In the new Critical Reading, Writing, and Speaking (CRWS) sequence, which paralleled English 102 in the 2020-2021 academic year, information literacy was deliberately integrated into courses to encourage students to learn information literacy theory and skills in a scaffolded approach across their years at Dominican (Dominican University, "Core Curriculum"). In the CRWS curriculum, information literacy is one of six learning outcomes and covers the basics of finding, evaluating, and integrating information and sources. The library instruction program also provides traditional "one-shot" sessions for classes on a variety of topics. These sessions often include activities that focus on information literacy theory and skills development as well as demonstrations of the library resources. This shift from teaching database searching to more heavily focusing on the theories behind information and digital literacy brings information to the forefront for students and helps them better understand the value of information literacy at the college level and beyond.

At least 42% of undergraduate students in Fall 2021 at Dominican were first-generation students (Dominican University, 2021; Tugade, 2021). A shift to helping students understand their information needs, such as how to read a syllabus and what types of resources their assignments require, has become part of the library curriculum as well. Helping students understand that much of what they will do for college may not be the traditional research paper, but will still include research, has also been a shift as more teaching faculty accept a variety of sources beyond the books and journal articles traditionally listed as citations. For first-generation students, the research efforts that instructors require – and the library where this research takes place – can be both mystifying and intimidating. One way to demystify the library is to invite first-generation students into the library space for events that are tangentially related to research and more directly related to the familiar concepts of community, family, and culture. Programming like the Día de los Muertos celebration achieves this goal.

Another technique to make the library more inviting and less mysterious for first-generation Latine students is to offer instruction sessions in Spanish. For example, in the more advanced Spanish classes, such as Business Spanish and Introduction to Hispanic Literature, librarians can introduce the students to the library resources and methods for researching, while also integrating specific library terms in Spanish to help students become more familiar with these words and concepts. This type of instruction for the Spanish classes and the native Spanish speakers on campus enhances their academic experience and bridges the gap between the library and the student. Offering library services in Spanish is one way that Latine-serving institutions can embrace and enhance the language skills of their students (Garcia, 2019).

Another way that Rebecca Crown Library staff and faculty support potential and incoming students from diverse backgrounds is to connect with local high schools and interact directly with future college students. Considering that almost 90% of Dominican University first-year, first-time students are from Illinois, and many of them attend high school only a few miles from campus, the library has hosted local high school students to experience college-level research and instruction (Dominican University, 2021). Trinity High School, another Sinsinawa Dominican-sponsored institution located only a few blocks from the university, visited the library many times before the pandemic for library instruction, reciprocal use of the databases, and one-on-one research consultations (GreatSchools, "Trinity High School"). Rebecca Crown Library has also welcomed students from William Howard Taft High School, which is a public school within the Chicago Public Schools system (Illinois Report Card, "Taft High School"). One goal for these visits is that the students receive an introduction to the demands of college-level research. Another goal is to make the possibility of attending college a more tangible one for the students – especially potential first-generation students. During these visits, librarians and the library instruction team see firsthand at what level high schoolers are engaging with information literacy and research. These mutually beneficial visits were suspended in the 2020-2021 and 2021-2022 academic years, but we intend to resume them when possible.

There are many ways that library staff and faculty can connect with Dominican students, now and in the future. Recognizing that

Dominican is an HSI with a large population of first-generation students is one step to better understanding how to meet the needs of our students. Another step is to design plans that enhance the Spanish language through library instruction: create more instructional materials, including videos, in Spanish; resume offering in-person high school visits from local high schools with large Latine populations; provide more library instruction for Spanish-language classes; and offer workshops in Spanish as an alternative to English. Just like collection development decisions and library programming, instruction services at Rebecca Crown Library aim to enhance and support students' Latine identities and language preferences to create a more inclusive and welcoming community.

Día de los Muertos: Cultural Background and Significance at Dominican University

Día de los Muertos has its roots in Pre-Columbian cultures and beliefs. Before the Spanish arrived in what is today Mexico, the Aztec gave offerings to their deceased ancestors as part of their death rituals. After the Spanish started to exert their own religious practices on the indigenous population, the celebration morphed to incorporate Roman Catholic beliefs and practices, creating a deeply religious, syncretic tradition. Traditionally, the cultural practice of honoring our ancestors involves an ofrenda, also known as an offering or home altar, which honors the memory and the spirits of those who have passed on. The ofrenda includes objects like photographs, incense, candles, flowers, sugar skulls, and food. As with All Saints' Day and All Souls' Day in the Roman Catholic Church, the indigenous celebrations on November 1 and 2 focus on people's connections with their ancestors. These celebrations honor the lives of the deceased by recognizing death as not a sad occasion, but as part of the natural cycle of life, a recognition that those who have gone before are still part of the community. The celebration also embraces local traditions, so Día de los Muertos events and ofrendas vary from community to community across Mexico and the United States.

Dominican University has held a celebration to honor and maintain the expansive traditions of Día de Los Muertos since 2015. When Día de los Muertos was first introduced to the campus community by a University Ministry intern and a collective of students, the altar and its representation were met with hesitation. Certain members of the upper administration worried that some elements on the altar would scare or intimidate individuals on campus, but early organizers realized that student involvement and ownership of the program would prove its value to the campus community. That first year marked student-driven efforts to create the ofrenda that continue to this day: the tradition that students develop and build the ofrenda; the practice of recruiting administrative, staff, and faculty support; and the circulation of the historical background of the Día de los Muertos practice throughout the community. Today, university faculty, staff, administrators, and students work across many departments to develop and implement the Día de los Muertos program. Campus partners include the Nutrition and Dietetics program, the Dominican University Performing Arts Center (DUPAC), the Center for Cultural Liberation (CCL), and the WeatherTech Innovation Lab (WIL) in Rebecca Crown Library.

Although Día de Los Muertos is notably recognized as a Latine celebration, the organizers of the event rely on the universal elements that the tradition holds – the celebration of the lives of those departed – to curate a theme that resonates with Dominican community members and to make the event accessible for them. While not all Dominican students, Latine or otherwise, practice the cultural traditions of assembling an ofrenda, the presence of this significant and recognizable cultural practice is an invitation to participate in whatever way feels appropriate to them. Notably, student organizers have helped the campus partners develop this traditional practice into a more contemporary and personal experience. In addition to honoring deceased family members, students also use this practice to reflect on social events that they feel compelled to mourn and honor. Examples of such events include the shooting in Pittsburgh's Tree of Life synagogue, the Black Lives Matter movement and the loss of Black and Brown lives to police violence, DACA and the suffering of immigrants, and the coronavirus pandemic and the unprecedented loss of life caused by the spread of the virus.

The WeatherTech Innovation Lab and the 2020 Día de los Muertos Celebration

The WeatherTech Innovation Lab (WIL), located in the new Learning Commons, opened in the fall semester of 2020. The WIL is both a makerspace and a technologies lab where students are encouraged to "drop in" to the multidisciplinary space and learn how to work with emerging and interactive technologies. The WIL is the fulcrum for the programming and instruction sessions that the Learning Commons Librarian administers. The greater Learning Commons, a site of experiential learning and peer-to-peer support, promotes collaboration and cooperation among students as they engage with the university's rigorous curriculum. By creating a central, visible, accessible, and student-centered space for collaborative learning, the Learning Commons improves students' academic and social self-concepts. Beyond merely destigmatizing support-seeking behavior, the departments that comprise the Learning Commons – including the Rebecca Crown Library – aim to build an inclusive intellectual community for inquiry, dialogue, exploration, and innovation on campus.

A vibrant demonstration of this model was the WIL's collaboration with University Ministry, the Dominican University Performing Arts Center (DUPAC), and the Nutrition and Dietetics program for the 2020 Día de los Muertos ofrenda blessing and pop-up exhibit, built around the theme "Spirit de la Comunidad." DUPAC contributed their design and artistic talents to the program by painting sugar skull puppets that were placed on display in the WIL. University Ministry and their student volunteers constructed the ofrenda and the programming for the blessing, and Nutrition and Dietetics students, who manage a weekly three-course meal service as part of their curriculum, organized a dinner event inspired by the ofrenda theme (see Figure 2).

Figure 2 The ofrenda and pop-up exhibit in the WeatherTech Innovation Lab in November 2020.

The WIL's first pop-up exhibit manifested during the pandemic as an opportunity to help University Ministry keep their yearly celebration alive and offered an alternative space for building the physical altar as well as the technical expertise to create a virtual programming event. Considering campus restrictions due to the coronavirus pandemic, University Ministry staff were exploring options for curating a virtual ofrenda and event. The WIL team offered to create a pop-up exhibit in the innovation lab to complement the virtual programming that University Ministry developed. The pop-up exhibit provided appointment-only observation of and interaction with the Día de los Muertos celebratory practices for resident students and other members of the campus community.

The pop-up exhibit itself emerged from brainstorming sessions held by University Ministry. Originally, their team pitched the idea of a virtual ofrenda that would showcase departed loved ones from the Dominican community through photo submissions and a curated Prezi presentation. The WIL team counteroffered to use this virtual ofrenda as an anchor for an in-person pop-up exhibit in the innovation lab. In the end, the WIL staff projected the virtual ofrenda presentation onto the lab's center wall, which is visible from the Learning Commons, and filled the surrounding space with a physical ofrenda, puppets, and festive décor to create a more immersive experience that visitors could enjoy either in person or virtually, from the comfort of their home (Dominican Ministry, 2020). A QR code on display in the WIL linked to the virtual ofrenda, enabling members of the campus community who had not yet viewed the ofrenda to access it on their mobile devices. This program impacted students on campus through its presence in the WIL and reached students and their families at home through the virtual, online format provided by University Ministry.

To complement and enhance the altar and virtual ofrenda, the Learning Commons Librarian and student Lab Assistants created a Día de Los Muertos research guide that presented reference and monographic resources on the subject, available through the library in various formats (see Figure 3 and Figure 4). It listed online recipes for Día de los Muertos celebrations and offered contextual information about the celebration and its history (Rebecca Crown Library, "Día de los Muertos"). The research guide also invited collaboration from the library's instruction, reference, and technical services units. The Instructional Services Unit offered support to the Lab Assistants in the curation of materials and content layout. In recognition of the students who led

Figure 3 Día de los Muertos research guide in English.

Figure 4 Día de los Muertos research guide in Spanish.

the development of the 2020 Día de los Muertos program, a student worker in the Access Services Unit translated the research guide into Spanish and a graduate assistant in the Technical Services Unit edited and formatted the translation within the research guide. This collaborative effort resulted in a research guide that offered historical background and traditional practices, recipes, participative activities for students on campus or at home, and a Spanish-language translation that students could share with their family without the additional labor of translating the resource themselves (Rebecca Crown Library, "Día de los Muertos Español").

Program Model for the 2021 Día de los Muertos Celebration

Rebecca Crown Library staff and faculty, led by the Learning Commons Librarian, recognized the success of the 2020 pop-up exhibit and ofrenda and planned to make the 2021 program another inclusive, student-led event. Our first step was to introduce students to the Día de los Muertos celebration. Two months prior to the event, the WIL team hosted an open call with University Ministry for two brainstorming sessions. The call invited participants to attend a tour of Chicago's National Museum of Mexican Art (NMMA) to view, discuss, and draw inspiration from the museum's annual Día de los Muertos exhibition, called "Día de Muertos – A Time to Grieve and Remember." The open call also sought volunteers to craft together the ofrenda at the end of October.

The purpose of the tour at the NMMA was to explore the history of Día de los Muertos through its origins in indigenous communities. Sharing this narrative helped our HSI community view the practice of Día de los Muertos as a tool to recognize and dismantle neocolonial systems of oppression. The tour served as a catalyst and a bridge for members of the Dominican community to better understand the various parts of the traditional Día de los Muertos altar. Therefore, the open call was a crucial element of curating the 2021 altar because it invited the knowing and unknowing to reflect and work together, sharing an understanding that this is a sacred practice.

The organizers, led by University Ministry and the Learning Commons Librarian, held three brainstorming sessions to discuss a potential theme for the ofrenda, unpack immediate takeaways from the tour, plan activities that appealed to the student population, and set a timeline for the construction of the ofrenda. During the brainstorming sessions, conversation leaders inquired about people's feelings associated with the Día de los Muertos celebration and worked with attendees to center the traditions and origins of the event. Those familiar with the celebration readily shared their experiences and suggested resources the organizers could consider. Some of the participants repeated what they had learned from the library's research guide or what most impressed them about the museum tour, while others disclosed their inexperience but also expressed a willingness to contribute.

The brainstorming sessions created active support and increased participation from students, staff, and faculty to be present for the many preparatory tasks leading up to the celebration. They also created a time and space for all participants to reflect on the grief they were carrying. Participants explored how to create space to mourn and heal together as a community. Finally, an overarching goal of these sessions was to discuss potential themes for the ofrenda that would help students express their collective grief while welcoming others unfamiliar with this practice. Rooted in these conversations, participants crafted the theme for 2021: "Nuestras Pérdidas y Esperanzas" or "Our Losses and Our Hopes."

These conversations and subsequent outreach to other campus partners led to a larger, cross-campus event that featured four ofrendas in four different campus buildings: the Learning Commons in Rebecca Crown Library, the second-floor alcove in Lewis Memorial Hall, the Center for Cultural Liberation in Mazzuchelli Hall, and the atrium in Parmer Hall, which is the campus center for the health sciences (see Appendix A). The WIL staff developed a Canva zine that described the locations and explained the "Nuestras Pérdidas y Esperanzas" theme. It included a Spotify playlist, called Angelitos y Airwaves, and referred people to the library's research guide for additional information. A QR code posted at each ofrenda also directed in-person visitors to the research guide on their mobile devices. On the day of the blessing, the connection among the four ofrendas was further emphasized spatially, visually, spiritually, and aurally by the music of a local mariachi band that progressed from one altar to the next, leading the crowd

Figure 5 Procession with mariachi band and other participants during the ofrenda blessing in the Learning Commons in November 2021.

of participants to each ofrenda via song (see Figure 5). A local pastor, who was the University Ministry intern that introduced the Día de los Muertos practice to Dominican, proclaimed a blessing at each stop.

Dominican University is a HSI, but that does not mean that every student who enters the library and Learning Commons is familiar with Día de los Muertos traditions. On the contrary, many students who utilize the library space do not practice or recognize this event in their own homes or community spaces. This factor created an opportunity for the Learning Commons Librarian and the campus partners to introduce the 2021 pop-up exhibit and ofrenda to students who have never celebrated this event. As such, we intentionally created an opportunity for them to share this newfound experience with their friends and families in multiple ways. One month prior to the event, an email to students invited them to participate in the celebration (see Appendix B). It requested the creation and display of artwork representative of Día de los Muertos; invited a contribution of photographs of their loved ones; and encouraged campus community members to contribute their favorite family recipes or a symbol of their favorite food. Participants also had the option of placing physical photos or mementos on any of the ofrendas on campus or submitting them digitally to be displayed in the WIL's pop-up exhibit. Organizers advertised the event via Rebecca Crown Library and University Ministry social media accounts, on Dominican's student intranet site, and in several announcements via email to students, staff, and faculty. To make the ofrendas reflective of the Dominican community, participation across the university was a crucial element in the curation of the ofrendas and the pop-up exhibit. Contributions from the campus community were compiled and published in two Canva slideshows, one for the recipes and accompanying memories for a Día de Los Muertos dinner event organized by the Nutrition and Dietetics students (Rebecca Crown Library, "Recipes y Recuerdos"), and the other for the digital photographs of loved ones who had recently passed (Rebecca Crown Library, "Memorial").

In keeping with the pop-up exhibit model of 2020, the weeklong Día de los Muertos pop-up exhibit commenced on the day of the ofrenda blessing, November 2, 2021. The WIL team, less encumbered by pandemic scheduling and staffing restraints, curated the ofrenda on a larger scale and displayed photos and mementos delivered in person by students, staff, and faculty (see Figure 6). The projection equipment in the innovation lab projected images of the digital photos submitted

Figure 6   The ofrenda and pop-up exhibit in the WeatherTech Innovation Lab in November 2021.

by the community on a loop during that week. Día de los Muertos décor filled the lab's space to create an immersive and interactive environment. The DUPAC once again displayed their Día de los Muertos puppets. Student-created objects were also on display in the lab: artwork relating to Día de los Muertos, sugar skull paintings made by Department of Theatre Arts and Music students, and painted, 3D-printed models of sugar skulls and alebrijes. Library student workers updated the Día de los Muertos research guide and a graduate assistant in the Technical Services Unit converted it into zine form in Canva (Rebecca Crown Library, "Zine"). The Rebecca Crown Library website also featured links to the research guide and the pop-up exhibit on its homepage in the weeks leading up to November 2.

Many of the objects on display were designed and created by students who attended one of the WIL's two in-person workshops, held one week before the pop-up exhibit opened: 3D Print & Paint Calaveras y Alebrijes and Face Mask Sugar Skull Painting. The 3D Print & Paint Calaveras y Alebrijes workshop was the innovation lab's most popular 3D printing workshop of the fall semester with 32 students in attendance (see Figure 7). Materials for the event were: acrylic paint, paintbrushes, palettes, and printed models of sugar skulls and alebrijes in the forms of an owl, a wolf, and a dog. WIL staff located the 3D models on Thingiverse and printed them prior to the workshop. During

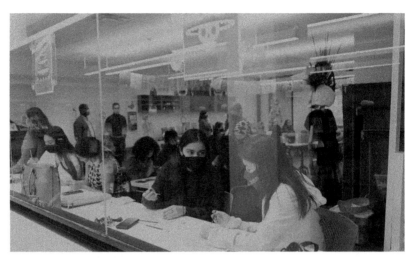

Figure 7 Students gather in the WeatherTech Innovation Lab to paint sugar skulls in October 2021.

the workshop, reference photos of sugar skulls and alebrijes were offered to the students and the 3D printer was available for students who wanted to print out additional models. These pedagogical and creative activities intentionally emphasized cultural competency and supported the university's entire student population through the promotion of information literacy, community building, and inclusivity.

Conclusion

The creative, collaborative, and cross-campus partnerships, led by the Rebecca Crown Library and University Ministry teams, resulted in a substantial turnout of over 60 attendees at the 2021 ofrenda blessing, and several news outlets covered the event, including online editions of the Chicago Tribune (Petlicki, 2021) and the Wednesday Journal of Oak Park and River Forest (Tugade, 2021). The success of the event recalls and reemphasizes Garcia's recommendations to HSIs to develop programs and curricula that are grounded in justice and equity, and to preserve the Spanish language by maintaining and enhancing cultural and linguistic customs. At the heart of the 2021 Día de los Muertos celebration were the student-centered and student-led brainstorming sessions, which clearly resulted in a successful and inclusive program, echoing the advice of the Association of American Colleges & Universities to develop common intellectual experiences and learning communities within the academic library (Murray, 2015).

Throughout the 2020 and 2021 Día de los Muertos celebrations at Dominican University, it was vital to mindfully and respectfully maintain the traditions held to the indigenous practice of Día de los Muertos, and to create space for dialogue to combat gatekeeping by Dominican leadership. While it is important for employees at HSIs to meet Latine students' expectations of representation, it is equally important to provide them space and grant them ownership to demonstrate what self-representation looks like for them. The Día de los Muertos programming exemplifies an inclusive, student-centered experience that aims to bring diverse groups and diverse talents together to create a shared vision. This practice, rooted in tradition yet untethered to spark further creativity and growth, helps us illuminate our shared humanity.

The broader adoption of this culture-enhancing program model, together with an increase in Spanish-language acquisitions, instruction, and research guides, will create an active and engaged community in and around Rebecca Crown Library, where our students will be empowered to take ownership of their visions and aspirations.

References

Bladek, M. (2019). Latino students and the academic library: A primer for action. *The Journal of Academic Librarianship, 45*(1), 50-57. https://doi. org/10.1016/j.acalib.2018.12.001

Contreras, F. and Contreras, G. J. (2015). Raising the bar for Hispanic-Serving Institutions: An analysis of college completion and success rate. *Journal of Hispanic Higher Education, 14*(2), 151-170. https://doi. org/10.1177/1538192715572892

Core Curriculum. Dominican University. Retrieved December 8, 2021, from https:// www.dom.edu/academics/core-curriculum

Dabbour, K. S., & Ballard, J. D. (2011). Information literacy and US Latino college students: A cross cultural analysis. *New Library World, 112*(7/8), 347-364. https://doi.org/10.1108/03074801111150477

Dominican Ministry. (2020, November 2). *Día de muertos altar blessing* [Video]. YouTube. https://www.youtube.com/watch?v=Zp1VOZMOjHA&t=2s

Dominican University. (2021). *Student profile: Fall 2021*. https://www.dom. edu/sites/default/files/pdfs/about/OIE/Fall%202021%20Student%20 Profiles_FINAL.pdf

Garcia, G. A. (2017). Defined by outcomes or culture? Constructing an organizational identity for Hispanic serving institutions. *American Educational Research Journal, 54*(1S), 111S-134S. https://doi.org/10.3102/0002831216669779

Garcia, G. A. (2019). Becoming Hispanic-Serving Institutions: Opportunities for colleges and universities. Johns Hopkins University Press.

Love, E. (2007). Building bridges: Cultivating partnerships between libraries and minority student services. *Education Libraries, 30*(1), 13-19.

Love, E. & Edwards, M. B. (2009). Forging inroads between libraries and academic, multicultural and student services. *Reference Services Review, 37*(1), 20-29. https://doi.org/10.1108/00907320910934968

Taft High School (7-12). *Illinois Report Card*. Retrieved December 9, 2021, from https://www.illinoisreportcard.com/school.aspx?source=studentcharacteristics&-source2=stude ntdemographics&Schoolid=150162990250043

Maloney, M. M. (2012). Cultivating community, promoting inclusivity: Collections as fulcrum for targeted outreach. *New Library World, 113*(5/6), 281-289. https://doi.org/10.1108/03074801211226364

Montiel-Overall, P., Nuñez, A. V., & Reyes-Escudero, V. (2016). *Latinos in libraries, museums, and archives: Cultural competence in action! An asset-based approach.* Rowman & Littlefield Publishers, Inc.

Murray, A. (2015). Academic libraries and high-impact practices for student retention: Library deans' perspectives. portal: *Libraries and the Academy, 15*(3), 471-487. https://doi.org/10.1353/pla.2015.0027

Petlicki, M. (2021, November 8). Ancient and modern Día de los Muertos traditions celebrated at Dominican University. *Chicago Tribune.* https://www.chicagotribune.com/suburbs/river-forest/ct-rfl-dia-muertos-dominican-tl-1111-20211108-voinxg2zxfdonnns4wqpruf4ri-story.html

Rebecca Crown Library. (n.d.) *Día de los Muertos*. Dominican University. https://research.dom.edu/diadelosmuertos

Rebecca Crown Library. (n.d.) *Día de los Muertos Español*. Dominican University. https://research.dom.edu/diadelosmuertosespanol

Rebecca Crown Library. (2021). *Día de los Muertos: Memorial*. Dominican University. https://www.canva.com/design/DAEugUQTb8A/mvAs1oojsmv-VFniZxtboBw/view?utm_content=DAEugUQTb8A&utm_campaign=designshare&utm_medium=link&utm_source=sharebutton

Rebecca Crown Library. (2021). *Día de los Muertos: Recipes y Recuerdos*. Dominican University. https://www.canva.com/design/DAEum2K4hhc/6rKV1bONQCvoaoXb1gnHgg/view?utm_content=DAEum-2K4hhc&utm_campaign=designshare&utm_medium=link&utm_source=sharebutton#1

Rebecca Crown Library. (2021). *Día de los Muertos: Zine*. Dominican University. https://www.canva.com/design/DAEtTkGiCeQ/aJMM71OjtEiXSP6oS6tKXQ/view?utm_content=DAEtTkGiCeQ&utm_campaign=designshare&utm_medium=link&utm_source=sharebutton#1

Trinity High School. *GreatSchools*. Retrieved December 8, 2021, from https://www.greatschools.org/illinois/river-forest/4447-Trinity-High-School/#Students

Tugade, F. A. (2021, November 2). Dominican's festival of four 'ofrendas.' *Wednesday Journal*. https://www.oakpark.com/2021/11/02/dominicans-festival-of-four-ofrendas/

Tugade, F. A. (2021, December 1). The road to success for 1st generation college students. *Wednesday Journal*. https://www.oakpark.com/2021/12/01/the-road-to-success-for-1st-generation-college- students/

Walter, S. (2005). Moving beyond collections: Academic library outreach to multicultural student centers. *Reference Services Review, 33*(4), 438-458. https://doi.org/10.1353/pla.2015.0027

Appendix A

The blessings of the four ofrendas took place at 11:30am on Monday, November 2, 2021. Each stop during the procession is noted below.

1. Meet at Parmer Hall Atrium and bless the altar
2. Mariachi begin playing at Parmer Hall Atrium and lead the group to the WeatherTech Innovation Lab
3. Enter the WeatherTech Innovation Lab for a song and bless the altar
4. Mariachi walk up the library staircase and lead the group to the Center for Cultural Liberation
5. Enter the Center for Cultural Liberation for a song and bless the altar
6. Mariachi led the group to the Lewis Memorial Hall Alcove for a final prayer and bless the altar
7. Procession ends at University Ministry offices where the community gatherers for tamales, pan de muerto, and champurrado

Appendix B

Open Invitation for 2021 Ofrenda Contributions

The following Open Invitation was a Google Submission Form that was emailed to the university community and promoted across campus. This approach invited the Dominican University community to participate in the ofrenda project in a variety of ways. Significantly, the Open Invitation encouraged students, faculty, and staff to submit content that reflected the diversity of our community.

Dear Dominican Family,

As in years past, our celebrations of the cultural traditions of Latine/a/o communities in the United States and Latin America continue! We are pleased to share that this year's theme of the ofrenda will focus on "Nuestras Pérdidas y Esperanzas; Our Losses and Our Hopes." This year we will be showcasing 4 Altars and will be in the following locations:

1. 2nd floor Lewis Alcove

2. Parmer Atrium

3. Weathertech Innovation Lab (WIL)

4. Center for Cultural Liberation (CCL)

We are looking for multiple submissions that will help us celebrate and honor all walks of life and expressions in our DU Community:

Digital/Physical Photos: We welcome the memory of your loved one, please bring a physical photo at any one of these altars beginning Monday, November 1st. Digital photos will be portrayed in the Innovation Lab. The blessing will take place on Tuesday, November 2nd at 12pm. People should gather for the blessing of the altars in the Parmer Atrium. Mariachis will then lead us to the WIL, then the 2nd floor

Lewis Alcove, and end in the CCL, followed by convivencia in the Ministry Center. We will be serving tamales!

Artwork: The Innovation Lab is holding an open call for art to be displayed as a part of this year's Pop-Up Exhibit. Día de los Muertos is a celebration of life and loved ones, artists are invited to submit work that reflects such spirit and themes. Your work will be publicly displayed during the week of November 1st–5th in the Innovation Lab, located in Rebecca Crown Library. Please submit your artwork the week of October 25th. For questions you may have, please email InnovationLab@dom.edu.

Recipes y Recuerdos: We recognize that food is at the heart of faith, culture, and relationship. Favorite foods are one item that people place on their ofrendas in order to remember those they love who have died. You're invited to symbolically bring food to our shared DU altars through story. Please share a specific food that reminds you of a person you'll be remembering at our celebrations and tell us why it makes you think of that person.

Thank you for your willingness to consider submitting a remembrance or artwork as part of the 2021 Día de los Muertos Altars at Dominican University! We thank you for your thoughtful and respectful contributions to this sacred space and practice.

Section 3
Establishing and Growing Representative Collections

Collaborating through Collections
The Male Success Initiative, Fullerton, Men of Color Collection

Anthony Davis Jr.

Introduction

Academic libraries seeking ways to directly impact retention and success for underrepresented students should consider outreach through access and technical services. Cross-divisional collaborations between libraries and campus retention programs in student affairs can provide opportunities for libraries to have an impact on Hispanic students and other students of color. At California State University, Fullerton (CSUF), a Hispanic Serving Institution, the Male Success Initiative (MSI), Fullerton program and the CSUF Pollak Library are partnering on a $15,000 faculty intramural Research, Scholarship, and Creative Activity Grant to build a circulating collection for the MSI, Fullerton Center. This chapter describes the creation of the MSI, Fullerton Men of Color Collection and explores the ways that cross-divisional partnerships based on collections can expand the library's impact on diversity, equity, and inclusion and bolster campus retention strategies for young men of color.

California State University, Fullerton

Among the largest campuses in the nation's largest public university system (California State University, 2021), California State University, Fullerton ranks No. 3 in the nation for baccalaureate degrees awarded to underrepresented students (California State University Fullerton, 2021). As a Hispanic Serving Institution (HSI) and Asian American and Native American Pacific-Islander Serving (AANAPISI) eligible institution, the university has intrinsically incorporated support for diversity into its mission and institutional strategic plan.

CSUF has over 41,000 students: 46% Hispanic/Latinx, 20% Asian, 18% White, 3% Multi-racial, 2% African-American; .2% Pacific Islander, .1% Native American, 58% female, 41% male, 48% underrepresented, and 31% first-generation students.

Founded in 1957 in Orange County, CA, the university has 55 bachelor's programs, 55 master's programs with doctoral programs in Education and Nursing Practice. The CSU libraries operate as a 23-campus consortium. Pollak Library is also an affiliate of the Statewide California Electronic Library Consortium.

MSI-Fullerton

The California State University, Fullerton MSI supports the retention and academic success of all undergraduate students who self-identify as men of color: African-American, American Indian, Asian-American/Pacific Islander, Hispanic/Latino, multiracial men, and men of trans experience. Originally starting in 2013 as an African-American male leadership institute to improve outcomes and narrow the achievement gap for African-American men, the program expanded in 2014 to support all men of color (Male Success Initiative, 2020).

To increase retention and graduation rates, MSI-Fullerton has tailored academic and career counseling and programming that not only builds community between the brothers but also validates their sense of belonging. MSI is also a scholar's program (MSI-Scholars) that awards scholarships to encourage retention while also allowing any man of color from the Cal State Fullerton community to join and participate (MSI-Fellows). While much of the programming is geared to the first-year experience, students often participate as upperclassmen up to graduation.

There are currently 66 MSI-Scholars and 17 MSI-Fellows. The MSI community is 42% Hispanic/Latino, 27% African-American, 10% Asian-American, 4% Multi-racial, 1% Native Hawaiian/Pacific Islander, and 1% White. The program has a 93.5% retention rate and an average GPA of 3.2.

The MSI-Fullerton Center opened in 2019 where, in addition to staff offices, they have a shared multi-purpose student study space where we plan to make the Men of Color Collection available.

The Men of Color Collection

Unlike other departmental library case studies, instead of making a previously existing collection accessible, we started the Men of Color Collection from scratch. We had to come up with a list of books to buy and furniture to put it on, so these needed to be done before the acquisition, cataloging, and circulation of the collection could be performed. But starting from nothing, all considerations around the collection had to be planned concurrently. We held bi-weekly meetings with the MSI-Fullerton staff to determine a process for collection development and met with leaders in Access Services, Acquisitions, and Cataloging and Metadata Services as needed to prepare for the workflow once the collection development decisions were made.

Process

Being approached by the Director of the Male Success Initiative (MSI), Fullerton program to help set up a satellite collection inside the MSI Center was an intriguing prospect. I wasn't particularly familiar with the work nor am I an expert on diversity. As a Copyright & Policy Librarian and faculty member, I serve as the campus intellectual property policy analyst with responsibilities in technical services for the licensing of electronic resources. Aside from selecting databases for inclusion into the Pollak Library's collection, I have no prior collection development experience. Rosemary Farr, a colleague in a staff position in interlibrary loan, informed me she was looking for diversity projects to support. I told her about the opportunity to collaborate with the MSI program and she joined me in working on the project.

Together, we went to the MSI-Fullerton Center and had a meeting with the Director and his staff. We started to hash out some rough ideas about what kind of collection he'd like to create and how we were going to go about it. At that time, we determined that the collection would relate to all men of color, masculinity, and brotherhood, developed around the department's guiding framework, the four MSI-Fullerton Pillars of Potential (Male Success Initiative, 2021):

1. Academic Coaching/Tailored Mentoring

2. L.E.E.D.-Leadership. Engagement. Enrichment. & Development.

3. Career Trajectory

4. Gender and Masculinity

Shortly afterward, I spoke with the Associate Dean for Collection Processing and Services. Based on our conversation, she agreed that the unit would provide acquisitions and discovery support for the MSI-Fullerton Collection if we could secure the funding. This was a tremendous in-kind gift, leveraging the library's technical services workflow to process, purchase, and provide metadata and discovery services for the collection.

Responding to a call for proposals, we applied and were awarded a faculty Research, Scholarship and Creative Activity grant of $15,000, an intramural grant from the Cal State Fullerton Office of Research. The MSI-Fullerton Men of Color Collection project would require high amounts of collaboration and coordination between the MSI Director and his staff and the Pollak Library. As Principle Investigator (PI) of the grant, I was the primary go-between and project manager. The MSI Director was Co-PI and Rosemary was Senior Personnel.

Literature Review: Male Success Initiatives

Writing about multicultural outreach, Walter and Eodice (2007) said, "collaboration with student affairs professionals must also be grounded in the language found in their literature and practice" (p. 220). One of the challenges of robust collaboration is the time it takes to familiarize oneself with the language, mission, and strategy of the partner organization. Over the past 25 years, many universities have begun male success summits, institutes, initiatives, and centers to counter the abysmal statistics in retention and degree attainment for African-American males and other men of color (Williams, 2014, pp. 122-25).

To familiarize myself with underrepresented male retention efforts, I attended the Academic Impressions conference, Comprehensive Student Retention Strategies for Men of Color (Brooms, Moore, & Patton, 2021). From that conference, I gleaned that practitioners in the field focus on successes not deficit narratives (Harper, 2014, p.135). The dominant strategy is to reveal and build up enough positives in the young men to outweigh the risk factors and challenges they will face.

One of the presenters and facilitators, Dr. Derrick Brooms at the University of Tennessee, Knoxville, has published extensively on his work with retention programs for African-American and Latino men. In his co-authored book, Empowering Men of Color on Campus, the authors (Brooms, Clark, & Smith, 2018) suggest taking a "strengths-based approach" (2018, p. 21). Rather than think of these students as the problem, one can choose to see their value as a community and to the community. In doing so, the authors challenge "educators and practitioners to affirm the communities students bring with them to college and to cultivate communities on our campuses that will lead to students' success" (2018, p.5).

In seeing community as a form of capital, the authors built upon Tara Yosso's Community Cultural Wealth Model, a critical race theory that shifts focus from the poverty and disadvantages of marginalized communities to highlight the knowledge, abilities, and navigational prowess of students of color (Yosso, 2005). There is significant social, cultural, academic, and leadership capital among young men of color (Brooms et al., 2018, pp. 67-89).

Social capital also resides in the idea of brotherhood. Men in the MSI program refer to each other as brothers and the MSI Director wanted brotherhood built into the collection so that concepts of masculinity and gender could be explored as a community rather than in isolation. Brotherhood also reduces competition by building trust and a shared language among men of different races. "Black and Latino males often come from communities that pit them against one another. Linguistic capital is a powerful tool that can be used to deconstruct the negative messages they receive about one another and motivate them to work together to achieve success" (Brooms, et al., 2018, p. 22).

Men of color are also placed in competition with women of color (Gordon & Henery, 2014, p. 22; Harper, 2014, p.131). Because Black women have statistically outperformed Black men in educational attainment, little attention has been paid to them while Black male success scholarship and programming has proliferated (Harper, p.133). Despite the fact that Black women face many of the same issues on campus as Black men, Black male research has overshadowed research concerning all other racial groups as well as Black women who continue to be marginalized and underserved (Harper, p.137).

In the excellent work, Men of Color in Higher Education: New Foundations for Developing Models for Success edited by Ronald Williams (2014), scholars apply feminist theory to examine men of color and the barriers to success they experience under the oppression of patriarchy. As a librarian working on the development of the MSI Collection, it was helpful to understand the unique challenges of each of the four major racial categories in the academic setting.

Sáenz and Bukoski's (2014) chapter on Masculinity through a Latino Male Lens makes the challenges of Latino masculinity in the first-year experience salient. Highlighting how Latino men entering college face a "border-crossing" (p.105), they explain the dilemma of machismo as the students transition from high school to the college context. These young men may forgo asking for help believing that they must do it all themselves (pp.100-102). At risk of being lured away to be a provider for their families, it is vital that they experience community in the first year and find successful mentors, peers, and models for engagement (pp.108-109).

Asian American and Pacific Islander (AAPI) students are lumped together, but come from 48 different ethnic groups with 300 different languages (Teranishi & Pazich, 2014, pp. 39-40). Despite being from different regions with different social and academic characteristics, these subgroups face a common "model minority" myth that they may internalize and try to live up to, an impossibility since a model minority doesn't exist (p. 49). They are also weighed down by stereotypes that they are more introverted, apologetic, and perpetual foreigners lacking the aggressive traits that characterize masculine gender performance (p. 38). AAPI students need support to transcend the model minority myth and the freedom to acknowledge the social and cultural differences that impact them in their pursuit of degree attainment.

Native Americans and Alaska Natives face the invisibility of their culture and historical erasure perpetuated by a treaty-breaking United States government (Bitsóí & Lee, 2014). Respect for indigenous perspectives and setting up a "home away from home" (p. 71) is crucial for support of the indigenous students who may not see the attainment of a four-year degree as the measure of success in their community (pp. 62-63).

Under the narrative of crisis, African-American males may be framed as a homogenous group characterized by incarceration, unemployment, lack of education, and a general disinterest in academic success (Gordon & Henery, 2014, p.1; Harper, 2014). Instead of framing African-American experiences on these deficit-based narratives, interventions need to be designed based on the experiences of those who succeeded (Harper, 2014, p.128). Programs also need to focus on African-American men as gendered beings (pp.128-129).

Utilizing the Black feminist theory of intersectionality (Teranishi & Pazich, 2014, pp. 35-36), an additional challenge emerges that anyone within any of these groups may come from different ethnicities, social classes, sexual identities and orientations, or immigration statuses. Any collection we would build would have to be nuanced and responsive to the unique challenges of persistence that any of these men faced.

In addition, the collection would need to acknowledge that what all young men have in common is that they are all searching for a path to respectability (Gordon & Henery, 2014, pp. 24-28). They need to be respected for who they *are and who they will become. Young men will pursue respect, legally or illegally* (Sáenz and Bukoski, 2014, p. 87), in an effort to attain the typical markers of success associated with capitalism or merely through reputational means that glorify antisocial behavior (Gordon & Henery, 2014, pp. 24-28). This is why respected men of color role models in the academy are vital to retention efforts. They present an alternate path to being respected that may not be readily available in the community or through popular media (Sáenz and Bukoski, 2014, pp. 108-109).

With this understanding, we were able to apply these values to the collection effort and formulate an aspirational statement of purpose that we used in our grant application:

The MSI Collection Project seeks to support the MSI brotherhood with a tailored, discoverable physical collection in the MSI Center and a complimentary electronic collection through the Pollak Library's online catalog, OneSearch. The goal of any library collection is to reflect the diversity of the community served. The physical collection will transform the MSI Center into a space that reflects the brothers' unique cultural experiences and encourages them to realize their full potential. Like all modern academic libraries, it will seek to make learning visible and empower the students to engage with questions of profession and identity in a campus center that validates their sense of belonging.

Outreach to Departmental Libraries

At the University of New Mexico, Sharon Moynahan (1999) saw the potential for the catalogers to do outreach, recommending "insourcing" the cataloging of departmental collections by having catalogers travel to departmental libraries to capture the collection data and make it available to the campus population, a strategy to increase the library's standing on campus and fight cuts due to limited budgets. Her work details three case studies of cataloger outreach to a Native American Studies Department reading room, the Clark Field Archive Library in the Department of Anthropology, and a special library within the Alliance for Transportation Institute.

At Southern Connecticut State University, Toce and Schofield (2011) illuminated the potential for technical service librarians to perform outreach in unique and meaningful ways, distinguished from public services, with several examples of technical service librarians creatively participating in the academic community to raise the profile of the library across the institution.

At Grand Valley State University, Roth and Daniels (2015) described how "back of the house" staff stepped forward to partner with other organizations on campus. "Through both deliberate partnerships and chance encounters" (p. 437) small departmental libraries incorporating materials into standing workflows increase discoverability exponentially. They made collections accessible for the Office of Undergrad Research and Scholarship, the Women's Center, the Faculty Teaching and Learning Center, the Office of Student Life, and the Annis Water Resource Institute. Department collections were cataloged into the integrated library system (ILS). Each location developed their own loan rules and some installed a local instance of the ILS for circulation.

Elguindi & Sandler (2013) championed using the ILS as a tool for collaboration with campus partners at American University. Conceiving of the library ILS as a campus-wide system, they were able to catalog five existing partner collections, both book and media collections as well as audiovisual and computer equipment. "Although it is a complex undertaking that can be full of politics and additional work for what may be an already busy cataloging staff, bringing student affairs and departmental collections into the library's ILS is a major form of outreach that can be performed by the technical services area of the library" (p. 295).

Laura Turner (2017) at San Diego State University found success making collections accessible for the Hoehn print study room, the Joan B. Kroc Institute for Peace and Justice, and the United Front Multicultural and Women's Center library through the main library's ILS. She writes,

"This type of arrangement requires a collaborative mindset and good communication to build strong and lasting partnerships" (p. 61).

Not every example of outreach was successful. Evans and Tilton (2010) documented the need to undo integration and expunge departmental library records from the ILS at Bowling Green State University. These changes were requested by the departmental libraries because of user confusion over differences in hours of operation, challenges with consortia agreements, and in some cases, these small libraries just couldn't keep up with the increased demand that exposure through the ILS brings with it. In these cases, dismantling integration and switching to a closed catalog was a better solution for some collections. The authors documented how, in answer to a politically sensitive situation, instead of performing an ILS integration, they created and implemented a separate catalog using WordPress Multi-User software. This enabled the Theater Studies Department to catalog and circulate a prestigious video collection independent of the main library.

There is ample precedent for collaborations between academic libraries and other student services, especially with Writing Centers (Ferer, 2012) where close collaborations between the library and writing center staff have flourished. LeMire and Bellestro (2019) documented how they had success at Texas A&M implementing a LibraryThing catalog for a Veterans Resource Center textbook collection. With Student Affairs, as the aforementioned case studies attest, LGBT+, multicultural student centers, women's centers, and career services (Holislister, 2005) have all benefited from academic library collections collaborations.

A greater degree of collaboration is necessary for successful outreach to multicultural student service centers, especially for underrepresented students. At the University of Arizona, Elaina Norlin (2001) highlights the necessity for "switching from passive to active mode" to perform outreach to minority students that find coming into the library overwhelming. Aguilar and Keating (2009) describe innovative outreach at the University of New Mexico Libraries through their SOS program. Their case study illustrates the importance of meeting students in their space and reflects the nuanced outreach to American Indian Student Services by three American Indian Librarians, "American Indian students are happy to see someone from their community working at the University Libraries SOS program table" (p. 23). While these examples are rooted in public service outreach, the strategies are applicable to technical service outreach as well.

Librarians wishing to perform outreach through departmental collections should expect to have a high level of engagement and collaboration, especially when performing outreach to services focused on retention and academic success for students of color. These student services may not have the skills that we possess for collection development, cataloging, and making collections accessible. Librarians performing outreach through collections will find their skill sets are complementary to student services professionals and through collaboration, there is a high likelihood of raising the profile of the library as a vital player for diversity on campus (Walter & Eodice, 2007, pp. 221-222).

I struggled to find examples of librarians helping departments start their own libraries, but Suzanne Bell in her survey of outreach to departmental libraries mentioned one, the Cleveland Clinic, a medical research organization that provided training and support for departments wishing to start their own collections (Bell, 1995, p.184).

Collection Development

The development of the initial booklist for the MSI-Fullerton Men of Color Collection was conceived as an interdisciplinary community building exercise where we would ask relevant members of the CSU Fullerton community for titles they wished to share or felt would go well in the collection. While the Library would generate the booklist, the Director of the MSI program would give final approval of all titles for inclusion in the collection. This decision was based on the fact that the Director worked directly with the MSI students and would have a better sense of what works would be most beneficial.

We developed a book suggestion form using Qualtrics that was shared with Ethnic Studies faculty, Pollak Library faculty and staff, multicultural center staff, and the MSI students. The form featured an invitation to participate in the inaugural Men of Color Collection and allowed participants to suggest up to ten titles: fiction, non-fiction, poetry, biography, any category of work as long as it aligned with at least one of the pillars. Initially, we did not get many responses, but what we did get was high-quality. I approached faculty and library subject experts directly including experts in African-American studies, AAPI studies,

Chicana and Chicano Studies, the Career Center, and the Center for Boys and Men and received responses directly over email. While not everyone approached had time to develop a list, we received many high-quality contributions this way. We asked the MSI brothers directly in their University 100 Course: Foundations for College Success and Lifelong Learning- BROTHERHOOD section, integrating it into the class as an assignment to provide at least three book titles they wished to share with their cohort. Finally, Rosemary and I looked at bibliographies and reviews to compile a comprehensive list. Our goal was 500 titles.

We were successful in getting the students involved with the collection development through the book suggestion form we developed. We expected a high amount of student engagement to come from the MSI Collection. As soon as the men heard a library was being built, they approached the Director about starting a book club. Anticipating that the social and communal aspects of the collection would allow the brothers to learn from each other, we took their title suggestions seriously knowing they were more likely to enjoy materials that others among their cohort valued. We were also hopeful that, consistent with other examples found in the literature (Elguindi & Sandler, 2013, p. 304), many of these resources were not represented in the Pollak Library's current collection. At the same time, duplication with the main library was not our chief concern. It was more important to us to have the right titles in the space, so if titles were held at the Pollak Library, we still purchased them for the MSI Collection.

The data from that survey was extremely helpful in not only building anticipation for the collection among the MSI cohort, but also allowing us to see what works the students were familiar with and what they wanted to share with their MSI brothers. While many high-quality titles were suggested, there was a visible deficit in what they knew in regards to works based on their own culture. As a result, the Director and his team expressed a desire to lean into the MSI student's thirst for knowledge and build a collection that was more reflective of their heritage and, following an asset-based approach, provided culturally familiar models of academic and career success.

While there would be some classic "men of color" texts, because of the age and historical context of our users, we felt the collection should be primarily made up of contemporary works with all four pillars addressed and a multicultural model where all students could see themselves and their community validated. As it was important that all our racial groups could see themselves represented in the collection, Joseph Diaz's (1994) excellent chapter on Collection Development for Multicultural Studies was a helpful map as it provided a model that addresses both the range of race and the necessity of queer collections for our gay men and men of trans experience.

While race and ethnicity might, as one would imagine, be foremost in consideration for inclusion in the collection, the four pillars of the program were determinative. Yet some things we selected didn't fit neatly into any of the pillars and many works fell into more than one category.

Academic Coaching/Tailored Mentoring: We looked for works that were likely to help students succeed in college. Books with strategies for surviving in college would add to their navigational capital, especially when they, for example, spoke from the Latino male perspective. But we did not exclude authors just because they were not men or of color. We simply prioritized survival guides that were for students of color when available.

L.E.E.D.-Leadership. Engagement. Enrichment. & Development: We looked for examples of leadership among men of color, especially when they had to walk a path through environmental challenges, for example, from the street to the boardroom. A lot of business leadership titles fell into this category along with self-help titles that were not overly faddish.

Career Trajectory: Declaring Your Potential: We looked for works that would encourage career exploration and examples of men of color in different career paths. For example, World War C: Lessons from the Covid-19 Pandemic and How to Prepare for the Next One by Sanjay Gupta shows the Indian-American doctor in scrubs on the cover and addresses a contemporary topic from their lives. We looked for positive examples of men of color operating in all the colleges: arts (especially novels and poetry), business, teaching, health, engineering, science and the social sciences. Some scholarly texts were also included so those that might want to explore life in the academy could also find examples.

Gender and Masculinity: Building Brotherhood through a Sense of Belonging: We looked for works exploring models of masculinity among men of color and themes of fatherhood. Works exploring gender and sexual orientation also fell under this pillar.

We built a spreadsheet of authors and titles with links to Goodreads, Kirkus, and other types of reviews, along with any notes we thought might be relevant. The Director went patiently through each title, read reviews, and approved or disapproved of every title. In the end, almost everything we suggested was approved by the Director, although it was interesting what the Director didn't select and what ideas he found harmful or too much of a fad. It was an opportunity to share librarian ethics derived from the ALA Bill of Rights and to listen to the expertise of the Director and the staff that had direct engagement with the students. Through the process, we came to a mutual understanding of what the collection should look like.

In all, we were able to develop a list of 500 titles for inclusion into the inaugural MSI-Fullerton Men of Color Collection.

Furniture

The Director of the Center hired an interior designer to help us determine how best to fit a small collection into the center space, planning for the initial collection of 500 books. The interior designer suggested a piece of furniture that was more credenza-like for the main room. She designed a plan with a long entryway table with bookends on the top shelf, several levels of shelves, and a more relaxed, informal library appearance that would transform the MSI-Fullerton Center into a welcoming space for communal browsing and socializing around the collection. There were also mounted shelving and display shelves set against the walls. It was an altogether modern design and we were all in agreement over the direction she suggested.

Currently, we have purchased the furniture and are getting final estimates from the university physical plant to have the mounted shelving installed. I walked over to the MSI-Fullerton Center with the Library's Facilities Coordinator and we discussed the plan for furniture and fire and safety requirements. He and I plan to build the furniture together.

Acquisitions and Cataloging

We worked with our Collection Development Librarian and Acquisitions staff to obtain access and training for GOBI, the integrated library system used to purchase books. Through the GOBI interface, as the Director approved titles, we placed the items in a folder for the acquisitions staff to place the book orders. Librarians that are unfamiliar with technical services should be aware that it can take several months for items to arrive, be stamped, and cataloged. In addition, not everything was available through GOBI and we had to work out alternatives with acquisitions staff to purchase books from individual vendors like Amazon.

The cataloging & metadata unit is classifying the collection under a unique local collection title field to identify the MSI-Fullerton Collection. This field will allow adding electronic titles owned by the Pollak Library to the MSI-Fullerton Collection, allowing related titles to be discoverable through the Primo interface that serves as the Library's discovery layer. As the MSI Collection will be discoverable by all faculty and students of the CSUF community, we anticipate visits to the MSI Center by some that may not know about the MSI program or the center space. After discussing alternatives, it was decided that the collection will be shelved using Library of Congress Classification. On the item records that the cataloging & metadata unit are creating, there will be virtual book plates embedded with hot-links to the MSI-Fullerton Center website.

Access and Technical Services

When I presented the MSI Collection Project to the Access and Technical Services units, I did not know if the Library would choose to have it discoverable in the ILS or to use a separate database. The Head of Circulation desired to use our Alma Unified Library Management System because it has the functionality to easily create a separate library for circulation. The separate library in Alma required setting up separate loan rules, hours, and location information. This will allow the MSI-Fullerton Center to circulate and check in materials from the center. In addition, a small Meescan station is being purchased for the Center for self-checkout for the MSI students. The Director decided that while the MSI Collection will be discoverable by the campus community they will only circulate to the MSI-brothers. Community users will see the items as non-circulating in the catalog but may read them in the MSI Center where all are welcome. This will require a list of the MSI-cohort to be delivered to the Head of Circulation each fall to set up the authorizations.

Memorandum of Understanding

Since the beginning of the project, sustainability was always a part of the conversation. To that end, in collaboration with the Associate

Dean, we are developing a memorandum of understanding (MOU) between MSI-Fullerton and the Pollak Library. The MOU will detail the relationship between the two partners by explicitly stating the areas of responsibility necessary to maintain the collection and make it sustainable. We plan to have Rosemary serve as a permanent liaison to the collection.

Future Plans

As previously expressed in our statement of purpose, a supplemental electronic collection is also being planned. We will replicate the book process and conduct searches against the Pollak Library's catalog for titles we already own that are available electronically in the Pollak Library's collection. These will be discoverable as MSI Collection titles through the use of the local collection title field in the catalog record. Quantitative and qualitative collection assessment will also need to be performed in order to determine the efficacy of the collection and the sustainability of the program. Finally, a ribbon-cutting ceremony is being planned for the fall 2022 semester after all the books have been cataloged and installed in the center.

Conclusion

As a librarian/faculty ally, I was invited to attend the California State University Young Males of Color Conference (California State University, 2022) in Sacramento and spend time with the MSI Fullerton students and staff over three days. At the conference, students and practitioners from across the CSU system gathered to hear presentations from male success students, both current and former, and nationally recognized experts from men of color success initiatives at peer institutions.

Listening to their stories made me realize that the books we were adding to the collection went beyond the abstraction of a list of titles. This work is all about people, some who immigrated from Mexico, some who overcame gangs and incarceration, and some who came from affluent backgrounds where they were one of the few students of color in their high schools or college programs. Everyone had family stories, whether it was overcoming parental abandonment and foster care or appreciating a supportive grandparent or a lesbian mother that pushed them to go on to college and reach a potential they never imagined for themselves. Regardless of where they came from, each member of the community was engaged in an effort to reshape masculinity beyond toxicity and share support with navigating the academy.

Over the course of the conference, I was able to make some personal connections and when they heard I was a librarian working on a collection for the MSI program, a few suggested books they thought might be right for the Men of Color Collection, some of which, I'm proud to say, were already on our list. Other leaders in cultural resource centers wanted to replicate our library program in their spaces.

Engaging male students of color through collections goes beyond providing support for their research. It's an opportunity to participate as an ally and leverage academic librarianship to serve a vital but vulnerable population of students. Academic libraries have the potential to support young men of color for who they are, both as individuals and as a brotherhood, and to have a lasting impact up to and beyond degree attainment. This type of engagement creates ways for brothers to find community in an academic context that is too often predisposed to see them through harmful stereotypes and deficit narratives. Within the collection, they can experience the validation of their culture, their leadership, their ambitions, and especially, what they bring to the academic community as men of color.

References

Aguilar, P., & Keating, K. (2009). Satellite outreach services program to under-represented students: being in their space, not on MySpace. *The Reference Librarian, 50*(1), 14–28. https://doi.org/10.1080/02763870802546365

Atkinson, H. C. (1983). A brief for the other side. *Journal of Academic Librarianship, 9*(4), 200-201.

Bell, S. S. (1995). Integrating access to formal and informal collections: What is important and what succeeds. *The Journal of Academic Librarianship, 21*(3), 181–186. https://doi.org/10.1016/0099-1333(95)90037-3

Bitsói, L. L., & Lee, L. L. (2014). Ahistoricism in the Native American experience. In R. Williams (Ed.), *Men of color in higher education : new foundations for developing models for success* (pp.55-84). Stylus Publishing, LLC.

Brooms, D., Clark, J., & Smith, M. (2018). Empowering men of color on campus : building student community in higher education. Rutgers University Press.

Brooms, D., Moore, J., & Patton, J. (2021 January, 27-28). *Comprehensive student retention strategies for men of color* [Conference presentation]. United States. https://www.academicimpressions.com/comprehensive-student-retention-strategies-for-men-of-color/

California State University. (2021, March). California State University fact book. Retrieved March 6, 2022, from https://www.calstate.edu/csu-system/about-the-csu/facts-about-the-csu/Documents/facts2021.pdf

California State University, Fullerton. (2021). Fact sheet. Retrieved March 6, 2022, from http://www.fullerton.edu/about/default.aspx#facts

California State University Young Males of Color Consortium. (2022 April, 6-7). *Beyond the rhetoric: eradicating opportunity and equity gaps for males of color.* [conference presentation]3rd Annual Conference. Sacramento, CA, United States. https://csuymoc.org/conference22/

Diaz, J.R. (1994) Collection development in multicultural studies. In Riggs, D. E. & Tarin, P. A. (Eds.)., *Cultural diversity in libraries* (pp.185-198). Neal-Schuman.

Elguindi, A.C., & Sandler, A. M. (2013). The ILS as outreach: Cataloging campus partner collections. *Cataloging & Classification Quarterly, 51*(1-3), 291-310. https://doi:10.1080/01639374.2012.722589

Evans, G., & Tilton, K. (2011). Creating an un-library catalog. *Library Resources & Technical Services, 55*(1), 45–53. https://doi.org/10.5860/lrts.55n1.45

Ferer, E. (2012). Working together: Library and writing center collaboration. *Reference Services Review, 40*(4), 543–557. https://doi.org/10.1108/00907321211277350

Gordon, E. T. & Henery, C. (2014). The problem of patriarchy. In R. Williams (Ed.), *Men of color in higher education : new foundations for developing models for success* (pp.1-34). Stylus Publishing, LLC.

Harper, S. (2014). (Re)setting the agenda for college men of color : Lessons learned from a 15-year movement to improve Black male student success. In R. Williams (Ed.), *Men of color in higher education : New foundations for developing models for success* (pp.116-143). Stylus Publishing, LLC.

Hollister, C. (2005). Bringing information literacy to career services. *Reference Services Review, 33*(1), 104–111. https://doi.org/10.1108/00907320510581414

LeMire, S., & Mosbo Ballestro, J. (2019). Insourcing library outreach: Engaging technical services in outreach to student organizations. *College & Undergraduate Libraries, 26*(2), 149-161. https://doi.org/10.1080/10691316.2019.1636442

Male Success Initiative. (2021). *MSI-Fullerton pillars of potential*. California State University, Fullerton. Retrieved March 6, 2022, from http://www.fullerton.edu/msi/programs/pop.php

Male Success Initiative. (2020). *History*. California State University, Fullerton. Retrieved March 6, 2022, from https://www.fullerton.edu/msi/about/history.php

Maloney, M. M. (2012). Cultivating community, promoting inclusivity: Collections as fulcrum for targeted outreach. *New Library World, 113*(5/6), 281–289. https://doi.org/10.1108/03074801211226364

Norlin, E. (2001). University goes back to basics to reach minority students. *American Libraries* (Chicago, Ill.), *32*(7), 60–62. https://www.jstor.org/stable/25645998

Roth, P. J., & Daniels, J. D. (2015). 'Flip this house': 'back of the house' library staff engaging the wider campus community. In Bernhardt, B. R., Hinds, L. H., and Strauch, K. P. (Eds.). *Where Do We Go From Here?: Charleston Conference Proceedings, 2015*, (pp.437-442). Purdue University Press.

Sáenz, V. B. & Bukoski B. E. (2014). Masculinity : through a Latino male lens. In R. Williams (Ed.), *Men of color in higher education : new foundations for developing models for success* (pp.85-115). Stylus Publishing, LLC.

Seal, R. A. (1986) Academic branch libraries. *Advances in Librarianship, 14*(1), 175-209.

Shkolnik, L.S. (1991). The continuing debate over academic branch libraries. *College & Research Libraries, 52*, 343-351.

Suozzi, P. A., & Kerbel, S. S. (1992). The organizational misfits. *College & Research Libraries, 53*(6), 513–522. https://doi.org/10.5860/crl_53_06_513

Teranishi, R.T., & Pazich, L.B. (2014). Intersectionality. In R. Williams (Ed.), *Men of color in higher education : new foundations for developing models for success* (pp.35-54). Stylus Publishing, LLC.

Toce, J., & Schofield, C. (2011). Technical service outreach strategies for academic libraries. *Technical Services Quarterly, 28*(3): 312–321. Retrieved from http://dx.doi.org/10.1080/07317131.2011.571638

Turner, L.S. (2017). Embracing satellite libraries in academia. *Collection Building, 36*(2), 58–62. https://doi.org/10.1108/CB-12-2016-0034

Walter, S., & Eodice, M. (2005). Meeting the student learning imperative: Supporting and sustaining collaboration between academic libraries and student services programs. *Research Strategies, 20*(4), 219–225. https://doi.org/10.1016/j.resstr.2006.11.001

Watts, T. D. (1983). A brief for centralized library collections. *Journal of Academic Librarianship, 9*(4), 196-197.

Williams, R. (Ed.). (2014). Men of color in higher education : New foundations for developing models for success. Stylus Publishing, LLC.

Yosso, T. (2005). Whose culture has capital? A critical race theory discussion of community cultural wealth. *Race, Ethnicity and Education, 8*(1), 69–91. https://doi.org/10.1080/1361332052000341006

Dusting off the Stacks
Building a Representative Collection in a Small HSI

Caitlin Archer-Helke

You got this job at a Hispanic Serving Institution (HSI). You're excited, and nervous, and even with your skills and your background, you aren't quite sure how to get started—because getting started is hard, right? And the collections are old and dusty, and your fellow librarians, if indeed there are any, aren't particularly skilled or interested in decolonial collection development or representative texts or whatever you're choosing to call it. GOBI's selection aids don't seem that great, and you're not really sure where else to look. Oh, and your budget kinda sucks, too. What on earth to do?

No fear, for I, your colleague from another library, was once also a terrified baby collection developer at a small, barely staffed HSI. Saint Xavier University (SXU), where I had worked as the User Services Librarian since 2018 and where I served as the Interim Director, is a small liberal arts institution on the far southwest side of Chicago. Ours is a diverse student body, a crosscut of Chicago's own plurality of cultures and ethnicities. We are an HSI, and many of our students are first-generation college students. Many are also first-generation Americans, ranging from Mexican American to Polish American, and from Palestinian American to Irish American. Chicago is a city of varied and fascinating histories, and my students are understandably drawn to its stories, which are so often their own as well. Indeed, SXU is an old Chicago institution. It was founded by the Sisters of Mercy in 1846 and officially chartered in 1847 (Clough, 1997, p. 2-3), well before the

Great Chicago Fire. We have long ties to Chicago and to the South Side, though I can't say I felt that our collections sufficiently reflected our positionality on the South Side.

As I started my job as a user services librarian, fumbling along with my postcolonial theories of collection development, I found resources that have helped me curate an increasingly representative collection (at least in my areas) while dealing with perpetual understaffing and an eternally shoestring budget. It's worth noting that I do not have education in every area for which I collect. As a User Services Librarian I collected for all social sciences, all humanities, all arts-related programs, most area studies programs (including gender studies, Middle Eastern Studies, and African American Studies), and education and adjacent areas. As Interim Director, however, I collect for the entire library, including business, nursing, and computer science. I have been able to leverage the tools I found not only to help me collect in the areas where I have gained expertise—such as social sciences or gender studies—but also in areas like business, where I have spent considerably less time. I've also got ideas of ways to make my collection—and yours, too—better, but we'll get to those later.

First, you're going to want to get your collection philosophy in order. That's different from your institutional collection development policy, and from whatever external pressure—budget, faculty, administration, your boss—you may face. Instead, it's your own philosophical approach to curating a collection. My first master's degree is in Spanish, with an emphasis on colonial Latin American and Early Modern Iberian texts, and my philosophy is drawn heavily from the theorists Aníbal Quijano's "Coloniality of Power, Eurocentrism, and Latin America" (2000) and Walter Mignolo's "The Geopolitics of Knowledge and the Colonial Difference" (2002). Additionally, I've gleaned information and positionality from Gayatri Chakravorty Spivak's eternal question, "Can the Subaltern Speak?" (1988). Together, these have helped me forge my collection curation philosophy, and have driven (and drive) me to seek out input from my stakeholders. Know your own philosophy, so you can work with it as well as with institutional policies. You'll need both.

My own philosophy is both intangible—I know it when I see it, which is probably a terrible way to engage in anything—and regimented. Like every other academic librarian, I build collections to support curricular goals. In many ways, I have adapted a decolonial framework for building these collections. If in the past specific voices (generally those of white men) have been privileged, I will seek out other voices. Much of my work closely dovetails with that described by Rachel Blume and Allyson Roylance (2020) as they speak of intentionality in collections and of what they call "'authentic authorship,'" which they define as "a term which refers to the correlation between author and subject area, and seeks to share views on history, culture, and experience through a genuine lens" (p. 1). In addition to a decolonial framework, I try to build on something a bit less tangible: I want engaging collections filled with books that, while scholarly, are also accessible and readable. Many of my students are Chicago Public School (CPS) graduates, coming to us from schools on the South and West Sides of the city. CPS, at a systemic level, lacks librarians: "Roughly 80% of the 514 district-run schools in the CPS system are without a librarian" (Inklebarger, 2019). Schools with librarians are largely located on the city's wealthier North Side, while South and West Side schools are largely without librarians and, often, without school libraries as well (Moreno, 2017, Westerberg, 2019, Li, 2016). I need to provide material that will be accessible and engaging enough for a student to want to spend time with it, and I need that material to reflect lived experiences and contemporary realties. Throughout this chapter, I will explore some of the resources and tools I have found helpful as I strive to decolonize my library's holdings.

If your director is anything like mine, you'll be pointed toward GOBI as an invaluable resource. I don't want to downplay GOBI; it's indeed useful, and you can and should make use of it, if it is the platform your library uses. However, especially after listening to Robin Bradford and Becky Spratford's amazing presentation at the 2021 Illinois Library Association Conference, *Actively Anti-Racist Library Service to Leisure Readers*, it's been increasingly clear to me that GOBI really doesn't cut it. We get little in the way of tailored guidance, and, let's face it, their recommendations are often downright terrible. (*American Dirt* just isn't an essential representative text, for my library or yours.)

If your library utilizes Baker & Taylor or Ingram as your book-buying platform, you may have somewhat better tools than GOBI's selection advice. However, these tools may also tilt toward the popular rather than the scholastic, making them less useful for us than for our public library peers. And, while I would argue that we should put together our own resources—like this book—that requires time. And for many of us, time is in short supply.

Time is an issue when it comes to building the networks that will help you serve your patrons, too, but it isn't entirely insurmountable. You have two built in networks already: students and faculty. Faculty are experts in their areas and can often suggest titles (although said titles sometimes date back to the professor's time in grad school, or are related to their own most recent publication). Students are experts in their lived experiences, and that, for any librarian striving toward a representative collection, is essential knowledge. I was fortunate to begin building relationships with students ahead of the COVID-19 pandemic and was able to organically move conversations toward what my students needed and wanted to see represented on our shelves. I have, at times, asked students directly what they wanted or needed to see on our shelves, since what they had found thus far spoke neither to their lives nor needs.

This directness won't work for every person—it's far too blunt for that—but, at least sometimes, I have gotten everything from lists of books to lists of scholars the student has read and with whom they identify. It's then my job to go forth and seek out those voices. While hanging out with students in their spaces I have learned not only about their feral cat rescue programs but also about their dreams and interests—which have helped me to direct my collection development in useful directions. When I visit the little art gallery in our institution, I always take time to talk to the student worker, who is usually an art student. Their interests in art, whether video games or photography or protest art, allow me to target material that will speak to their needs. In those halcyon pre-COVID days, when I had a famous candy bowl and my office was open to any student who wanted to hang out, whether they had a reference question, I hosted accidental parties that generally included students telling me, often without realizing what they were doing, about their passions, their interests, and what they couldn't find in our collections. I have yet to figure out how to rebuild this sort of easy-going community life in a time of COVID-19, but I'm sure there is a way to create something similar.

In the meantime, I have also used heritage and history months to great advantage in collection development, speaking with students, student organizations, and student government about what they would like to see on a Latinx Heritage Month display or a Pride Display or a Black History Month display or an Arab Heritage Month display. Their input has not only given them a feeling of ownership over the displays in question, and therefore over the collection itself, but it has provided me with invaluable information on their interests—and on their expertise. Our students are the experts on their own lives. They know their families' stories and carry them to school. We need their expertise to build a solid collection.

I was able to sort my students' requests and interests into categories: decoloniality here, border crossings there, a special place for Chicago writers over yonder. Once I had those requests, it was time for me to track material down. Occasionally my students gave me scholar names and monograph titles, but it was more common to hear about interests and broad topics than to get a scholar's name or publisher. I had little money, little time for professional development, and little resources in the way of library colleagues in my institution. So, I turned to resources beyond my institution, and, indeed, often beyond academe itself.

You may have heard, before this, that Twitter is a great resource for librarians. I'd heard it many times and had ignored it for years before finally signing up in 2019. I am therefore able to tell you, from my own experience, that Twitter can be a great networking tool. It doesn't require as much time as hunting down trainings, and you can curate your lists to help you find people studying and writing about what you need to know. I began following librarians doing work I found interesting and librarians with whom I enjoyed interacting. I followed my mentor and sought out her extensive connections. And, finally, I regularly went looking for scholars of color. I've found them in a variety of ways: the scholar and author David Bowles, for example, wrote *They Call Me Güero*, a middle grade novel in verse which won multiple youth literature awards, including a Pura Belpré Honor. Ilan Stavans publishes a lot of material in the areas in which I have always collected. Each writer and artist and scholar I found on Twitter, in turn, led me to additional writers and scholars and artists, whose work I could then seek out for my students.

Publishers also tend to have social media presences, and publishers—specifically specialized presses, academic presses, and imprints—can be incredibly useful for you as you build your representative library collection. My students are intensely interested in reading not only about other minoritized people in Chicago but also from people whose experiences are similar to their own. (Erika Sánchez's 2017 *I Am Not Your Perfect Mexican Daughter*, which I have purchased in both English and Spanish-language translation, is one example—as is José

Olivarez's 2018 *Citizen Illegal*.) The University of Illinois Press publishes several series focusing directly on the sort of material my students want, including the series *Latinos in Chicago and the Midwest*. It is a wide-ranging scholarly series, and while many of the books focus on the Puerto Rican and Mexican American experience in Chicago, others look at everything from Latinx farmers in the Midwest to representations of Latinx people in American media. Providing my students with material of direct interest to them not only enables them to study histories they find interesting and engaging but also reminds all of us—including me and their faculty—that history is not made exclusively by wealthy white people, and that cities like Chicago owe a great deal to all our citizens.

As librarians, we have a tendency to rely on reviews when we're deciding what to purchase. And reviews can be fantastic! I am quite fond of a good capsule review in *Kirkus* or *Publishers Weekly* or *Library Journal*. Unfortunately, our beloved capsules will not always cover the material we need. Nor will they always give the same levels of care to material by or about BIPOC creators—which means that, once again, it is time for us to find additional review sources. I have found that *Bitch* makes a concentrated effort to provide reviews of representative texts and employs reviewers of color. *ΓIYAΙΙ*, largely a literary magazine, includes reviews of works by Black authors, including Afro-Latinx authors. You will find your own sources, but it is, when you've got a bit of time, worth the effort to look.

Professional organizations and listservs can be a big help to you, although there, too, you will need to curate. I have been a member of REFORMA National since I was a graduate student, and it often provides essential information and support, as well as a finger on the pulse of services to Spanish-speaking patrons throughout the country. (While many of my students do speak Spanish at home, most have no desire to speak it with me. They do, however, enjoy reading leisure material in Spanish.) The American Library Association has some excellent resources, such as the Pura Belpré Award. Most of these resources do not require membership, which can be helpful if your institution, like so many libraries, does not cover professional membership fees (Comanda et al., 2021). Overall, I have found my local library association, Illinois Library Association, to be of more direct assistance—perhaps because it is built by other librarians in Illinois. Your local association may be essential for you too—or it may, at least, provide you with opportunities to meet other library staff working with Hispanic students. Don't discount those networking opportunities. Finally, if you are building collections of youth material for preservice educators—one of my favorite pieces of collection development—you'll find a wealth of organizations to help. There are, to name just a few, the Pura Belpré Awards, the Américas Award, the Tómas Rivera Book Award, and the We Need Diverse Books organization, all of which will be invaluable resources to anyone trying to build a representative collection in youth and young adult material.

What to do about funds for collection development? This is tricky and will depend on multiple factors. For the most part, my students dislike eBooks and will actively look for printed monographs. In a way, this makes my job easier: print monographs are often half the price of their eBook counterparts, or even less. (This is less useful when we were locked down due to the COVID-19 pandemic.) Your students may or may not feel differently, although if you, like me, collect for youth materials, you may not have much of a choice. (GOBI offers few or no youth materials in eBook formats, and Amazon does not license eBooks to libraries.) If you have some leeway in your purchasing, you may want to price out books. Where can you get the best discount? Can someone negotiate a better discount with your current vender? Finally, depending on how old and sad your collection is, you may want to look into grants, such the Humanities Collections and Reference Resources grant offered by the National Endowment for the Humanities. This is, again, a massive time commitment, which is why I have yet to attempt it myself. Do not undertake it alone. Look for help from your institution and from other library staffers, assuming you are not solo. (Your circulation clerk, for example, will have expertise you do not. I know mine do.) Then budget out what you can do and build from there.

Curating your collection is about much more than purchasing material that reflects our diverse world and our current scholarship. It is also about maintaining those stacks, and about weeding out material that is no longer current (or just doesn't circulate). Weeding can be a touchy topic in libraries: some of us (including me) love to weed, while others find it depressing. It generally requires a deft hand and a lot of explanation. Your library will likely have rules for weeding, and you will want to familiarize yourself with them. You may also want to approach with rationale for conducting a good summer weed. The shelves will be easier to navigate; it will be less difficult to find material students and faculty want. Prepare your talking points in advance, and be ready to explain and, if necessary, to negotiate. Your work as a curator involves pulling unneeded material off those shelves just as it includes bringing in new material.

Those of us working in small schools with little or no support can often feel very alone, and the thought of building collections to adequately represent our students and our worlds can be daunting. I felt very alone when I first started. But there are resources available to you, and many of them are much easier and much less expensive than seeking out professional development opportunities. Others are closer at hand: listservs like that from REFORMA have been essential for me, as has my local library association, the Illinois Library Association. Seek out your own network, on Twitter or Instagram or TikTok. Talk to your students and help them help you. And, most of all, enjoy the curation of your beautiful new collection.

References

Blume, R., & Roylance, A. (2020). Decolonization in collection development: Developing an authentic authorship workflow. *The Journal of Academic Librarianship*, 46(5). https://doi.org/10.1016/j.acalib.2020.102175

Bowles, D. (2018). *They call me Güero: A border kid's poems.* Cinco Puntos Press

Bradford, R., & Spratford, B. (2021, October 12). *Actively anti-racist library service to leisure readers: Foundations* [Conference session]. Illinois Library Association 2021 Annual Conference (Virtual).

Clough, J., RSM. (1997). *First in Chicago: A history of Saint Xavier University.* Saint Xavier University. https://collections.carli.illinois.edu/digital/collection/sxu_books/id/451/rec/1

Comanda, B., Wilkinson, J., Bradham, F., Koziura, A., & Seale, M. (2021). Service ceiling: The high cost of professional development for academic librarians. *In the Library With the Lead Pipe.* https://www.inthelibrarywiththeleadpipe.org/2021/service-ceiling/

Inklebarger, T. (November 8, 2019). How the CPS strike affected Chicago school librarians: What the 11-day strike could mean for the city's school librarians going forward. *American Libraries.* https://americanlibrariesmagazine.org/2019/11/08/cps-strike-affected-chicago-school-librarians/

Li, A. (November 16, 2016). School librarians, shelved: CPS cuts further drain library resources for students. *South Side Weekly.* https://southsideweekly.com/school-librarians-shelved/

Mignolo, W. (2002). The geopolitics of knowledge and the colonial difference. *The South Atlantic Quarterly*, 101(1), 57-96.

Moreno, N. (September 4, 2017). Information literacy lost: Most CPS schools no longer have librarians. *Chicago Tribune.* https://www.chicagotribune.com/news/ct-cps-librarian-cuts-met-20170902-story.html

National Endowment for the Humanities. (n.d.). *Humanities collections and reference resources.* Accessed March 31, 2022. https://www.neh.gov/grants/preservation/humanities-collections-and-reference-resources

Olivarez, J. (2018). *Citizen illegal.* Haymarket Press.

Quijano, A. (2000.) Coloniality of power, Eurocentrism, and Latin America. (M. Ennis, translator.) *Nepantla: Views from the South, 1*(3), 533-580. https://muse.jhu.edu/article/23906

Sánchez, E. (2017). *I am not your perfect Mexican daughter.* Alfred A. Knopf.

Sánchez, E. (2018). *Yo no soy tu perfecta hija méxicana.* (G. Romero Saldaña, trans.) Vintage Español (Original work published 2017).

Spivak, G.C. (1988). Can the subaltern speak? In C. Nelson and L. Grossberg (Eds), *Marxism and the interpretation of culture.* University of Illinois Press.

University of Illinois Press. (n.d.). *Latinos in Chicago and the Midwest.* Retrieved March 31 2022. https://www.press.uillinois.edu/books/find_books.php?type=series&search=lcm&page=1

Westerberg, L. (2019, November 13) Our work is not done: The need for more librarians in Chicago Public Schools. *The Chicago Union Teacher, 83*(2). https://www.ctulocal1.org/chicago-union-teacher/2019/11/our-work-is-not-done-the-need-for-more-librarians-in-chicago-public-schools/

Decolonizing the Library

Building a Collection that Reflects the Student Body at Bronx Community College

Nelson Santana

Author Statement

Being an academic librarian coupled with my personal identity as a Latin American and Caribbean, I understand firsthand the importance of diversity, inclusion, equity, and accessibility especially within libraries, archives, and academia. Diversity is a critical component both of my personal identity and professional career. Providing a diverse, inclusive, equitable, and accessible environment is critical in librarianship and this is especially true in my area of collection development where I work closely with multiple internal and external stakeholders including students, faculty, staff, and overall, the Bronx Community College (BCC) community. Since my arrival at BCC—a Hispanic-Serving Institution (HSI)—I have attended multiple events focused on diversity, equity, and inclusion including CUNY's Ethnic Studies Town Hall on September 16, 2020, as well as the NASIG and Ideal '19 conferences in 2019; the themes for both conferences focused on diversity, equity, inclusion, and accessibility. As chair of the Library/Liaison Committee at BCC, I am in constant dialogue with faculty across campus. I also conduct library and information instruction classes where I engage in conversation with students and include student voices through my reference work. In the following pages, I will detail my work to foster a more diverse library collection at Bronx Community College of the City University of New York. More specifically, this project will detail my efforts in building a more diverse, equitable, inclusive, and accessible library collection.

I want to thank a few individuals for making this work possible. I presented versions of this paper at several conferences and meetings including the LXIII Annual Conference of the Seminar on the Acquisition of Latin American Library Materials: Sites/Cites, Texts, Voices in Critical Librarianship: Decolonizing Libraries and Archives (2019); the Sixth Annual Bronx Community College Faculty Day: Reflections on Diversity: Sharing Scholarship, Teaching, and Creative Works (2019); and the Diversity and Collection Development event panel, sponsored by the Community and Junior College Libraries Section (CJCLS) (2022). I also want to thank my cohort colleagues and mentor from the CUNY Faculty Fellowship Publication Program for providing feedback during this fellowship program in 2021. I also thank Amaury Rodríguez who provided feedback. Lastly, I thank the editors of this invaluable volume, Isabel Soto-Luna and Sommer Browning for their support and patience during the editorial process.

Correspondence concerning this chapter should be addressed to Nelson Santana at nelson.santana02@bcc.cuny.edu

Introduction

As most librarians and people in the realm of librarianship are aware, fostering relationships is key, and this is especially true in collection development. Librarians must be creative, flexible, be able to think on their feet and outside the box as a means to grow the library's collection. This work focuses on the Bronx Community College Library and the work that I have been doing as Collection Development Librarian.

Librarians have been at the forefront of initiatives that promote diversity, equity, inclusivity, and accessibility. My purpose with this interdisciplinary project is to build upon the existing scholarship with my own intervention, which partly is contributing to the debate on decolonizing the library. The aim of this project is fourfold. First, this chapter will acquaint readers with Bronx Community College, the Bronx Community College Library, and related matters such as the respective histories of these two entities and user demographics. Second, by highlighting the collection development work at the BCC Library—including specific examples of the work I am doing—I hope to provide a model that other libraries and repositories can emulate to successfully decolonize their libraries, thus creating more diverse, equitable, inclusive, and accessible repositories. Thus, this chapter will serve as a manual or case study of the work the collection development librarian at a Hispanic-Serving Institution has been doing since their arrival in 2017 and in doing so, I will share measures I have taken at BCC to decolonize the library and provide a more diverse, equitable, inclusive, and accessible space for our population of users. Thirdly, this chapter will provide actionable steps and firsthand examples that information professionals can undertake to implement a successful donation strategy. The fourth objective of this chapter is to situate the decolonization of the library within the landscape of decolonization and decolonial movements as noted by previous scholars—especially scholars of color—acquainting or reacquainting information professionals with the works of these thinkers. Subsequently, this chapter will engage in conversation with different methodologies and schools of thought that tackle colonization and the isms (e.g. racism, sexism, etc.).

Bronx Community College

Established in 1957, Bronx Community College (BCC) opened its doors in 1959 with 125 students (*History and Architecture*). *Originally located at the former Bronx High School of Science at Creston Avenue and 184th Street*, BCC's operations moved on multiple occasions. Present-day BCC stands on 45 acres with 34 buildings. As the only community college in the United States designated as a National Historic Landmark, BCC is home to the United States' first and oldest Hall of Fame: The Hall of Fame for Great Americans. This landmark made national headlines in recent years due to the removal of the statues of Confederate Civil War combatants Robert E. Lee and Stonewall Jackson in the aftermath of massive protests that took place in Charlottesville, Virginia in 2017 (*BCC to Remove Confederate Statue at Bronx Hall of Fame*). *Thus, Bronx Community College has a storied legacy.*

The story of Bronx Community College is one linked to the struggles of people of color, as BCC's founding occurred during the Civil Rights Movement in the United States. About a decade after BCC's founding, academic institutions across the nation began an academic reckoning, with students and faculty clamoring for Black and Latino studies curriculums. Both Black and Latino/a/x students as well as allies spearheaded protests that continue to have ripple effects to this day. In her book, *The Black Revolution on Campus* (2014), Martha Biondi places student activists front and center, where she convincingly argues that students played a pivotal role in the Black Freedom movement, helping to shape and transform American higher education across schools. Similar to Black students, faculty, and staff, Latino/a/x individuals—especially Chicano/a/x and Puerto Ricans—pushed for their own histories to be archived, documented, and disseminated.

BCC is part of The City University of New York (CUNY), which has the distinction of being the largest urban university system in the United States. Originally established in 1847 as the Free Academy and known colloquially as "The Poor Man's Harvard," CUNY's first college was re-christened the City College of New York (CCNY). The original location of CCNY is the current location of a Baruch College building on 23rd Street and Lexington Avenue. In 1961, several public institutions united under the banner of The City University of New York (Van Nort). Today, eleven senior colleges, seven community colleges, and seven professional institutions across 25 campuses makeup CUNY. As per their website, CUNY serves more than 275,000 degree-seeking students each year (The CUNY Story: A Brief History), with nearly one-third of Hispanic/Latino/Latinx origin. A testament to the large concentration of Hispanic/Latino/Latinx community of students, as well as the advocacy of Latin American-descended people and allies, CUNY is home to several centers and institutes that document, preserve, make accessible, and conduct research on several groups of people who trace their ancestry back to Latin America. Some of these institutes include the Centro de Estudios Puertorriqueños at Hunter College established in 1973, the CUNY Dominican Studies Institute at City College established in 1992, the CUNY Mexican Studies Institute at Lehman College established in 2012, and the Haitian Studies Institute at Brooklyn College established in 2016 (Aponte and Santana, 183-184).

Student Demographics

Even before delving into the decolonization of the library, it is important to understand user demographics—in this case, student demographics—in relation to the setting. BCC is one of several City University of New York colleges designated as Hispanic-Serving Institutions (HSIs). Nearly half of CUNY schools have this designation, and BCC is one of four CUNY schools with more than 59% of Latinx/Hispanic students. BCC students who identify as Latino/a/x/Hispanic comprise 59% of the total population, with more than half tracing their ancestry to the Dominican Republic. Approximately 34.4% of students identify as Black, non-Hispanic, with 6.1% identifying as other. BCC's student body mirrors the neighborhood's population. Although slightly more than half of students are U.S.-born, the largest number of foreign-born students were born in the Dominican Republic.

According to statistics from BCC's Office of Institutional Research, more than half of incoming students enrolled at BCC in fall 2016 were foreign-born. Of the total 1,255 incoming freshmen, only 426 were born in the United States. It should be noted, however, that some of these 426 people are probably the children or grandchildren of immigrants. In fall 2016, 413 (or 32.9%) of incoming freshmen identified as being from the Dominican Republic. In addition, 364 (or 29%) of students speak Spanish. Most BCC students are English speakers while most students speak more than one language including Bengali, French, Arabic, Akan, and Creole. More than one-third of the population speaks Spanish. Additionally, BCC is home to students who have been impacted by the justice system in the U.S. Notable former BCC students include Guinean immigrant Amodou Diallo and U.S.-born Kalief Browder, who lost their lives because of police brutality and a racially biased justice system.

Bronx Community College Library

Although Bronx Community College was formally established in 1957, it was not until 16 years later in 1973 when the Bronx Community College Library was formalized. Since its founding, the BCC Library has been housed in multiple on-campus locations including Meister Hall, Sage Hall, and its current location at North Hall and Library. In 2012, BCC's Library opened its doors in a new state-of-the-art facility comprised of three floors. Although the building where the library is located contains classrooms used by departments throughout campus, two of the three floors are devoted to the library with two classrooms: one classroom equipped with computers for use by library faculty who teach information literacy courses and the second classroom known as the Law Library classroom. The BCC Library is equipped with more than 200 computers, 12 study rooms, and multiple service areas including the BCC Archives and Technology Services, a unit that provides and makes available technology support to BCC's community of users.

Decolonizing the Mind

Diversity, equity, inclusion, and accessibility are important to all facets of society, including the library. To diversify the library and make it more equitable, inclusive, and accessible, one must work to decolonize it. The decolonization of the library requires that one decolonize the mind first and foremost. Decolonizing the Library requires the rejection of Eurocentric notions or at the very least understanding that western culture is not superior to other cultures. This does not mean that one must flat-out reject and erase all western thinking including Eurocentric writing and culture such as some of the most controversial works ever written.

Many people, especially people of color, will continue to feel uncomfortable when reading passages from classic texts such as Mark Twain's *The Adventures of Huckleberry Finn* (1884) and J.D. Salinger's *The Catcher in the Rye* (1951), each considered the "Great American Novel" at one point in time. Works considered the "Great American Novel" provide a snapshot of U.S. culture, politics, and the average U.S. citizen—albeit White—during a specific period in the country's history. Many of the literary works that are or were considered the "Great American Novel" were written by individuals who were a product of their time, and it has been debated whether many of these works and/or the authors were racist. F. Scott Fitzgerald, author of *The Great Gatsby* (1925), for instance, has been accused of producing antisemitic literature that at one point had to be removed by editors from different publications (Flood). In a March 2, 2021, letter, Dr. Seuss Enterprises, L.P.—the children's entertainment company that manages the Dr. Seuss brand—noted that they made the decision to cease publication and licensing of several books written by the famed children's author due to racist and insensitive images (Statement from Dr. Seuss Enterprises). According to the statement, "These books portray people in ways that are hurtful and wrong." Although the following statement may seem counterintuitive, it is not really a paradox: decolonizing the library does not entail the removal of all western or European-centered texts, because this would be a disservice to libraries across the world, including the Bronx Community College community. Are we as a society in the twenty-first century, going to regress by censoring books? Would this act not be similar to removing all speeches, manifestos, audio and video footage created during the dictatorships of individuals like Adolf Hitler, Rafael Trujillo, and Benito Mussolini? Are we not doomed to repeat history if we erase and forget all the events that transpired in the past?

This chapter is grounded in the theoretical framework of the decoloniality school of thought, which challenges the centrality and perceived notion that Western (European) culture is superior in comparison to non-Western culture. As noted by Catherine E. Walsh and Walter D. Mignolo, "Each of us, endorsing and embracing decoloniality, is responsible for our own decolonial liberation" (Mignolo and Walsh, 10). In essence, decoloniality aims to untangle, deconstruct, and allow us to understand colonization and its legacy. Emerging in Latin America, decoloniality considers questions pertaining to race, class, gender, and ethnic studies, although some scholars have argued that decoloniality has blind spots for gender analysis. One of the most appealing aspects of decoloniality is that this theoretical framework interconnects diverse voices of the colonial experience at the global level, considering a multitude of scholars and engaging with the scholarship of scholars in the Americas, South Africa, South Asia, the Caribbean, and Eastern Europe, for instance. Scholars sometimes conflate decoloniality with decolonization, postcolonialism, and even postmodernism, which share commonalities, but are inherently different. Part of my theoretical framework—more specifically, the phrase "decolonizing the library"—derives from Kenyan postcolonial theorist Ngũgĩ wa Thiong'o's seminal text *Decolonising the Mind: The Politics of Language in African Literature* (1986), which many scholars who use the term "decolonize the library," often fail to mention. Although I acknowledge postcolonial theorists such as Thiong'o and members of the Subaltern Studies Group, their influential scholarship focuses exclusively on South Africa, India and South Asia, and for the most part ignore the Americas. Hence, my divergence from decolonization and postcolonialism schools of thought.

Decolonization calls for dialogue between the colonized, the colonizer and their descendants. In his anti-imperialist magnum opus, Thiong'o calls for linguistic decolonization, asking African authors to abandon the language of the colonizer and urging them to write in African languages. *Decolonizing the Mind* served as a farewell to the English language, as most literary works that Thiong'o produced afterward were written in Gĩkũyũ, a language spoken today by approximately seven million Kenyans, which not coincidentally is the primary language spoken by the Kikuyu people—the largest ethnic group in Kenya.

Thiong'o's position on calling for the eradication of the colonizer's language, especially as a process of cleansing to decolonize the mind is a noble idea, yet it is too idealistic. First, there is value in utilizing the language of the colonizer. English, French, and Spanish, for example, allow people in different regions of the world to communicate with one another, hence, in this sense, language is a unifying factor. Second, unlike the vast continent of Africa—where there are over 3,000 ethnic groups and at least 2,000 languages spoken—in the western hemisphere, many ethnic groups along with their culture and cultural elements such as their language, have perished, unfortunately. Although I understand Thiong'o's suggestion that we should reject the language of the colonizer and speak those of our ancestors, this idealistic idea is impractical in most of the Western Hemisphere. This model may work for people who speak Náhuatl or the six million Mayan people in the Americas, as well as the Cherokee or Navajo nations. However, this idea is not practical in places like the Caribbean or among populations that only speak English or one of the Romance languages.

If Thiong'o offers a starting point to decolonize the library, where do we go from there? Many thinkers have discussed steps toward decolonization. In fact, there is an extensive literature devoted to both decolonial and postcolonial studies. Simply put, decolonization involves the act of undoing colonialism. Then, how do we decolonize the library? The conversation starts with the dismantling of a Eurocentric lens, meaning that rather than placing Western or European values at the center, we place them side-by-side in dialogue with non-Western views. Although not scholars of the Latin American decoloniality school of thought, the works of Martinique-born intellectuals Aimé Césaire and Frantz Fanon are fundamental to discussions regarding the decolonization of libraries. Fanon notes that no colonized person is ever truly at home, with the reality being that their situation as a colonized "other" prevents them from attaining their goals (Fanon). Césaire, who greatly influenced Fanon, blames European and Western civilization for the decadence of society, noting that "colonialist Europe has grafted modern abuse onto ancient injustice, hateful racism onto old inequality" (Césaire 11).

Bringing the conversation back to librarianship, one of the fascinating aspects pertinent to this discipline—but not unique nor exclusive to the profession—is that several scholars of librarianship apply different theoretical frameworks and use different terms, with many of these scholars regularly challenging the structures of oppression and the isms within the profession (e.g. White privilege, transphobia, racism, sexism, ableism,). For instance, some scholars have applied Kimberly Crenshaw's intersectionality lens to examine knowledge organization (Fox) or the experience of women of color at the reference desk (Chou and Pho); others are participating in anti-racist initiatives to create more inclusive libraries (Conner-Gaten, Caragher, and Drake); some are disrupting the profession through Critical Race Theory (Leung and López-McKnight; Walker); and others are applying a decolonial lens to challenge and dismantle the systems of oppression. Although many of these scholars use different terminologies and apply different methodologies, essentially, they are challenging the Eurocentric or Western nature of librarianship, combating racism, White privilege, and using critical lenses to challenge the systems of oppression that have historically been in place within librarianship.

Just as important as individuals writing about their own histories, experiences, and effectively working to effect change, allies can and are playing an important role as well. One of the most prestigious journals to focus on the management and development of library collections is *Collection Management*. Realizing that *Collection Management* had not recently published on the challenges related to Native American studies and tribal libraries, Susanne Clement and Judith Nixon both decided to edit a special edition on the topic (Clement and Nixon, 123). Both editors understood they did not have the personal nor professional experience to produce this work and subsequently they reached out to colleagues who are Indigenous and Native American.

Many excellent works devoted to the decolonization of repositories (libraries, archives, special collections, etc.) have emerged in past three decades. Unfortunately, many of these scholars and information professionals do not use the work of their peers in other regions of the world, although they do focus on their own lived experience, an important component of decolonization. The truth is that it is nearly impossible to do justice to this type of work. Hence, I do not aim to provide readers with a comprehensive or authoritative work on decolonization, decoloniality, or anything related to movements against colonial and imperial structures. I do hope, however, to provide readers unfamiliar with these terms, conversations, and debates, with some food for thought or at the very least a starting point for a reading list on the matter.

Decolonizing the Library at Bronx Community College

Accommodating everyone within the public sphere of the library requires negotiation. The library is a space of contestation among different groups of users at varying levels: culturally, ethnically, academically, professionally, and so forth. Whether or not administrators and key stakeholders are willing to admit it, diverse groups of users compete every day for the library's resources. Our Bronx Community College Library is no exception. At this two-year institution of higher learning, a diverse community of users—comprised primarily of students—converges with an end-result of obtaining an associate's degree, certificate, or to learn the English language via programs such as CUNY's Language Immersion Program (CLIP) (*CUNY Language Immersion Program*).

The Library is both a physical and mental place that must be decolonized. As noted by Aisha Conner-Gaten, Kristyn Caragher, and Tracy Drake:

> Librarianship and collection development practices, along with the publishing industry, work in tandem to marginalize Black and other non-Black people of color by not publishing Black and non-Black creators of color and by not collecting materials by Black and non-Black creators of color. (Conner-Gaten, Caragher, & Drake, 2017, p. 152)

The process or work of decolonization must be undertaken collectively. Decolonization involves consultation with scholars, students, community members and stakeholders. If the first step in decolonizing the library involves the very act of acknowledging that the library needs to be decolonized, then logically, the second step is to begin decolonizing the library through action. At Bronx Community College, I noticed there are specific populations of students, thus I have made it my goal to ensure that these populations are reflected in the library's collection by acquiring resources that reflect the lived experience of these groups.

Librarians, especially BCC's collection development librarian, are tasked with acquiring appropriate resources to support the more than 40 academic programs at BCC. It is of the utmost importance to grow a library's collection that speaks to the diversity of the college's student body. BCC's population includes students who represent more than 100 countries as well as LGBTQIA students, and some formerly incarcerated people. A crucial component in the journey of these students is to have access to a collection of library resources that not only support their studies, but also resources that reflect their own background. Being exposed to reading material that students can relate to serves as an empowering mechanism that in the long term will enrich their lives and impact their studies in a positive manner, thus enriching the BCC community. There are many ways to empower students and one such way is by providing students with resources that they are interested in reading, comprising of leisure readings, topics of interest to them as well as reading material in the native language of immigrant students, for instance.

Collection development is the process of developing a library's collection of resources. This process is essential to the college and university academic curriculum. Without consistent analysis and evaluation of collection development, support for the school curriculum collapses.

As collection development librarian, my role is to continuously evaluate and develop our library's collection. I take great pride in this task because it affords me the opportunity to shape the intellectual culture at Bronx Community College (BCC). I do not simply order books and databases; I consistently evaluate the library's resources and update the collection accordingly to ensure that the collection of resources supports BCC's curriculum. Thus, collection development comprises of (1) collection analysis, which entails assessing in a truthful manner the strengths and weaknesses of the collection; (2) weeding the current collection, which involves making decisions pertinent to whether the library should keep or remove resources from the library's collection; and (3) deciding what resources to add to the collection including books or databases, classic texts, or any resources that directly support BCC's curriculum. Although we as librarians—especially collection development librarians—must work toward providing unwavering support toward the school curriculum, I argue that it is of paramount importance to incorporate diversity, equity, inclusion, and accessibility analysis into collection development to create a bibliographic collection of resources that represents the student body.

Building a Collection through Donations

When one arrives at a new institution, it is important to acquaint oneself with the culture of that institution. Prior to my arrival, the Bronx Community College Library had an established culture of book donations, as some students who complete courses are inclined to donate copies of books they use for their coursework. Additionally, some members of the faculty are compelled to make book donations, including books for which they have written reviews or books in their possession they no longer have use for and prefer donating to the library. Therefore, one way I have continued to grow our collection of physical books is by maintaining and continuing to foster relationships established by my predecessor and current colleagues who have been at BCC prior to my arrival.

Establishing rapport with one's community is a crucial component of the library. During difficult times such as when budget cuts are looming, it is of the utmost importance for librarians to establish relationships and build upon these relationships to grow the library's collection of resources. One of the most efficient ways to grow the library's collection is by reaching out to potential donors, thus establishing new relationships, and/or by building upon relationships that one has already established. Fortunately for me, the BCC Library had established an unofficial donation policy with students and faculty who regularly donate books, including BCC's college president. Although the library does not have an official donation policy, collection development is guided by the Bronx Community College Library Collection Development Policy (*Bronx Community College Collection Development Policy*).

In addition to students, faculty, staff, and authors, BCC librarians lead by example as they generously donate new books to the library where they work. Some of our donations are unsolicited, coming from individuals who believe in giving back or by sharing their scholarship with the BCC community.

Fostering relationships is critical to collection development, especially for seeking donations. During my time at BCC and prior to my arrival, I have made it one of my goals to foster relationships with information professionals, scholars, authors, activists, and members of the community. Over the years, I have sustained relationships with individuals and institutions such as the Museum of Modern Art (MoMA), the John Simon Guggenheim Memorial Foundation, and the CUNY Dominican Studies Institute. Reaching out to friends and colleagues in my list of contacts has led to more than 1,600 book donations to the BCC Library since my arrival in 2017.

Prior to the COVID-19 pandemic the BCC Library's budget had been in decline. With the untimely arrival of the pandemic, budget cuts were accelerated across the college, impacting the library at extreme levels. As of spring 2022, the library was operating at nearly 50% personnel capacity; at one point the library lost all part-time staff in 2020, months after the COVID-19 outbreak. In addition to the loss of part-time personnel and hiring freeze, we saw the decimation of the library's book budget. Throughout the college and the CUNY system, funds previously allocated for Other Than Personnel Services (OTPS) became unavailable, as funding agencies retracted the capital. Much of BCC's budget comes by way of New York State. Some of the funding for book purchases derives from New York States' Coordinated Collection Development Aid (CCDA), a grant funded by the New York State government, providing aid to academic libraries that meet specific guidelines.

Although some funding has been allocated during this time, the budget pales in comparison to previous years. Prior to the pandemic, the book budget surpassed $100,000 in some years. However, said book budget has been on a sharp decline in recent years, with the pandemic creating a direr situation. Therefore, it is always a wise choice to establish a stream of donations.

Weeding Donated Materials

Cultivating a culture of giving can be one of the most rewarding aspects of collection development. Sadly, not every item that enters one's library should make it to the library's collection of resources. Most collection development policies include wording that revolves around weeding: the process of analyzing the collection and removing items that may no longer serve the community of users. For example, in the summer of 2019, BCC's Department of Nursing began its reaccreditation process, prompting a site visit from the New York State Education Department, Office of the Professions in conjunction with the Accreditation Commission for Education in Nursing (ACEN). During this process, we removed titles from the collection that were older than seven years, given that Nursing is a field that is changing rapidly, and outdated or inaccurate information can put any program's accreditation in jeopardy.

Building and Sustaining Relationships Via Conferences

Relationship-building is a process that extends beyond one's library and, along with being genuinely kind to others, can lead to unexpected book donations. I am active in several library and non-library-focused associations including a few entities within the American Library Association (ALA): the Library Association of the City University of New York (LACUNY), the Seminar on the Acquisition of Latin American Library Materials (SALALM), and the Dominican Studies Association (DSA). Founded in 1956, SALALM is the preeminent association for worldwide repositories involving Latin American collections. Over the years, I have fostered relationships with numerous SALALM members. Two individuals with whom I have sustained a relationship are librarian Joseph Holub from the University of Pennsylvania and Patrick Gavilanes from Gavilanes Books from Indoamerica. I met Mr. Gavilanes through Professor Holub at the yearly SALALM conference, an annual gathering that I have attended since 2014—except for the 2017 conference. Mr. Gavilanes is a charismatic librero (book vendor). I mention Mr. Gavilanes and his bookstore because he was kind enough to donate several Dominican Studies-related books to me; books that I subsequently donated to the BCC Library.

Further Challenges Brought by the COVID-19 Pandemic

In the introduction of this section, I discussed several challenges brought upon by the COVID-19 pandemic—challenges mostly linked to budgetary constraints. Similar to campuses, libraries, and most business entities across the United States, the BCC Library closed to the public for a period of 17 months. One concern this situation presented involved the acquisition of books. Due to the library's closure, books purchased prior to the pandemic arrived at the college, yet those same books remained in a location outside the library for several months. Equivalently, donations could not be shipped to the college. Instead, I had books shipped to my home address. Another issue compounded by the global pandemic pertains to delays in cataloging donated materials. Books donated weeks prior to the pandemic as well as those donated in the middle of the pandemic have yet to be cataloged because of a few factors, including the backlog of books, mixture of remote and in-person work modality, and preference toward cataloging titles that are purchased with the approved budget.

Fostering and Sustaining a Relationship with the CUNY Dominican Studies Institute Library to Secure a Culture of Giving

BCC has one of the most diverse student bodies in academia. One of the first things I noticed upon my arrival was that the college is home to a significant population of students who trace their ancestry to the Dominican Republic. Consequently, it was only fitting to connect with potential donors that have an interest in Latin American materials. Upon my arrival at BCC, two of the first people I reached out to were Chief Librarian Sarah Aponte from the CUNY Dominican Studies Institute Library (CUNY DSI) and Mrs. Bienvenida Castillo Byrd. They each donated 80 and 53 books, respectively. Nearly all books donated by Mrs. Castillo Byrd and Professor Aponte fall within the field of Dominican Studies.

In fall 2019, I received a correspondence from Professor Sarah Aponte. In her message she asked me if an interest existed within the BCC Library to accept duplicate copies of materials for which the Dominican Library sought to find a new home. Fortunately, Professor Aponte's staff compiled a list of the books, journals, and audiovisual content, using Excel. This thoughtful action allowed me to view the titles that were up for donation. The earliest books in the collection had been published in 1944, while the most recent monographs were published in the twenty-first century. Not only did I accept the donation, but I also rented a U-Haul truck and along with my colleague, Mr. Darren Chase, paid a visit to the CUNY DSI to collect the donation. In total, the donated collection included 476 books, 216 individual journal titles, 15 magazine issues, four DVDs, and two VHS cassettes, making this the single largest donation of materials since my arrival at BCC.

It is difficult to gauge the magnitude of donations without context. Therefore, I will attempt to put the donations made to the BCC Library—since my arrival—into perspective by contrasting the number of books donated to the number of books acquired through our yearly book budget. Some years our book budget tops $100,000, while on other occasions, the budget is significantly reduced. If we assume that the average monograph costs $100, then a $60,000 budget would allow me to purchase 600 books. If the average book costs $50, a $60,000 budget would allow me to purchase 1,200 books. When possible, I purchase books in hardbound or cloth format, and although expensive, these have a longer shelf life due to their durability. The two donations made by the CUNY Dominican Studies Institute Library provided the Bronx Community College Library with the equivalent of a year's worth of books. Furthermore, adding the CUNY DSI Library's donation of 556 books to the total amount of books donated by individuals and institutions since my arrival in 2017, surpasses 1,600 books.

To this day, I continue to work with colleagues to accept individual and institutional donations from the Museum of Modern Art (MoMA), the John Simon Guggenheim Memorial Foundation, the Consulate General of India, and many more generous partners. Through a combination of purchases and donations, we are building a collection that speaks to our student body and to the curriculum.

Donations: Best Practices

Regularly pursuing donations is an excellent way to grow one's collection as donations complement book purchases. These are some best practices when seeking donations:

Be sure to request the donor's contact information. However, be mindful that a donor may not want to disclose their name and contact information. Therefore, it is important to request this information in a respectful manner, but also let the donor know from the onset that it is optional to share this information.

> Be honest with the donor. Inform the donor that if a donated item is contaminated or in poor condition, library staff will not add the material to the collection. If the library has the same edition of the item, it is likely the library will not add the work to its collection. If it is deemed that the item is in good condition, library personnel may choose to donate the material.

> The person tasked with managing donations should create a system that documents all donations. It is highly recommended that one uses a program such as Microsoft Excel. Although alternate software such as Microsoft Word can be useful, an Excel spreadsheet provides one with more options for data management.

Library personnel should always send the donor a deed of gift and/or thank you letter that acknowledges their donation. It is advisable to include a list of all donated items since donors appreciate the gesture. Thank you letters may not always be possible due to circumstances beyond one's control such as when the donor does not provide their contact information or instances when the donor wishes to remain anonymous.

Collections for Students with Justice System Involvement and Carceral Studies

Developing and managing a library's collection requires one to work diligently to close the gaps that exist within our collection to ensure that we avoid creating archival silences as forewarned by conscientious scholars Michel-Rolph Trouillot and Marissa Fuentes. Both have written extensively about how the narratives of the underprivileged have been silenced by the historical record in favor of the records of elites. One of the perks of being a librarian is having the opportunity to interact with students on a regular basis. One population of students that we as information professionals encounter regularly at BCC are formerly incarcerated students. BCC has spearheaded several initiatives to tend to the needs of these students, including the establishment of the Kalief Browder Memorial Scholarship, established for formerly incarcerated students who are enrolled full-time at BCC. This scholarship is named in honor of Kalief Browder, who "spent three years at Rikers Island without ever being convicted of a crime" while enduring close to three years in solitary confinement (Gonnerman). Unfortunately, Browder passed away in 2015, but his legacy is endless. In 2017, the documentary, TIME: The Kalief Browder Story, premiered, and a year later it won a 2018 Peabody Award. BCC is aware of this student population and this scholarship is one initiative that acknowledges the presence of students with justice system involvement. All student populations at BCC are important and we (faculty, staff, etc.) must be able to provide the support that our students need.

In addition to supporting the Criminal Justice degree program, Paralegal Studies degree, and Paralegal Certificate, it is critical to develop a collection that speaks directly to students with an interest in Carceral Studies. Similar to scholars of Ethnic Studies such as Black and Latino/a/x studies programs, scholars and authors of Carceral Studies come from diverse backgrounds. The role of criminalization, the carceral state, and punishment go together and are all crucial to this area of inquiry. But just as important, these works speak directly to our population of formerly incarcerated students. For centuries, the lives of law enforcement and people of color in the United States have been intertwined through race, criminalization, and the Carceral State. In recent decades and in differing ways, scholars have correlated the institution of slavery to the Carceral State, if not writing off the latter as a continuation of the former. In *The Condemnation of Blackness: Race, Crime, and the Making of Modern America* (2010), Khalil Gibran

Muhammad writes about "the idea of black criminality in the making of modern urban America." One of Muhammad's major arguments is that today's modern urban America was shaped by the idea of Black criminality in the United States.

Initially I was a bit surprised when I realized that some crucial texts in Carceral Studies were not in the collection prior to my arrival. Michelle Alexander's *New Jim Crow: Mass Incarceration in the Age of Colorblindness* (2010) was certainly one of the books in our collection due to the debates and discussions it continues to generate. *The New Jim Crow* is still banned in several prisons across the United States. The last time I checked, the three copies at the BCC Library had been checked-out more than 100 times—a testament to the popularity of this text.

Having the ability to be able to read a book about one's experience or learning about a history that involves one, is very empowering. As Michelle Alexander notes in *The New Jim Crow*, people who are criminalized automatically become ineligible for life for public housing, educational benefits, welfare benefits, and other variations of government assistance, as many of our students at BCC are aware. The simple act of making these works available to our community of users allows us to empower our students. My goal is to ensure that our collection nurtures all our students.

Documenting Requests, Acquisitions, and Donations

There are multiple ways I engage the process of collection development to acquire titles. The BCC library subscribes to Choice Reviews, a publication that has been providing academic reviews of titles and electronic resources for more than 50 years, with approximately 2,400 academic libraries currently using this resource. I also take into consideration recommended titles from entities and platforms such as GOBI's Spotlight lists, the "Outstanding Reference Sources List" compiled yearly by the Reference & User Services Association (RUSA), National Book Awards, as well as Pulitzer and Nobel prize-winning authors. Additionally, I constantly seek recent and classic publications via a mixture of different means, which include conference attendance, subscribing to listservs, and more methods.

When I started at BCC in 2017, one of the earliest initiatives that I implemented involved the creation of a Microsoft Excel spreadsheet. This spreadsheet allows me to collate a list of book titles whether these are requests from faculty, staff, or students. Most of these titles, however, are books I have added based on the collection development strategies that I have learned to implement over the years as a librarian.

The color-coded Excel spreadsheet file that I named, "Bronx Community College Acquisitions Requests," contains the following information: book title, author, ISBN, year published, publisher, call number, price, department under which the book would fall under, the Library of Congress Classification, format (e.g. hardcover, paperback, e-book), date requested, date request was input, the corresponding librarian liaison, and the person who made the request (typically a faculty or staff from outside the library). Having a color-coded system allows me to keep track of specific title recommendations, special requests, and even the format. When discussing the color-coded system, I am referring to the "Fill-Color" feature within Excel, which, basically turns the background color of cells into the specified color. For example, the color "Blue, Accent 1" is used for textbooks; entries with a "Light Blue" color were previously requested; "Orange, Accent 2, Lighter 40%" are books that have yet to be published; entries in "Purple" are titles I plan to order the next time I place a purchase. In addition to this master spreadsheet, I have a second Excel file titled, "2017-2022 Book Acquisitions," wherein I copy titles from the original spreadsheet and paste them onto this different spreadsheet as titles arrive to our library. There is another step, however, as I use yellow highlight to distinguish these arrivals.

Conclusion

Students should have access to resources that relate to their own lived experiences. If we think about it for a moment, traditionally, the histories and literatures that students have been exposed to in the United States educational system are the histories and literatures of White U.S. Americans and Europeans. Historically, the voices of women and people of color have remained silent in favor of White, male narratives. Given the advent of "history from below" or the movement to tell a more inclusive social history, the 1960s saw the rise in telling the histories of people of color, thus paving the way for an increase in the visibility and recognition of people of color where their stories would be written, read, disseminated, and dissected. Some of the largest populations at BCC are foreign-born students, especially those who are African-born or born in Latin America, with the largest ethnic group deriving from the Dominican Republic. It would be a disservice to ignore any of BCC's populations.

By decolonizing the library, we are also diversifying the collection to reflect our student population. Diversification and decolonization go hand-in-hand with one another. Part of the strength of a library's collection is found in the extent of its diversity. Yes, I argue that being exposed to resources pertinent to one's background is an empowering endeavor. However, being exposed to the culture of another person and reading about the experiences of individuals from a different part of the world can be enriching for our intellectual growth. Not only is this enriching because we learn about someone else or another culture, but the experience is enriching and fulfilling because if we read carefully, we will notice commonalities between ourselves and those people that we initially viewed as different from us. That is the beauty of diversity.

Just as one easily celebrates one's accomplishments, it is important to note deficiencies in one's scholarship as well as initiatives that may not be successful. For instance, one of the issues with this work pertains to it not fully being a case study of the Bronx Community College Library. Thus, no data pertinent to collection development at Bronx Community College was collected and analyzed for this study. Consequently, having an understanding of the aforementioned, I intend to do a follow-up to this chapter by surveying Bronx Community College Library users.

In this chapter, I outlined specific initiatives that can be undertaken to ensure successful collection development guided by diversity, equity, inclusion, and accessibility. These efforts include participation and attendance at professional development meetings and events; initiatives that engage and include active participation from BCC stakeholders; and initiatives that foster relationships with sister institutions and individual donors such as the CUNY Dominican Studies Institute. My expectation is that this chapter will provide a framework and model examples for others to emulate my work, critique it, and improve upon it. Lastly, this chapter provided readers with a starting point for engaging with works that utilize theoretical frameworks in the realm of decoloniality, Critical Race Theory, and related schools of thought, situating the library within the landscape of decolonization and decolonial movements as noted by scholars of color.

Bronx Community College Acquisitions Requests (2017; Since Nelson Santana's Arrival)

LEGEND
Ordered
We Own It
DVD/CD
On Order
Special Request
Order Next Time
Out of Print
Previously Requested
Eliminated from Previous Order
Not yet published
Adding to Books Bundle
Reference
E-book

Title	Author	ISBN	Year	Publisher	Call #	CUNY	Price	Dept.	LC Class.	Format	Req. Date	Date Input	Librarian	Professor	Notes

Figure 1

References

Alexander, M. (2010). *The New Jim Crow: Mass incarceration in the age of color-blindness.* The New Press.

Aponte, S. & Santana, N. (2019). The CUNY Dominican Studies Institute Library: Bringing the community to the academic library. In G.A. Williams & J.L. Krentz (Eds.), *Latin American collection concepts: Essays on libraries, collaborations and new approaches* (pp. 183-195). McFarland & Company, Inc.

BCC to remove Confederate statue at Bronx Hall of Fame. (2017, August 17). Norwood News. Retrieved February 28, 2022, from https://www.norwood-news.org/bcc-remove-confederate-statue-bronx-hall-fame/.

Biondi, M. (2014). *The Black revolution on campus.* University of California Press.

Bronx Community College Library Collection Development Policy. Bronx Community College. (n.d.). Retrieved February 25, 2022, from http://www.bcc.cuny.edu/wp-content/uploads/2018/04/library_collection-devpolicy.pdf.

Césaire, A. (1972) *Discourse on Colonialism.* Monthly Review Press.

Chou, R.L. & Pho, A. (2017) Intersectionality at the reference desk: Lived experiences of women of color librarians. In M.T. Accardi (Ed.), *The Feminist Reference Desk: Concepts, Critiques, and Conversations* (pp. 225-252) Library Juice Press.

Clement, Susanne K. & Judith M. Nixon. (2017). Sharing knowledge and smashing stereotypes: Representing Native American, First Nation, and Indigenous realities in library collections. *Collection Management, 42*(3-4), 123, 2017. https://doi.org/10.1080/01462679.2017.1392806

Conner-Gaten, A., Caragher, J., & Drake, T. (2017). Collections decoded: Reflections and strategies for anti-racist collection development. In Baudino, F., Hart, K., & Johnson, Carolyn, Brick & Click: *An Academic Library Conference*, 3 Nov. 2017, Northwest Missouri State University, Maryville, Missouri.

Crenshaw, K, Gotanda, N.T., Peller, G., & Thomas, K. (1995). *Critical Race Theory: The key writings that formed the movement.* New Press.

CUNY Language Immersion Program (CLIP). The City University of New York. (n.d.). Retrieved February 25, 2022, from https://www.cuny.edu/academics/academic-programs/model-programs/cuny-college-transition-programs/cuny-language-immersion-program-clip/.

The CUNY story: A brief history. The City University of New York. (n.d.) Retrieved March 1, 2022, from https://www.cuny.edu/about/history/.

Drollinger, T., Comer, L. B., & Warrington, P. T. (2006). Development and validation of the active empathetic listening scale. *Psychology & Marketing, 23*(2), 161-180. https://doi.org/10.1002/mar.20105

Fanon, F. (1986). *Black skin, white masks.* Pluto Press.

Fitzgerald, F.S. (1925). *The great Gatsby.* Charles Scribner's Sons.

Flood, A. (2014, May 1). F Scott Fitzgerald stories published uncensored for the first time. *The Guardian.* Retrieved February 25, 2022, from https://www.theguardian.com/books/2014/may/01/f-scott-fitzgerald-stories-uncensored-sexual-innuendo-drug.

Fox, M.J. (2016). "Priorities of arrangement" or a "hierarchy of oppressions"?: Perspectives on intersectionality in knowledge organization. *Knowledge Organization 43*(5), 373-383.

Fuentes, M.J. (2010) Power and historical figuring: Rachael Pringle Polgreen's troubled archive. *Gender and History 22*(3), 564-584.

Fuentes, M.J. (2016). *Dispossessed lives: Enslaved women, violence, and the archive.* University of Pennsylvania Press.

Furst, J., Willoughby Nason, J., & Sandow, N. (Creators). (2017). *TIME: The Kalief Browder Story.* [TV series]. The Cinemart. The Weinstein Company. Netflix.

Gonnerman, J. (2015, June 7). Kalief Browder, 1993-2015. *The New Yorker.* Retrieved on February 20, 2022, from https://www.newyorker.com/news/news-desk/kalief-browder-1993-2015.

Hall of Fame for Great Americans. Bronx Community College. Retrieved March 2, 2022, from https://site.bcc.cuny.edu/HallOfFame/.

History and architecture. Bronx Community College. (n.d.) Retrieved March 2, 2022, from http://www.bcc.cuny.edu/about-bcc/history-architecture/.

Leung, S.Y, & López-McKnight, J. (2021). *Knowledge justice: Disrupting library and information studies through Critical Race Theory.* The MIT Press.

Mignolo, W.D., & Walsh, C.E. (2018). *Decoloniality: Concepts, analytics, praxis.* Duke University Press.

Muhammad, K.G. (2010). *The condemnation of blackness: Race, crime, and the making of modern urban America.* Harvard University Press.

Salinger, J.D. (1951). *The catcher in the rye.* Little, Brown and Company.

Statement from Dr. Seuss Enterprises. Seussville. (2021, March 2). Retrieved February 25, 2022, from https://www.seussville.com/statement-from-dr-seuss-enterprises/.

Thiong'o, N. (1986). *Decolonising the mind: The politics of language in African literature.* J. Currey.

Trouillot, M.R. (1995). *Silencing the past: Power and the production of history.* Beacon Press.

Twain, M. (1844). *The adventures of Huckleberry Finn.* Chatto & Windus / Charles L. Webster and Company.

Van Nort, S.C. (2007). *The City College of New York.* Arcadia Press.

Walker, S. (2015). Critical Race Theory and the recruitment, retention and promotion of a librarian of color. In R. Hankins & M. Juárez, *Where are all the librarians of color?: The experiences of people of color in academia* (pp. 135-160). Library Juice Press.

Section 4
Archives, Research, and Heritage

Archives, Libraries, and Pedagogy at the California State University, Los Angeles

Azalea Camacho
Mario H. Ramirez
Lettycia Terrones

Introduction

Situated at the gateways to East Los Angeles and the San Gabriel Valley, the California State University, Los Angeles (Cal State LA) sits at the heart of multiple immigrant, BIPOC, and activists histories and communities that contribute greatly to the makeup of its students and their experiential diversity. Home to long standing Latinx, Asian American, and Armenian communities, the region is a beacon for the rich tapestry of BIPOC and immigrant life in the greater Los Angeles area, and the concomitant and dedicated effort to celebrate and nourish the many cultures and diasporas that have come to flourish here. Key to the endurance of these communities, even in the face of socio-political marginalization, racism, and attempts at their cultural erasure, has been their ongoing struggle to maintain a foothold in the region, and fight for the integrity and importance of their social, cultural, economic, and historical contributions to their neighborhoods and Los Angeles. This notwithstanding, communities in the area continue to grapple with numerous challenges that frustrate their success and which filter into the very fabric of communal life.

As inheritors of these rich yet complicated legacies, the students at Cal State LA, the bulk of whom are culled from the region, bring to the

campus and their studies unique needs and opportunities for recon-
ceptualizing the pedagogical endeavor, and for transforming the strategies used to engage and stimulate BIPOC, immigrant, and first-generation students at what is, ostensibly, a Hispanic and Minority Serving
Institution. Garcia and Okhidoi note, HSI's "must actively change their
curricula and programs to meet the needs of their diverse population,
including Latina/o, low income, and first-generation students" (Garcia
2015, p. 345). Veering away from a "deficit narrative," (Garcia, et al., 2019,
p. 751) which highlights what students lack as opposed to the experiential richness they bring to university life, HSI's are "responsible for fostering a sense of inclusion and intentionally facilitate positive group relations between students, faculty, and staff from diverse backgrounds,"
(Franco and Hernandez, 2018, p. 64) and for engendering an organizational framework "that is grounded in decolonization" and is organized
"for the empowerment and liberation of racially minoritized students"
(Garcia, 2018, p. 133). As an institution where the student body is close to
70% Latinx and predominantly immigrant, working-class, and first-generation Cal State LA's commitment to social justice is all the more key for
the development of pedagogies, services, and programming that are equitable and inclusive, and speak to the life experiences of our students.

The role of the university library, and more specifically special collections and archives and the work of instructional librarians, is to not
only uphold the core mission and values of the university in regard to
its student body, but to, moreover, push the boundaries of collaborative pedagogies as a means of centering the histories and learning
capabilities of students. As Latinx, immigrant, and working-class individuals ourselves, who have been active in our respective fields and
social justice movements for several decades now, this focus on the
communities and experiences of BIPOC and immigrant students has
been at the core of our collective work throughout our careers, and
is central to our efforts at Cal State LA. Our ongoing commitment is
to not only provide experiences and pedagogical materials that approach our students with an equity and intentionality, but, moreover,
to do this work while relating to and centering their lives, communities, and knowledges. We aim to do this in the development of special
collections and archives collections, workshops, courses, programming, and mentorship, and that of the instruction team's workshops,
instruction, and outreach. As Lumley (2020) asserts, "A fundamental goal of the library...must be to reassert its role as a democratic commons where the voices of all are encouraged to speak out and

be heard, especially those who recognize a need for resistance or change" (p. 483, 2020). Our positioning as Latinx faculty and librarians and archivists, historically deficient in the academy, yet instrumental towards the success of Latinx and other BIPOC students, (Vargas, et al., 2019; Adkins and Hussey, 2006) continues to be key to our commitment to embedding multiple perspectives and pedagogical approaches in the work of our library, and in our personal investment in supporting the students at Cal State LA.

In the following chapter, we will expand upon some of the pedagogical methods we have developed to engage our predominantly immigrant, Latinx, first generation, and undergraduate student body in archival and academic research. When confronted with the task of research, primary as well as secondary, this student population (which faces numerous socio-economic, cultural, and educational challenges) requires the creation of more innovative strategies that foreground their experiences and take into account the profound connections between community, memory, and geography that shape their histories, identities, and interests. Based on community archives principles and praxes, as well as library pedagogies and praxes that center social justice, our approach foregrounds the experiences of marginalized populations, and how the lives of students, their communities, and families are the fundamental basis for history making, research, and academic study.

Among the examples we will discuss include our Work It Out Wednesdays and LibraryLive! series on information literacy and research skills which feature student-led panels sharing insider strategies for accessing library resources and effective research help; mini-tutorials and lectures via Instagram on a number of information literacy topics; and collaborative teaching opportunities with campus partners such as the Center for Academic Success and the Educational Opportunity Program's transfer student support office. In addition, we will present a case study on how we embed archival instruction within undergraduate courses and syllabi as a means of cultivating an early engagement with the formation of community driven histories.

Mervyn M. Dymally: Bridgebuilder and History Maker, Public Events and Exhibition Project

This case study describes the Mervyn M. Dymally: Bridgebuilder and History Maker, Public Events and Exhibition Project at Cal State LA, which began in fall 2019 as a collaborative partnership between a disciplinary lecturer, an archivist, and undergraduate students. The partnership was founded on developing a project-based, active-learning experience through teaching history, archival practice, and primary source analysis. Together we explored various approaches to engage students beyond the classroom setting by embedding archival practice throughout a history course focused on the intersections of race and ethnicity with culture, gender, and socio-economic class in the United States. We integrated archival practice and primary source analysis by engaging students with the physical processing of the Mervyn M. Dymally (1926-2012) Papers. Dymally emigrated from Trinidad at the age of nineteen and became the first Black Lieutenant Governor of California (1975-1979) after serving in both the California State Assembly (1963-1966, 2002-2008) and State Senate (1967-1975). He later served for twelve years in the United States House of Representatives (1981-1993). Dymally is known for coalition building and challenging racial barriers by advancing equality and human rights. The collection includes over 300 record storage boxes of materials, consisting of legislative files, correspondence, committee and congressional files, press releases, speeches, photographs, awards, and ephemera.

Planning & Preparation

The initial planning for this course began in summer 2019 in preparation for the start of the 2019-2020 academic year. Two sections of the course worked on processing the correspondence and photographs of the Dymally Papers. Three special collections and archives instruction sessions were customized to include,

Session 1: Introduction to Special Collections & Archives

1. Overview of Special Collections & Archives
2. Conducting Research
3. Visiting
4. Guidelines
5. Tour of the Department

Session 2: Archival Processing

1. Preliminary Research

2. Biographical and Historical Research

3. Developing a Processing Plan

4. Inventory & Container List

5. Dymally: The First of His Kind Documentary

Session 3: Activity–Hands on Archival Processing

1. Organization of the collection

2. Rehousing

3. Labeling

Each instruction session was designed to build upon one another to prepare students for physical processing. However, the sessions in special collections and archives exceeded the three originally outlined due to the interest of the students and flexibility of the lecturer to adapt the syllabus to focus on the processing project. Initially, each student was to complete the archival processing of two record storage boxes of materials. However, students expressed interest in continuing to visit the archives to not only complete the two record storage boxes assigned to them, but to complete as many boxes as possible throughout the semester. Both sections of the course were scheduled once a week in the archives for the duration of the semester. The assignments for the course were created to assess the student's physical processing work in the archives. The midterm focused on the history of archival practice in the United States. The mid-semester reflection essay asked students to identify academic and real-life skills learned from processing the collection. The final exam was an analysis of a select group of primary sources discovered by students during processing sessions. Students also completed inventory worksheets for each box of materials and submitted an exhibit worksheet at the end of the course. The exhibit worksheet was used in the spring semester to curate a virtual exhibition. Special collections and archives staff compiled the data collected by student and included that in the container list of the finding aid.

Figure 1 Students processing the photographs from the Mervyn M. Dymally Papers.

Figure 2 Student reviewing photographs of Mervyn M. Dymally and Cesar Chavez.

Figure 3 Students processing the correspondence from the Mervyn M. Dymally Papers

Figure 4 Student processing reviewing the correspondence in the Mervyn M. Dymally Papers

The use of primary sources encouraged curiosity and inquiry-based learning and select course readings that covered the origins, growth, and challenges of archives enhanced student understanding of race and ethnicity in the nation. As students processed the collection, they constructed their own arguments based on original research and evidence to draw connections between primary sources and course readings. Through the semester length active learning experience, students met the following shared learning outcomes:

- Acquire primary source, information, visual, and digital literacy skills.

- Learn about collective memory, cultural heritage, and individual/cultural perspectives.

- Understanding archival processing and the importance of preservation.

- Develop historical thinking skills by learning about Dymally's role in Los Angeles, politics, and in the larger national landscape.

Pivot to Virtual Learning

In spring 2020, due to the COVID-19 pandemic, students were no longer able to physically process the collection in person. All courses were adapted to the virtual learning environment. The initial idea was to continue to build on the work of the students from the previous semester and integrate the curation process of developing an exhibition in an urban history course in spring 2020. However, a physical exhibition was no longer an option, the university library lacked the resources to support a virtual exhibit and public programming events. During this time the social sciences librarian joined the lecturer and archivist in preparation of an instruction session that included curation and label writing. Together they applied to the California Humanities Quick Grant and were granted the funds to move forward with the virtual exhibition and public programming project highlighting the student work and the life and legacy of Dymally. The Mervyn M. Dymally Bridgebuilder and History Maker, Public Events and Exhibition Project consisted of a three-part series: Virtual Exhibit Launch and Gallery Tour, Co-hosted Event with the Autry Museum of the American West, and Community Speaker Panel with Cal State LA Project Rebound and The Los Angeles Regional Reentry Partnership (LAARP).

We held two instruction sessions virtually introducing students to the Dymally Papers, curation, and caption writing. In addition, throughout the semester both the librarian and archivist visited the class to assist and provide feedback to the students on their captions. The student research and writing of the captions challenged them to write succinct and compelling content for a specific audience and purpose. Students in both courses became part of the collaborative process of making an archival collection accessible from inception to the curation of a virtual exhibition that will inspire knowledge creation, facilitate intentional dialogue, and produce research and scholarship opportunities for future students and faculty.

Outcome

What started as an instruction session inspired by the embedded archivist model moved beyond our expectations and continues to grow well into 2022. The driving force and success of the project was due to the genuine interest between the librarian, archivist, and lecturer to cultivate critical thinking, encourage inquiry-based learning, information literacy, and research skills among Cal State LA students. Students also related to Dymally's story as an alum of Cal State LA and the materials within his collection that documented the history of Los Angeles. They were able to recognize locations, people, and subjects they were familiar with from their own communities, such as ethnic studies, educational equity, state violence, and incarceration. Our students come from working-class and commuter backgrounds, are first-generation, are ethnically and racially diverse, and represent a varied range of academic skills. Through this project we aimed to provide students with a hands-on experience that will enhance and supplement their academic courses and develop transferable skills.

Throughout the course of the project students in the courses represented majors that ranged from history, math, technological sciences, electrical and civil engineering, criminal justice, and biological and cognitive sciences. Students enhanced their information literacy skills and improved their historical and critical thinking skills by analyzing primary sources. Through the midterm reflection essay course assignment students in both courses indicated that through archival processing they gained real-life skills, such as organizational methods, hierarchies and various measures used in data collection, collaboration and teamwork, and close attention to project details. Overall, students took part in the collaborative process of preserving and providing accessibility to an archival collection from inception to curation of a virtual exhibition, which will engage our campus community, facilitate intentional dialogue, and produce research and scholarship opportunities.

Engaged Pedagogy and Chicana Feminist Epistemology and Information Literacy

This section of the chapter describes the culturally sustaining pedagogical approaches and philosophy that guide the information literacy (IL) initiatives that I, Lettycia Terrones, have developed at California State University Library in my role as learning and instruction services librarian. Chicana Feminist Epistemology (CFE) and Engaged Pedagogy (EP) practices of care deeply ground the methodology taken in the development of these initiatives. The delivery of these initiatives and

our students' response to them confirm the power in the pedagogical impact both CFE and EP have on our student demographic. CFE, as
Calderón et al. (2012) remind us, unfolds from Chicana philosopher Gloria Anzaldúa's "powerful insights [that] speak directly to our work as
Chicana education scholars committed to anti-oppressive social justice research and guided by Chicana feminist epistemological frameworks" (Calderón et al., 2012, p. 514). CFE not only weaves a critique of
dominations, including the critique of "dominate research paradigms,"
it also boldly orients our work as educators as being "both spiritual
and intellectual, [requiring] deep introspection and a vision for something different" (p. 514). In Teaching to Transgress: Education as the
Practice of Freedom, bell hooks (1994) similarly foreground the spiritual aspects of EP, stating that "those of us who teach [as a practice
of freedom] also believe that there is an aspect of our vocation that is
sacred; [we] believe that our work is not merely to share information
but to share in the intellectual and spiritual growth of our students"
(p. 13). The new IL initiatives unfolding strive to tap into the intersections where intellectual and the spiritual meet.

As feminist practices, both CFE and EP center the importance of connecting personal experience to the analytic process, particularly an
analytic process that critiques power dynamics in their analysis of social phenomena. CFE and EP pedagogy extends the feminist stand-
point that the "the personal is political" (Hanisch, 2006) in two distinct ways. EP not only "acknowledge[s] a connection between ideas
learned in university settings and those learned in life practices," it
further "emphasizes wellbeing" (hooks, 1994, p. 15). EP is critically attentive to teaching practices that cultivate grounds for "self-actualization that promotes" wellbeing for all those engaged in the learning process, teachers and students alike. An EP pedagogical approach
views teachers and students "as 'whole' human beings, striving not
just for knowledge in books, but knowledge about how to live in the
world" (hooks, 1994, p. 14-15). Like EP, CFE also capacitates a wholis-
tic understanding of students and teachers engaged in the learning
space, by drawing from personal experience as a "source of cultural
intuition ... derived from the background that we each bring to the research situation" (Bernal, 1998, p. 564).

Dolores Delgado Bernal (1998) articulated the role of cultural intuition
within Chicana Feminist Epistemology—an epistemology and social
justice critique of the world that "arises out of a unique social and
cultural history, and demonstrates that our experiences as Mexican

women are legitimate, appropriate, and effective in designing, conducting, and analyzing educational research" (p. 563). Delgado Bernal theorizes cultural intuition as a complex process emerging in the dynamic confluence between personal and collective experience, noting how the shared knowledges transferred generationally through "ancestral wisdom, community memory, and intuition influence one's own personal experiences" (p. 565). Cultural intuition as understood by CFE, necessarily concerns itself with the holistic wellbeing of teachers and students because it engages an analytical process that draws from Chicana feminist practices of care that "resist dominant epistemologies" that bring forward the lived experiences and histories of Chicanas (Bernal, 1998, p. 568). The reparative work of forwarding and recovering Chicana ways of knowing necessarily expands an ethic of care. This imperative to care about our students lives, to honor their diverse cultural knowledges, and to view their wellbeing as more than just academic success measured by completion rates, deeply orients the design and delivery of the IL initiatives I have developed at Cal State LA. By grounding in EP and CFE, these initiatives align with what Gina Ann Garcia (2019) recommends for creating "Latinx-enhancing" spaces as a charge of HSI universities by intentionally creating "spaces that not only recognize minoritized students' ways of knowing and begin, but enhance their sense of belonging, engagement, racial and ethnic identity, and personal knowledge of self" (p. 49-50).

From Personal Experience to A Wholistic Wellbeing Approach in IL

To describe how CFE and EP practices of care inform the methodology for developing and delivering initiatives at Cal State LA, I begin with a personal story that locates my investments, obligations, and accountability to the practices of care in teaching information literacy. I am the daughter of Rosario and Juventino Terrones. I grew up in the historically working-class and racially diverse neighborhood of Boyle Heights in East Los Angeles and attended California's public schools, including, Roosevelt High School, UC Berkeley, East Los Angeles Community College (ELAC), Cal State LA, and UCLA. As a first-generation, Chicana from an undocumented Mexican immigrant family, I understand my achievements in higher education as deeply non-individualistic, and profoundly tethered to kin. My parents' educational aspirations for my five siblings and me was forged in the fields tilled and harvested by my father's Bracero hands. It was manifested in my mother's heart and mind during the many hours she labored scrubbing floors, washing dishes, and caring for the children of her bosses. Between them, my parents, Rosario and Juventino Terrones, have a combined six years of rural classroom education. Yet they actualized educational experiences that have empowered all of their children to live lives less impacted by exploitation.

Cal State LA plays a significant role in this story. It was where my brother Humberto—the first of my siblings to attend college—enrolled after graduating from Roosevelt High School. My sister Teresa earned her Elementary School Teacher Credential at Cal State LA. I danced and practiced musical theatre in the studios and hallways of the physical education building as a middle-schooler in the Conservatory of Fine Arts program that took place Saturday mornings. When my tenth-grade class visited the campus, I was already familiar with the shining Solar Eagle I, and could tell my classmates the story about how this award-winning, solar-powered car was built by the hands and minds of Cal State LA's brilliant students and faculty in the School of Engineering and Technology.

Like many working-poor people, my family moved often and rented exclusively in the eastside. From these locations, the prominent black and gold letters atop Simpson Tower spelling "Cal State L.A." remained a visible marker, signifying to us that Cal State LA was attainable. We belonged at Cal State LA. The university remains material in my life and educational journey. I center myself in this way to emphasize the incalculable value that Cal State LA has and continues to have in shaping the many lives that comprise its thriving communities. I center in this way to illustrate my close affinity with our students and their lived experiences. My lived experiences as a working-class, first-generation, daughter of immigrants, and woman of color from East Los Angeles who has navigated a wide range of higher education institutions—as a student, librarian, educator, mentor, and leader—equip me with the technical and cultural skill set to support the educational success and aspirations of Cal State LA's students.

The many challenges I have faced as a racialized minority in academia have taught me the value of setting ambitious goals, cultivating excellence through diligent, dedicated, and attentive work, and deploying my intellectual and creative assets purposefully to serve the public good. My commitment to empowering students in higher education is informed by my conviction that our struggles for justice and dignity are worthy and realizable. It is our ethical imperative to amplify the ways in which race, ethnicity, class, gender, sexuality, ability, age, and citizenship status are all key to innovation and vitality. The rich complexity found in diverse and intersectional lives is indeed our greatest asset. The complex and multiple viewpoints and experiences found in our diversity activate our capacities to imagine new ways of orienting our social lives and, indeed, our hearts and minds. Beginning in this manner allows me to map a conceptual trajectory about the critical pedagogy that provides the vision for my IL work. This map traces the pedagogical imperatives that locate my obligations to critical pedagogies vis-à-vis IL.

James Baldwin's classic essay, "A Talk to Teachers," has profoundly shaped the ethical obligations I assume in my role as a librarian educator and teacher of information literacy. In it, Baldwin confronts the epistemic violence of anti-black racism in the American public school system. Presenting a reckoning for white publics, specifically the cultural and intellectual elites in charge of the institutions of American education, Baldwin describes the "paradox of education" (Baldwin, p. 17). Baldwin reminds us that despite what normative educational structures may purport in their discourse about the importance of intellectual inquiry, "no society is really anxious to have that kind of person around. What societies really, ideally, want is a citizenry which will simply obey the rules of society" (p. 18). Baldwin then shifts, presenting his readers with a warning and an ethical charge. American education and society will surely collapse if American education continues unchallenged in its anti-Black violence, its biopolitical management of Black students, and by extension minoritarian students. Baldwin's charge for the critical educator makes clear the obligations we all have to fight against the inertia of anti-Black epistemic violence. Our charge is to teach our students that they do not "have to be bound by the expediencies of any given administration, any given policy, any given morality; that [they have] the right and the necessity to examine everything" (p. 19). This is criticality and, indeed, a move central to intellectual inquiry. Criticality is deeply ethical because it advances critical thinking toward imagining and enacting a more just world.

Baldwin's pedagogical imperative aligns with Bernal's theory of cultural intuition and the epistemological perspective that activates the criticality Baldwin describes. In my development and delivery of IL initiatives, I deploy "cultural intuition" to critically examine and "question whose knowledge and realities are accepted as the foundation of knowledge, especially in the research process" (Bernal, 2020, p. 155). I model to our students moves criticality makes toward disrupting dominate normative epistemologies. Criticality "opens up possibilities for how we conduct research and how we reconceptualize what it means to teach and learn," and gives us all opportunities to rehearse and envision worlds that do not reproduce the violence of epistemological violence. (Bernal, 2020, p. 156). Moreover, as hooks (1994) reminds us engaged pedagogy (EP) views criticality or intellectual inquiry is not solely the domain of academic profession, where professionalization "within bourgeois educational structures" dismisses our pedagogical imperatives to the wholeness or wellbeing of our students and teachers (p. 16).

Often this dismissal of our students and teachers recurs at the site of language and the linguist diversity of racialized people. Jonathan Rosa and Nelson Flores (2017) theorize raciolinguistics as ideologies that "conflate certain racialized bodies with linguistic deficiency unrelated to any objective linguistic practices" (p. 177). How raciolinguistics operates in academia is especially important to my pedagogical approaches in developing and delivering IL initiatives at Cal State LA. Rather that positioning our students' linguist practices as well as their information literacy skills as assets from which to build on toward acquisition of so-called academic language and information literacy skills, I take a culturally relevant pedagogical approach. Gloria Ladson-Billings (1995) defines culturally relevant pedagogy as "a theoretical model that not only addresses student achievement but also helps students to accept and affirm their cultural identity while developing critical perspectives that challenge inequities that schools (and other institutions) perpetuate" (p. 469). My goal as a teacher is not to have our students understand their information literacy skills as always already measured against a proximity to "academic language," but to rather view their already existing criticality as an asset toward challenging dominate ideologies of standardized academic achievement. In the next section, I describe two IL initiatives I designed—Work It Out Wednesdays and LibraryLive!—to demonstrate how the culturally relevant education theories described above inform the EP practices of care and CFE cultural intuition I bring to my delivery of the programs and my engagement with our students.

Culturally Relevant IL at Cal State LA: Work It Out Wednesdays and LibraryLive!

Work It Out Wednesdays (WOW) is a weekly IL initiative that happens live every Wednesday at 11:30 am (PST) via Cal State LA Library's Instagram, @calstatelalibrary. A collaboration between myself and Kelsey Brown, the communications strategist and event coordinator at Cal State LA Library, WOW is an experimental teaching approach leveraging social media for the creation of non-traditional teaching spaces for information literacy instruction. WOW aligns with cognate literacy teaching approaches using "[d]igital platforms and social media [to] provide a unique way to bring affinity spaces together across" diverse locations and access points (Buffone & Jerasa, 2021, p. 10). During WOW, I deliver a 5–7-minute micro-lesson or info-blast on broad scope of information literacy skills and concepts. Each week's topics is directly informed by student reference questions that I engage in reference consultations as well as the questions students ask in our IL webinar sessions (LibraryLive!). I come into WOW with a brief outline of the day's topic which I use to launch into an improvised non-scripted mini-lesson based on the co-produced data (student generated questions engaged in reference and IL activities). Here, I rely on what Bernal theorizes in her description of cultural intuition to interpret and draw from this data and to address the IL needs students bring to research consultations and IL webinars. I draw from my personal experiences in education and the collective knowledges culled from my family and communities' experiencing of marginalization from normative educational systems to deliver WOW content.

Cal State LA's library instruction program has a robust approach to teaching operational skills for information literacy. This includes teaching students where to locate subject databases in our library catalog and website, how to use database tools to organize sources, including email, citation exporting, and PDF downloading management tools. I designed my WOW info-blasts to integrate the teaching of critical thinking strategies to support investigative moves required for research, what the Association of College and Research Libraries (ACRL) *Framework terms: "knowledge practices, which are demonstrations of ways in which learners can increase their understanding of these information literacy concepts, and...describe ways in which to address the affective, attitudinal, or valuing dimension of learning"* (ACRL 7-8). The conceptual aspects or knowledge practices of IL often prove more difficult to scaffold in traditional one-shot IL instruction.

and is less tangible because the traditional one-shot model of library instruction for information literacy does not allow for open-ended discussions and query posing.

The purpose of WOW, then, is to provide information "blasts" on information literacy concepts that center explanation and discussion of strategies for building critical thinking. For example, students are tasked with locating and incorporating peer-reviewed scholarly literature in their course papers. At WOW we have the opportunity to engage in sustained discussion around the concept and process of the peer-review process, the differences between empirical studies, literature reviews and theoretical articles, and the importance of building background knowledge on theoretical concepts and historical events to use in their development of course papers. Because WOW occurs live on Instagram, we are not focused on modeling how to use database platforms but can rather to take a deeper-dive to explain, for instance, how students can locate research methodologies in article abstracts to distinguish between types of scholarly articles, i.e., empirical studies, literature reviews, conceptual articles, etc. This is important because these concepts may be less tangible to address in traditional one-shot model of library instruction for information literacy where time constraints and the tailoring to specific course assignments may not allow for open-ended discussions and query posing. The purpose of Work It Out Wednesdays, then, is to provide information "blasts" on information literacy concepts that center explanation and discussion of strategies for building critical thinking. The images below capture some of our WOW live teaching performances.

Instagram: @calstatelalibrary

Additionally, WOW intentionally delivers "academic language" and the productions of scholarly production in ways that are approachable, low stakes, and easily accessible for students. I fashion my WOW teaching as performances as understood by Diana Taylor's (2003) concept of archive and repertoire, a performance studies theory that accounts for the transmission of knowledge through embodied performance or repertoire. As Taylor notes, the "ephemeral repertoire of embodied practice/knowledge … enacts embodied memory: performances, gestures, orality, movement, dance, singing—in short, all those acts usually thought of as ephemeral, nonpreducible knowledge" (p. 19-20). While we do upload (archive) WOW to the Cal State LA Instagram, these teaching performances are activated in an ephemeral repertoire. While their ephemeral and dynamic aspect may not be attributed the same authority, particularly at the site of disciplinary strongholds and canonical investments privileging writing systems over oral, visual, or otherwise performed systems, the response we receive from our students evidences their impact. As of April 18, 2022, 10:03 am (PST) our WOW program has 1406 total views, with a number of posts shared by views on their respective Instagram stories. However, WOW performances and shared content does not limit itself to strictly traditional IL skills and concepts. Woven into each WOW are messages that bring us back to the EP imperatives of teaching with care toward the holistic wellbeing of our students. I begin each WOW by directly addressing our students at Cal State LA with words of wisdom and kinship. These have included a meditation by Thích Nhất Hạnh titled "Flower Fresh," shout-outs to local artists and cultural workers in Boyle Heights, a neighborhood adjacent to our university, and sharing of resources toward the abolition of prisons.

!!!

!!!

This methodological shift toward everyday acts of care for our students further show up in our information literacy instruction delivery in LibraryLive! a research skills webinar series I launched in fall 2020. I developed LibraryLive!, to provide our students with synchronous and recorded Zoom workshops centered on foundational information literacy and research skills. Co-teaching LibraryLive! with Azalea Camacho, archivist and special collections librarian at Cal State LA has opened opportunities to weave in primary source instruction to our sessions. For example, one of our LibraryLive! sessions included students using concept mapping to evaluate primary sources from Compton Communicative Arts Academy (CCAA). Students practice formulating research questions around primary source materials. LibraryLive!, now in its fourth semester, occurs six times per semester and averages a student attendance of 50 at each session. LibraryLive! scaffolds student learning outcomes identified in the ACRL Framework for Information Literacy for Higher Education, including systematic gathering of information such as background resources, secondary sources, and primary sources, and reference consultation; use of databases to identify and apply scholarly literature by using keywords, subject terms, and research method descriptors; evaluation of scholarly literature and its citational use; and the analysis of readership, publication processes, and citational practices. LibraryLive! works with these outcomes that demonstrate standardized information literacy, but we do so by emphasizing peer-to-peer modeling in the building of these skills. For example, our "Level Up! Library Student Workers Share Tips and Resources" LibraryLive! webinar in fall 2021 built upon providing students with a general orientation to the Cal State LA Virtual Library, but from a student-centered perspective. Our panels of student presenters offered recommendations, resource sharing, and advice for leveraging library resources including Writing Wing tutoring, student research consultant reference, and special collections and archives internship advice to support our students' research skills and critical thinking dispositions. We also held a student panel featuring transfer students from the Educational Opportunity Program (EOP) speaking about their use of library resources such as reference consultation and library study spaces.

Conclusion

The through lines that connect our pedagogy and advocacy for the students at Cal State LA, are deeply rooted in the personal and professional experiences we bring to our work at the university library. Through the various workshops, instructional sessions, reference interviews, or forms of outreach we conduct, at the center is our commitment towards empowering a student population that reflects our own communities and families, and who require a much more engaged and progressive pedagogy. This community based and driven approach seeks to not only build research skills but to promote critical thinking. It goes beyond traditional library and archives instruction models that focus primarily on communicating the content of instruction, rather than integrating the intersectional lives and experiences of students and learners. Actively involving students in the pedagogical process and foregrounding the importance of their contributions, is critical towards making education and universities relevant to our student population.

Moving forward, our commitment towards modeling social justice and empathy in our pedagogy will be at the heart of the development of new instructional initiatives, and will continue to center and celebrate the lived experiences of the students at Cal State LA. In addition to building upon existing collaborations such as embedding primary source instruction into student coursework and dynamic outreach and instruction via Work It Out Wednesdays and LibraryLive!, we are also planning to cultivate the critical thinking skills of our students through credit bearing courses. These courses will explore the practice and principles of archival work, as well as the relationship between archives and race, gender, and information in contemporary society. Indeed, in the future, we anticipate building one of the only undergraduate minors in information science in the California State University system that trains underrepresented and minoritized students in the critical praxis of information studies. Our hope is that this will not only train a new and more diverse generation of library and archives professionals, but that it will further integrate the rich lives, experiences, and communities of Cal State LA students into the world of library and archives and, subsequently, change the field. This process of decolonization will not only serve to challenge hierarchies of knowledge, but also radically alter the fundamental premises of library and archives instruction, its content, and who it serves to empower.

References

Adkins, D., & Hussey, L. (2006). The library in the lives of Latino college students. *The Library Quarterly, 76*(4), 456-480.

Baldwin, James (1998) A talk to teachers. In T. Morrison (Ed.), *Collected Essays* (pp. 678-685). Library of America.

Bernal, D. D. (1998). Using a Chicana feminist epistemology in educational research. *Harvard Educational Review, 68*(4), 555-582.

Bernal, D. D. (2020). Disrupting epistemological boundaries: Reflections on feminista methodological and pedagogical interventions. *Aztlan: A Journal of Chicano Studies, 45*(1), 155-170.

Calderón, D., Bernal, D. D., Huber, L. P., Malagón, M., & Vélez, V. N. (2012). A Chicana feminist epistemology revisited: Cultivating ideas a generation later. *Harvard Educational Review, 82*(4), 513-539.

Framework for Information Literacy for Higher Education. (2015, February 9). American Library Association. http://www.ala.org/acrl/standards/ilframework

Franco, M. A., & Hernández, S. (2018). Assessing the capacity of Hispanic serving institutions to serve Latinx students: Moving beyond compositional diversity. *New Directions for Institutional Research, 2018*(177), 57-71.

Garcia, G. A. (2018). Decolonizing Hispanic-serving institutions: A framework for organizing. *Journal of Hispanic Higher Education, 17*(2), 132-147.

Garcia, G. A., & Okhidoi, O. (2015). Culturally relevant practices that "serve" students at a Hispanic Serving Institution. *Innovative Higher Education, 40*(4), 345-357.

Garcia, G. A., Núñez, A. M., & Sansone, V. A. (2019). Toward a multidimensional conceptual framework for understanding "servingness" in Hispanic-serving institutions: A synthesis of the research. *Review of Educational Research*, *89*(5), 745-784.

hooks, b. (1994). *Teaching to transgress*. Routledge.

Lumley, R. M. (2016). *The Academic Library and Social Justice: A Q-Study of Librarian Attitudes*. [Doctoral dissertation, California State University-San Bernadino]. https://scholarworks.lib.csusb.edu/etd/418/

Rosa, J., & Flores, N. (2017). Do you hear what I hear? Raciolinguistic ideologies and culturally sustaining pedagogies. In D. Paris and H.S. Alim (Eds.), *Culturally sustaining pedagogies: Teaching and learning for justice in a changing world* (pp. 175-190). Teachers College Press.

Centro Library and Archives Bring Resources for Students and Educators in Hispanic Serving Institutions

Elizabeth Taveras Rivera
Raquel M. Ortiz Rodriguez
Anibal Arocho

Introduction

Too frequently, colleges and universities that become Hispanic Serving Institutions (HSI) earn their federal designation as a non-intentional byproduct of enrollment shifts (Flores, 2014). In the past fifty years, Latinx college students have become the fastest-growing population. "Hispanic enrollment in higher education is expected to exceed 4.4 million students by 2025, far surpassing the growth rate of any other racial-ethnic group" (*2021 Fact Sheet: Hispanic Higher Education and Hispanic-Serving Institutions*, 2021, p. 1). Their growth has created a path for predominantly white institutions (PWIs) to become HSIs. In HSI, Latinx students represent 25% or higher of the student body (Excelencia in Education, 2020).

Earning an HSI designation does not necessarily result in visible changes in the institution. Specifically, few of the institutions that are now counted in the HSI list have updated their mission statements to reflect their new designation (Contreras et al., in Flores, 2014). Historically Black Colleges and Universities (HBCUs) and Tribal Colleges and Universities (TCUs) are explicit in their mission to support their students of color (Flores, 2014). Their mission statements reflect a development process, integrate the community's feedback, and seek to address the learning community's needs through the institution's short and long-term goals (Contreras et al., in Flores, 2014). For example, in its mission statement, Howard University states its goal to support the needs of its Black students. Specifically, they seek to "provide an educational experience of exceptional quality...with particular emphasis upon educational opportunities for Black students." Their core values emphasize "the development of scholars and professionals who drive change and engage in scholarship that provides solutions to contemporary global problems, particularly ones impacting the African Diaspora" (*Mission & Core Values | Howard University*, n.d.). Diné College, a tribal institution, states that its mission is to "encourage Navajo youth to become contributing members of the Navajo Nation and the world" (About Diné College, n.d.). Its current Strategic Goals focus on promoting the sustainability of "the institution's Diné identity...[through the] increase use and application of language, history and culture campus-wide" (About Diné College, n.d.).

Faculty and staff at institutions with missions that do not include a focus on students of color may not a) understand the needs of Latinx students, b) have built capacity among its teaching and administrative staff to support Latinx students' retention and graduation rates, or c) have addressed curricular barriers that exclude the contributions of Latinx peoples in the United States, such as the Puerto Rican community which established enclaves as early as the mid-1800s, in the teaching of content (Flores, 2014).

When an institution of higher education is designated as an HSI, it is eligible for additional federal funding through "grants under the Title V and Title III, Part A, Programs" (*Hispanic Association of Colleges and Universities—HSI Definition*, n.d.). According to the Hispanic Association of Colleges and Universities (HACU), HSI began to receive Title III and Title V funding in 1995, with federal grant awards totaling over $10 million, a sum that grew to almost $150 million by 2020 (*About HACU–Hispanic Association of Colleges and Universities*, n.d.). In 2019, appropriation for Title V awards was $124,415,000 (*Funding Status—Title V Developing Hispanic-Serving Institutions Program*, 2020). While not all institutions apply for grants, many of the colleges that comprise the City University of New York (CUNY) system have benefited from federal funding for programming related to supporting the retention, longevity, and graduation rates of its Latinx student population.

The CUNY system predates the Civil War and has 25 junior and se-nior colleges spread throughout the five boroughs. Together, the col-leges serve over one-quarter of a million students (About CUNY, n.d.). CUNY's overarching mission is to "provide a public first-rate educa-tion to all students, regardless of means or background" (About CUNY, n.d.). Hunter College, one of CUNY's eleven senior colleges, had 23,193 full-time students in 2019 (*CUNY Hunter College | Data USA.*, *n.d.-b*). Al-most a third of the enrolled students are Latinx, less than one percent higher than the number of White students, yet, "white [students] re-ceived…1.42 times more" degrees than Latinx students, 2,171 to 1,525 degrees (*CUNY Hunter College | Data USA.* *(n.d.-a).* In 2020, white stu-dents at Hunter College had a 58.87% graduation rate, almost 10 per-cent above Latinx students (*CUNY Hunter College—Graduation, Trans-fer-out, and Retention Rate,* n.d.). The graduation rate of Latinx students was also significantly lower when compared with the other two largest minoritized student groups: "The graduation rate of Asian students is 60.57% [and the] rate of Black (Non-Hispanic) students is 52.47% (*CUNY Hunter College—Graduation, Transfer-out, and Retention Rate,* n.d.).

Centro: A History of Activism and Inclusion

The Center for Puerto Rican Studies (Centro) is the only research insti-tute dedicated to studying, preserving, and disseminating Puerto Ri-cans' history and culture within the United States (*History | Centro de Estudios Puertorriqueños*, 2009). Centro is the "oldest and largest Lati-no research and archival institution in the Northeast United States. The Centro's twofold mission is:

1. to collect, preserve and provide access to archival and library re-sources documenting the history and culture of Puerto Ricans; and

2. to produce, facilitate and disseminate interdisciplinary research about the diasporic experiences of Puerto Ricans and to link this scholarly inquiry to social action and policy debates" (*History | Centro de Estudios Puertorriqueños*, 2009).

The Center for Puerto Rican Studies was born out of the struggles of students, academics, and community supporters, many of whom lived the effects of deficit perspectives about the community in terms of limited economic, political, and educational opportunities. Student groups, such as the Puerto Rican Student Union on CUNY's campus-es, called for the creation of ethnic studies departments and the integration of the contributions of minoritized communities across curricula content. Students saw the establishment of institutes, such as Centro, as a means to dismantle systems of oppression based on racial and ethnic stereotypes. As part of the plan to support academics and develop strategies to bolster these new Puerto Rican studies programs, a library focused on collecting and disseminating new scholarship in Puerto Rican Studies was created (Pérez, 2009).

The demands of students, academics, and community supporters for representation in academia and for funding for the resources necessary to support a growing Puerto Rican student population led to the establishment of Centro. Centro carved out a space where the intellectual growth of the community through the documentation and exploration of what it means to be a member of the Puerto Rican diaspora was possible. At Centro, Puerto Rican scholars, students, and allies were able to inform change within educational institutions that had been limited by the singular story, the White male, cisgender story, which excluded and silenced the histories and contributions of minoritized peoples in the United States. Centro offers a space that continues to be academically rigorous, where the community can learn to be politically engaged and is in tune with the needs of the Puerto Rican community.

Centro Library and Archives Collections and Programming

With the full support of the Centro administration, a new librarian was hired in 1974; by this time, Centro held an extensive collection. The collection continued to grow in tandem with the programs and task forces established by Centro with input from different working groups and recommendations from scholars; the collection grew across subject areas, literary genres, and cultural materials. Through this growth, the collection began to attract students and researchers outside of the CUNY system. Today, the Centro's Library and Archives have grown to include over 18,000 books, 3,000 academic dissertations, 600 films and documentaries, 300 historical publications on microfilm, and 300 print journals.

Alongside the development of the library collection and through the work of the original Centro Oral Histories Task Force was the creation of the Centro Archives. The Centro Archives collects, preserves, and provides access to archival resources documenting the history and culture of Puerto Ricans, with an emphasis on the development of communities in the diaspora. The Centro Archives holds the personal papers of elected officials, community leaders, educators, and everyday citizens and the organizational records of community organizations, national organizations, governmental offices, and cultural institutions, totaling over 300 collections. Moreover, the Centro Library and Archives provide these primary and secondary source materials to higher education faculty and staff working on creating interdisciplinary studies about Puerto Ricans. These collections include but are not limited to:

The Pura Belpré Collection

The Pura Belpré Papers are an essential source for studying Puerto Rican children's literature and Puerto Rican folk tales and legends. They are valuable for examining relationships between the Puerto Rican community and a central institution like the New York Public Library. The materials include personal documents, financial statements from publishers, correspondence, manuscripts, flyers, clippings, photographs, and illustrations. In addition, there are both Spanish and English documents.

Pura Belpré was a renaissance woman. As the first New York Public Library Latina librarian, Belpré opened doors for many and created communities of readers. Thanks, in large part, to Belpré's efforts, the New York Public Library began addressing the needs of the growing Spanish-speaking community. She broke down barriers in the publishing world, publishing one of the first Latino children's picture books in the United States. During her lifetime Belpré published eight additional children's books and a young adult novel, published posthumously. As a folklorist, she researched, preserved, and shared countless Puerto Rican folktales. Furthermore, she helped establish an archive to collect original Puerto Rican documents and also helped to found several community organizations.

Belpré's activism was motivated by her commitment to educating her community. She was at the forefront of the long battle for bilingual services because bilingual activism was what Belpré did and who she was. And, towards the end of her career, as part of the South Bronx Library Project (SBLP) team, she brought library services and materials to children and adults who, for decades, had been ignored, abused, and beaten down. Through SBLP, Belpré also created a puppetry renaissance–a literary, artistic, and cultural celebration through puppets that became key in sharing Puerto Rican folktales all over New York City. She also elevated storytelling to an art form, dazzling children and adults with her dynamic telling of tales. Belpré filled people's minds and hearts with Puerto Rican pride by painting stories with her words.

Belpré wrote:

> I wish to be like Johnny Appleseed, who was known in the United States for planting apple seeds across the land. I had read about him in one of my books in Puerto Rico. And so, I wished to plant my story seeds across the land. (Unpublished papers, 1977)

The very first story Belpré planted, *Pérez and Martina*, was published in 1932. During her lifetime, she continued to plant story seeds. Belpré cultivated a garden of Puerto Rican folklore through activism and outreach. Her work blossomed as she delved deeper and integrated folklore from around the world. She shared the beauty and richness of Puerto Rican culture with tales handed down from generation to generation, created by many people, and shared through many voices. Belpré understood that no end-of-story seeds were waiting to be planted. She was brave. She had the courage to write her stories.

Cultural Ambassadors Program

The Puerto Rican Heritage Cultural Ambassadors Program makes history real, alive, tangible, and dynamic by sharing the value, importance, and joy of learning about Puerto Rican histories, stories, and culture. A Cultural Ambassador learns about, teaches, and celebrates Puerto Rican heritage by promoting historical recovery and civic engagement and promoting learning and teaching by celebrating heritage, historical recovery, and preservation activities.

The Cultural Ambassadors Program is made up of four modules that help people learn about Puerto Rican history and culture by using CENTRO's online collection of texts, posters, videos, and documentaries. All of our modules have a teaching guide and quiz.

- Module One: The History of Puerto Ricans in the U.S.
    - Part One: The Pioneers/Pioneros Documentary Series is made up of five documentaries. Pura Belpré, Storyteller (56 minutes), explores the life and work of Pura Belpré, New York

City's first Puerto Rican/Latina librarian and an ambassador for the New York Public Library's work with the Latino community. The Legacy of Frank Bonilla (53 minutes) traces the life of a pioneer in higher education from his humble roots in New York City to his days in combat during World War II to the founding of Centro. Clemente Soto Vélez: A Revolt through Letters (48 minutes) explores the life of Clemente Soto Vélez with an emphasis on his contributions to community-building, literacy and cultural identity, political activism, and his undying support for the arts. Plena is Work, Plena is Song (29 minutes) explores this original Puerto Rican musical form of storytelling song. AmeRícan Poet TATO LAVIERA (57 minutes) explores the life and legacy of Jesus Abraham "Tato" Laviera, emphasizing his extensive roots in community activism.

- Part Two: The History of Puerto Ricans in the US (after which the module is named) is a collection of seven essays (5-7 pages long) that provide a comprehensive overview of the Puerto Rican experience in the U.S. They explore labor migration and U.S. policies, Puerto Rican New York during the Inter-War Years, the Great Migration, and the themes of community, organizations, resistance, empowerment, and politics.

- Module Two: The Puerto Rican Voices is made up of ten short films that feature the contributions of Puerto Ricans throughout the United States—highlighting neighborhoods in New York, Chicago, Philadelphia, Boston, Hartford, Orlando, and Miami, among many others. These bilingual (English and Spanish) films bridge the Puerto Rican community's time and space, highlighting how the community's bonds are maintained across history, culture, and geography. In addition, the films explore themes such as Nuyorican poetry, the visual arts, and bilingual children's theater.

- Module Three: The Puerto Rico–US Socio-Economic Conditions uses Centro data reports to provide a socio-economic context regarding current realities on the Island and stateside communities and support comparative analysis. These reports feature timelines on Puerto Ricans' U.S. citizenship after the Jones Act, the economic crisis on the Island, and the impact of Hurricane Maria.

- Module Four: The Puerto Rican History is a fifteen-part video series by Dr. Teresita Levy of Fordham University that traces the history of Puerto Rico from the Taino people to Spanish colonial rule, highlighting pivotal moments of the last century and current events.

The Cultural Ambassador Program also includes Cultural Ambassador Junior materials that help facilitate classroom and community teaching and learning for educators and caregivers of children in Pre-K through 5th grade. Materials include author talks, maps, timelines, the Pura Belpré exhibit, seven panels about Belpré's career as a storyteller, author, recording artist, and puppeteer. Teacher guides, caregiver guides, and videos include CENTRO's Emmy-nominated animated film, *Cucarachita Martina's Musical Adventure*, a contemporary version of a classic Puerto Rican folktale that celebrates Pura Belpré's work and *plena*.

The Puerto Rican Heritage Poster Series

The Puerto Rican Heritage Poster Series documents the history of Puerto Rican migration and the experiences and contributions of Puerto Ricans to U.S. society. The Puerto Rican Heritage Poster Series offers an opportunity to engage students in an exploration of themes such as Puerto Rican cultural roots (1200 to the 1700s), migrant pioneers to the United States (1898-1930s), the Great Migration (1940s–Mid-1960s), political participation, and public service (1960s–2010s), and educational struggles, and institution building (1960s–2010s). In addition, three demographic and historical posters explore Taíno, Spanish and African Roots (2000 BC–1898), Puerto Rican Migrations to the United States and the Caribbean (1898–2012), and the geographic movement of the Puerto Rican diaspora in the United States using 2010 census data.

Centro Partnerships with Institution in Higher Education

In addition to building and maintaining the library and archival holdings, the Centro creates programming to support the diversification of the information science field and support programs dedicated to eradicating racial disparities in academia through partnerships with colleges in New York City, New York, and Lorrain, Ohio.

New York City partnerships include colleges from CUNY. Namely, Queens College Graduate School of Library and Information Studies (GSLIS) (Division of Library and Information Services Schools, n.d.)

and the Hunter College Mellon Mays Undergraduate Fellowship Program (MMUF).

Throughout the summer of 2019, the Centro Library and Archives was the host institution for the Advanced Archival Practice course offered by the Queens College GSLIS program. This course consisted of a practicum where students had hands-on experience with nine collections, including A.V. material, ephemera, personal papers, and organizational records. The Queens College GSLIS program is the only American Library Association accredited library science program in the CUNY system, and the diversity of CUNY is represented and encouraged in the recruitment practices of the GSLIS program and partnerships with research institutes such as Centro (Q.C. Demographics & Diversity Report, n.d.). Students from the GSLIS program were able to work directly with primary source materials to provide arrangements and descriptions of archival collections and gained a deeper understanding of how Puerto Ricans fit into the fabric of the history and culture of the United States.

The Andrew W. Mellon Foundation established the Hunter College Mellon Mays Undergraduate Fellowship Program (MMUF) in 1988 to achieve greater diversity in academia and eradicate racial disparities in the social sciences and the humanities. The program provides Hunter College undergraduate students from traditionally underrepresented backgrounds support structures, mentoring, and experiential opportunities. As part of the programming offered by the MMUF program, the Centro Library and Archives provides orientation workshops for students. These students have a wide range of research interests such as women & gender studies, political theory, philosophy, linguistics, anthropology, history, Caribbean identity, gender violence, African American studies, music, and Puerto Rican Studies. In addition, working with a mentor professor, Centro staff provide hands-on access to both primary and secondary source materials, and orientation regarding the use of archives in academic research for the development of Black and Puerto Rican studies programs across the 20th century. Students are able to acquire skills that will serve them in their future academic pursuits. For many MMUF students, Centro represents the first time they will be working with archival materials.

The impact of working with primary source materials is apparent through the conversations and questions that such work elicits. Students went beyond what was written in the syllabus and interrogated materials that served as evidence of growth, struggle, and the resilience of communities. In concrete terms, the work conducted by the Queens College GSLIS students had real and positive implications for the archives and their future patrons. These students successfully arranged and described nine collections. The work completed represents artifacts, documents, and photographs from the 20th century and documents a cross-section of individuals and entities within the Puerto Rican community. Students had their concepts of traditional archival work challenged by the unique nature of ethnic studies-related materials and saw first-hand the limitations that traditional protocols had when working with Centro's varied collections. The standard arrangement and description of documents and the processes that were taught as archival theory failed to capture the nuance, historical context, and external factors that need to be considered when preparing an archival collection for future research use. In a short period of time, students gained subject area knowledge and presented work and findings that will be appreciated for decades to come.

In 2019 the impact and use of Centro went beyond the New York area when Lorain County Community College began to offer the course HUMS 295G, Introduction to Puerto Rican Studies. This was the first time that a Puerto Rican Studies course had been offered at this institution or in the state of Ohio, at large. In this ten-week, three-credit course, students' study and analyze the Puerto Rican diaspora's racial, historical, linguistic, religious, social, and cultural realities, focusing on pertinent themes in Puerto Rican history, culture, literature, contemporary society, and politics. As part of the course work, students must complete the Puerto Rican Heritage Cultural Ambassador Course 1: History of Puerto Ricans in the USA. Upon completing all required coursework for HUMS 295G, students receive three credits from Lorain County Community College, a certificate of completion, and a designation as a Cultural Ambassador.

From its initial form, as a resource for the new and burgeoning Puerto Rican Studies programs in the late 1960s, to its current state as a specialized library and archive open to the general public, the Centro Library and Archives have worked to share collections that represent the community's resilience, activism, and creativity. By partnering with academic programs such as the GSLIS and mentoring programs such as the MMUF, Centro participates in the growing equity of the library and information science field and the future of ethnic studies at large, helping to dismantle deficit perspectives about people of color.

Our experience can help both newly-formed and established HSI meet the needs of Latinx students by building capacity among its teaching and administrative staff to increase Latinx students' representation in the curriculum with the goal of strengthening retention and graduation rates (Flores, 2014).

References

2021 Fact Sheet: Hispanic higher education and Hispanic-Serving Institutions (HSIs) Title of author or page?. (2021).

Title of page? HACU Office of Policy Analysis and Information. https://www.hacu.net/images/hacu/OPAI/2021_HSI_FactSheet.pdf

About CUNY. (n.d.). *The City University of New York*. Retrieved October 25, 2021, from https://www.cuny.edu/about/

About Diné College. (n.d.). *Diné College*. Retrieved October 12, 2021, from https://www.dinecollege.edu/about_dc/about-dc/

About HACU–Hispanic Association of Colleges and Universities. (n.d.). title of page? Retrieved October 25, 2021, from https://www.hacu.net/hacu/HACU_101.asp

About the Mellon Mays Undergraduate Fellowship Program: Hunter College. (n.d.).title of page? Retrieved October 31, 2021 from, https://hunter.cuny.edu/mellon/mmuf/about/

Belpré, P. "I wished to be like Johnny Appleseed." *Unpublished essay.* [1977] The Pura Belpré Papers, Archives of the Puerto Rican Diaspora. Centro de Estudios Puertorriqueños, Hunter College, CUNY.

CUNY Hunter College | Data USA. (n.d.-a).Title of page? Retrieved October 25, 2021, from https://datausa.io/profile/university/cuny-hunter-college/#enrollment—lots

CUNY Hunter College | Data USA. (n.d.-b).Title of page? Retrieved October 29, 2021, from https://datausa.io/profile/university/cuny-hunter-college/

CUNY Hunter College—Graduation, Transfer-out, and Retention Rate. (n.d.). *College Tuition Compare.* Retrieved October 12, 2021, from https://www.collegetuitioncompare.com/edu/190594/cuny-hunter-college/graduation/

Division of Library and Information Services Schools. (n.d.). Title of page?Retrieved October 31, 2021, from https://www.best-schools.info/division-of-library-and-information-services/.

Excelencia in Education. (2020). Hispanic-Serving Institutions: 2018 -19 Fact Sheet. https://files-eric-ed-gov.tc.idm.oclc.org/fulltext/ED607558.pdf

Flores Cailloux, L. (2014). Purposeful Hispanic-Serving Institution identity formation for Latino success: A conceptual model and plan to create a culture
supporting Latino student success at a predominantly White community
college planning to become a Hispanic-serving institution. [Doctoral
dissertation, University of Washington]. https://digital.lib.washington.
edu/researchworks/bitstream/handle/1773/26287/Cailloux_washing-
ton_0250E_12952.pdf

Funding status—Title V developing Hispanic-Serving Institutions program. (2020,
January 23). US Department of Education (ED). https://www2.ed.gov/pro-
grams/idueshsi/funding.html

Hispanic Association of Colleges and Universities—HSI definition. (n.d.)title of
page?. Retrieved October 25, 2021, from https://www.hacu.net/hacu/
HSI_Definition.asp

History.(2009, April). Centro de Estudios Puertorriqueños. Retrieval date? https://
centropr.hunter.cuny.edu/about/mission-history

Mission & core values. Howard University. (n.d.). Site name needs to come first,
then the title Retrieved October 12, 2021, from https://www2.howard.edu/
about/mission

Pérez, N. (2009). Two reading rooms and the librarian's office: The evolution of the
Centro Library and Archives. *Centro Journal*, 21(2), 198–219.

Site name? (n.d.). *QC Demographics & Diversity Report*. Retrieved October 31, 2021,
from https://www.collegefactual.com/colleges/cuny-queens-college/
student-life/diversity/

Transforming Digital Pedagogies with Heritage Speakers of Spanish
Collaborative Instruction and Latinx Archives

Sandy Enriquez*[1]
Covadonga Lamar Prieto*
Rachel Starry*
Andrea Hoff*
Krystal Boehlert*

humming ballads
corridos revolucionarios
instilling carnalismo
para nacer hermanos

Excerpt from "Concha Rivera," by Angela de Hoyos (1977)

Statement on Positionality and Terminology

In the spirit of transparency, and as part of a decolonial practice, we the authors wish to disclose our individual and collective positionalities. We recognize the importance of acknowledging our intersectional perspectives as part of the contextualization of this project. We also wish to acknowledge that we presently work on the ancestral

1   * equal authorship

lands of the Tongva, Cahuilla, Serrano, and Luiseño peoples, now called Riverside, California. In sharing our individual positionalities, we aim to make visible the ways our identities impact our work and our connections with the communities we serve. Sandy Enriquez is the Special Collections Public Services, Outreach, and Community Engagement Librarian at the University of California, Riverside (UCR or UC Riverside) Library. She is a first-generation, U.S.-born, Spanish and Quechua heritage speaker of Peruvian Andean descent. As part of the Special Collections and University Archives (SCUA) team, she provided instructional support and helped facilitate the use of digitized primary sources during the course. Covadonga Lamar Prieto is a recent immigrant to the U.S., first-generation college student, and first of her family to obtain a degree beyond high school. As a faculty member in the Department of Hispanic Studies in UCR, she teaches, serves, and conducts research focusing on California Spanish and those who speak it. Rachel Starry is the Digital Scholarship Librarian at UC Riverside Library. She is a white, cisgender woman with multiple degrees, who is a U.S.-born English speaker and beginner level Spanish speaker. As the Digital Scholarship Program lead, she contributed to digital scholarship instruction during the course. Andrea Hoff is the University Archivist at UC Riverside. She is a U.S.-born English speaker. She contributed instructional support regarding the use of Special Collections and University Archives as well as background and context about the Tomás Rivera archive during the course. Krystal Boehlert is a white, U.S.-born English speaker and beginner level Spanish speaker. As the Digital Initiatives Specialist in the Digital Library Division of the UC Riverside Library, she supports digitization and digital scholarship. For this course, she contributed to the technical infrastructure and digital scholarship instruction. Each of us brought our different perspectives in support of this course, which is reflected in our writing. We aspire to a collaborative working style that strengthens the project as a whole, and that cohesion is also reflected in this chapter. We acknowledge again that Spanish 130 was the result of the labor, approaches, and knowledge of everyone involved.

Likewise, we wish to acknowledge that there is no single terminology that effectively and equitably encompasses all peoples that we, within the context of Western or American culture, typically call "Latino" or "Latinx." Monolithic terms like these erase the intersectional realities, perspectives, and experiences of the people who originate from countries and diasporas within the North and South American territories.

We choose to use these recognizable terms in an effort to make this information accessible and searchable, but we want to acknowledge that these terminologies are complex and will continue to evolve past the printing of this work. This chapter utilizes "Latinx" in reference to peoples who have migrated, or descended, from ancestral lands in the Americas. Whenever possible, we aim to respect the terminology used by each individual or community to describe themselves. For instance, we use "Chicano/x" when speaking specifically within the context of the course, since the focus of that class was on Tomás Rivera who identified as Chicano. In the literature review, we use the same terminology as the authors we cite. Lastly, we utilize "Latinx/Chicanx" to be inclusive of all genders and identities, while acknowledging that this choice may privilege English-speakers due to this term's prevalence within a uniquely diasporic-U.S. context.

Introduction

Collaboration between different constituents in higher education is fundamental for developing inclusive digital pedagogies that aim to break the cycle of silencing of Latinx voices, among others, in both the archives and in broader academic conversations. This is the spirit in which we developed an inclusive research opportunity for undergraduate students at the University of California, Riverside. Through a quarter-long Spanish upper division course (SPN130 course designation, referred to informally in this chapter as Spanish 130), Latinx students majoring in Hispanic Studies were offered the chance of working with previously unpublished manuscripts and other materials from the Tomás Rivera Archive. While this chapter discusses the course as it was taught in Winter 2021, it continues to be revised and offered.

The year 2020 was historic for many reasons. On the one hand, it marked the first time Latinx and Chicanx students comprised the highest demographic (36%) from California to be admitted to the UC system (Cowan, 2020). At UCR specifically, that number rose to 41.8% of admitted undergraduate students identifying as either Chicano or Latino (Institutional Research, 2021). More than half of these students also identify as first-generation and are the first in their families to attend college. As such, the university has developed several outreach and service programs to meet the needs of students of the global majority, such as First-Year Experience Programs for students in the College of Humanities, Arts, and Social Sciences, as well as Costo Hall, which houses the campus student programs including Chicano Student Programs, Native American Student Programs, Undocumented Student Programs, LGBT Resource Center, and many others. In 2018, UCR welcomed its first full-time immigration lawyer to expand legal services for UCR's immigrant students (UCR News, 2018). Despite the success of enrollment, outreach, and additional services, the most recent statistics from 2016 indicate that approximately only 60% of admitted Chicano/Latino students graduate after four years (Graduation Rate Overall, 2020). These statistics indicate that the university must do more to serve and support Latinx students, particularly first-generation undergraduates. Unique offerings like Spanish 130, which combined hands-on pedagogy with curated library resources and a curriculum relevant to Chicanx student experiences, are one avenue we can explore to better support all Latinx students.

This case-study helps fill a gap in the literature regarding Latinx student engagement with archives and digital pedagogies centered on that engagement. It also serves as an example of a successful cross-departmental collaboration that called on the joint expertise of librarians, library staff, instructional designers, and faculty to design a learning experience specifically for Latinx students. We hope that in sharing our pedagogical approaches and experiences, we can encourage others to develop similar courses or projects that facilitate educational and culturally empowering experiences for underrepresented students.

Course Design

The development of the Spanish 130 course took place within the context of a new, collaborative program called "Teaching with R'Stuff." The R'Stuff program provided grant funding to faculty members as well as a cross-departmental support team that included archivists, librarians, instructional designers, and other library staff members. The program was a multi-unit collaboration between the UCR Library and XCITE, the Exploration Center for Innovative Teaching and Engagement at UCR. Teaching with R'Stuff was led initially by the Director of Teaching and Learning at UCR Library, Dani Brecher-Cook, and subsequently by our Primary Source Literacy Teaching Librarian, Robin Katz. The authors of this chapter formed the Spanish 130 team along with a colleague from XCITE, Samantha Eastman.

Applications for the pilot R'Stuff program, to run during the 2020-2021 academic year, were open to all faculty members and required that they incorporate a library collection into their instruction, whether a general collection or a notable collection from Special Collections and University Archives (SCUA). Applicants were also recommended to include a non-traditional research project in their proposed course in order to "create opportunities for undergraduate students to create substantive scholarly or creative projects, think through information ethics, and gain technical skills" (UC Riverside Library, n.d.).

The program was developed prior to the pandemic, and originally a core theme was the importance of location and materiality. The program steering committee had hoped that library workers, faculty members, and students would engage with each other closely on-site with the physical collection materials. Unfortunately, the pandemic required us to rethink the program entirely from a new virtual lens. We will speak to ways this shifted both our goals and implementation further below.

The R'Stuff program formalized assessment in the form of pre- and post-surveys of students, with anonymous feedback and self-assessments of learning outcomes conducted using Qualtrics. The purpose of the pre- and post-surveys were to gauge the efficacy of student engagement and identify areas for program revision. They asked students to self-identify their familiarity with the library's role in supporting their coursework and more specifically their comfort levels describing what archives and special collections were, as well as their comfort levels learning new digital tools in their classes. As the surveys were designed for program evaluation and internal use only and not subject to Institutional Review Board (IRB) oversight, we are unable to share specific results related to student responses.

We would also like to share some broader context for the creation of the Spanish 130 course, called Digital Dialectology, within the Hispanic Studies department at UCR. This course takes a revisionist approach to the traditional concept of dialectology, which is the study of different dialects of a language. The idea behind the course was to bring dialectology into the digital realm, but it is important to clarify the use of this terminology here. In some instances, particularly in common usage, the term "dialect" carries the implied colonial accusation of being a "lesser" variety of a language, as the term can be used pejoratively to identify such "lesser" varieties of a language spoken by underprivileged populations. This is not the case with the use of dialectology here. Spanish 130 reappropriates the terms "dialect" and "dialectology" to refer to the interaction between dialects. The concept of digital dialectology examines the use and uses of natural language and its dialects within a digital realm; it encompasses all human-machine, human-human, and machine-human interactions in which at least one of the elements of the communication system is digitally created, transmitted, or produced. The phrase digital dialectology also refers to the different interactions, relations, and links between two or more languages or dialects in the digital production by an individual. By examining digital materials, undergraduates engaged in a new form of communication with the works of Tomás Rivera and with the UCR Library and SCUA.

This course was designed for a group of 25 undergraduate students, all of whom are bilingual speakers of Spanish and English. In short, students received a set of scanned documents from the Tomás Rivera collections and were tasked with transcribing the materials, examining the contents and their iterations, and also creating an Airtable database and an Omeka digital exhibit page. The primary learning objective for this course was that students would develop their bilingual digital literacy. If "digital literacy" in general refers to students' ability to "understand and use information in multiple formats from a wide range of sources," (Gilster, 1997) approaching it from a bilingual perspective with digital media would be a step forward from most linguistics approaches. On the one hand, this idea of bilingual digital literacy immediately validates the speaking of Spanish in the United States as a source of knowledge, while at the same time it prompts questions about the standardization of the Spanish language in education. This concept also speaks to the erosion of the auctoritas of the sources and the re-evaluation of the ways in which knowledge is produced.

In more practical terms, digital dialectology and bilingual digital literacy are anchored in the lived experiences of our students. Tomás Rivera was the first Chicano chancellor within the University of California, and his works were written in both Spanish and English. The sources therefore speak to students in both the languages that they speak, and both the languages are at the same height of elaboration and elegance of expression. The bilingualism of Rivera's writings foresees a community of readers able to deeply engage with English and Spanish at the same time. The existence of the Tomás Rivera Archive thus provided a unique opportunity to create a community of digital practice in which students become the agents and subjects of their own sociolinguistic research project that in a way, echoes their own lived experiences.

In addition to working directly with archival materials, students were encouraged to develop skills with digital humanities tools and approaches. This course introduced students to the experience of documenting archival materials, organizing information, and creating digital exhibits to contextualize the archival materials for a broader audience. Working with two tools, Airtable and Omeka S, students had the opportunity to build critical digital competencies and collaboratively produce their own digital scholarship.

Background and Context

The Legacy of Dr. Tomás Rivera

It is difficult to find a figure whose importance looms larger in the history of UCR than Tomás Rivera. In many ways, his leadership helped UCR become one of the most diverse of the ten UC campuses. Tomás Rivera was chancellor at UC Riverside from 1979-1984. He was the first Chicano chancellor as well as the first person of color to serve in this role in the UC system. Rivera was a noted author and poet who often wrote about themes related to his upbringing as the son of migrant farmworkers. He was both an example and a strong proponent

Figure 1   Chancellor Tomás Rivera seated at desk, circa 1979-1984.

of social mobility through education (Hinojosa, 1988). Social mobility continues to be an important metric of success for UCR today (UCR News, 2021).

Rivera's upbringing played a critical role in his identity, especially as a writer and later in his role as chancellor. Rivera hailed from Crystal City, Texas. His parents were both migrant farm workers, and his family moved around throughout his childhood for work (Olivares, 1986, p. 7). He lived in many states throughout the Midwest, including Iowa, Minnesota, Wisconsin, Michigan, and North Dakota. He actually included migrant farm labor on his CV throughout his career, a fact which is cited throughout the literature on Rivera (Hinojosa, 1988, p. 64).

Rivera had experience working in education at multiple levels in multiple roles before becoming an administrator. He earned a BS in English Education and taught English and Spanish in high schools in Texas in the early part of his career. He then earned a Masters in both Educational Administration and Spanish Literature. In 1969, he completed a PhD in Romance Languages and Literatures. He became a professor at Sam Houston State University and University of Texas, San Antonio before becoming chancellor at UCR in 1979 (Rivera, 1988, pp. 54-55).

Rivera was in charge during a particularly difficult period for the university in terms of budget cuts. In 1982, several programs, including Black Studies and Chicano Studies came under scrutiny due to their low enrollment. UCR Dean David Warren's proposal to dissolve these programs was met with criticism from many student groups on campus. In November 1982, about 50 student protesters marched from the Bell Tower to a dining hall in University Commons where Chancellor Rivera was having lunch with a group of high-ranking UC officials from Berkeley. Rivera responded to the students' concerns saying, "My philosophy about the need and importance to develop minority communities is well-known. And I don't intend to back away from that" (Rodriguez, 1982, p. B-3). In the end, these programs were retained, and their retention remains an important part of Rivera's legacy.

Rivera died unexpectedly of a heart attack in 1984 while serving as chancellor, at 48 years of age (Kolb, 1984). His papers came to the library in 1985 as a result of an agreement between Interim Chancellor Daniel Aldrich and Rivera's widow, Concepción Rivera. The archive consists of almost 200 boxes in a wide variety of formats. It is the only collection at UCR that has its own dedicated room. An advisory committee was established in conjunction with the archive in the hope that the collection would be used to support research on Rivera and to promote his legacy (Martinez, 1992).

This Spanish 130 course allowed Rivera's legacy to come full-circle by providing Latinx students first-hand access to his letters, photos, and poetry manuscripts. The research opportunities built into this course were designed to encourage students to critically engage with the Tomás Rivera Archive. Students were invited to reflect on how their own lived experiences and cultural knowledge may influence their understanding and interpretation of Rivera's papers through facilitated talks, exercises, and activities. Encouraging this self-reflexive analysis helped break the barriers of exclusivity and whiteness that typically surround archival research. Instead, students were able to witness how their culture and language expertise provides a unique lens by which to navigate the archive. This became particularly important as they engaged with bilingual materials that originated from a Chicano perspective predating the use of Latinx, an identity with which many students align themselves today.

Research Landscape

To fully outline the contribution of this case-study to the disciplinary landscape, we should briefly discuss ways in which the relationship between libraries and the Latinx community has fluctuated significantly over time. For example, during the first World War, public libraries were tasked with the 'Americanization' and assimilation of Latinx immigrants (Flores & Pachon, 2008). Although outreach to Latinx communities would eventually evolve and improve through community engagement, bilingual services, and diverse collection development, caution and mistrust of the library would again resurface for some Latinx users with the USA Patriot Act of 2001 (Kravitz, 2003). Recently, Latinx opinions and perceptions of the library have shifted to a more positive light. The Pew Research Center found that in 2015, 75% of Hispanic people surveyed strongly agreed that libraries "give everyone a chance to succeed" and 71% felt libraries "improve quality of life in [the] community" (Brown & Lopez, 2015).

A survey of the academic literature on Latino perspectives of the library, drawn over a period of 35 years, finds that Latino users are consistently "looking for cultural and linguistic reinforcement; educational support, including study space; a space free of value judgments... and a space in which they can learn about those elements of their culture that conflict with the established order" (Adkins and Hussey, 2006, p. 460). Since those conclusions were drawn primarily from users of public libraries, Adkins and Hussey interviewed Latino college students to learn how their perspectives may be similar or may differ. Students generally reported positive associations with academic libraries, though some did experience alienation, yet the consensus was to dismiss the academic library as a "source of cultural reinforcement" since they experienced very little (if any) representation there, in contrast to public libraries which they felt were more "culturally relevant and responsive" (Adkins & Hussey, 2006, p. 476). This echoes a later study by Dallas Long (2011) which posits that Latino students have different expectations for academic libraries that, when unmet, may contribute to their lower rate of academic library use and proficiency compared to other ethnic groups. Long found that Latino undergraduates interpret libraries as spaces for cultural support based on their experiences in public libraries growing up. Since "students perceive libraries as cultural spaces, yet no attempts are made in academic libraries to engage Latino students culturally," they may be alienated and not wish to spend as much time in the library, which may help explain why Latino students are less likely to utilize the library than their white peers (Long, 2011, p. 511). This can be especially detrimental as research indicates that first-year students who use library services may be more likely to academically succeed, as demonstrated by higher grade point averages and higher rates of retention (Soria, Fransen, & Nackerud, 2013, p. 160).

This illuminates the reality that for many Latinx communities, and perhaps other BIPOC or underrepresented communities, public libraries are generally seen as more culturally supportive and engaged than academic libraries. This is not unintentional. From the elitism of early colonial colleges, to the manifest destiny enacted by land-grant colleges, academic libraries in the United States have traditionally functioned as sites of knowledge formation for, as well as exclusivity and conformity to, white, heteronormative, patriarchal power structures. The culture and structure of academia is changing, however, in no small part because of the activism and support of students, staff, and faculty of color (for one case-study example, see Santa-Ramirez, 2021). Affirmative programs and designations are also ways universities can be motivated to better serve and support underrepresented students. While the Hispanic-Serving Institution (HSI) designation only tracks student population percentages and does not include a mandate to serve Latinx students, other federal programs do exist to promote support of Latinx students. A significant one is Title V, the Developing Hispanic-Serving Institutions program, which aims to expand educational opportunities, improve academic attainment, enhance academic offerings, and generally help larger numbers of Hispanic students complete their degree programs (Santiago & Andrade, 2010, p. 5). Programs like this, coupled with the research indicating Latinx undergraduates would benefit from greater library engagement and representation, suggest that the academic library is a prime site for building Latinx student support services.

In particular, special collections and archives (hereafter abbreviated to "archives") are an under-utilized resource for Latinx student support within the academic library. While the historical absence of multicultural collections is often a consequence of the inherent whiteness and coloniality of archives, the field's gradual move towards social justice over the past four decades (see Punzalan & Caswell, 2016) indicates that these conditions are changing. This transition is exemplified by growing support among archival institutions for social justice-oriented initiatives like inclusive collecting, community archives, and post-custodial frameworks. However, it is not enough to simply acquire or preserve more diverse materials. Diverse materials must be put into connection with diverse audiences through culturally sensitive and empowering exchanges. Therefore, this transition towards diversifying the archive must occur alongside inclusive outreach and intentional instruction that specifically benefits underrepresented communities like Latinx students. Archives have unique holdings that can provide an important opportunity for Latinx students to engage with elements of their culture and history in tactile and creative ways.

As we diversify the collections and audiences we serve, we must also recognize that not all students respond and connect to archives in the same way. Students from marginalized backgrounds may have distinct interactions with materials that share their cultural, social, or ancestral roots. For instance, Vos and Guzman describe how a primary source literary workshop led one BIPOC student to feel an emotional connection to the archives after she learned how her hometown contributed to the civil rights movement (2019). Similarly, the "Transforming Knowledge/Transforming Libraries" project at the University of California, Irvine, which connected Ethnic Studies students with local community archives, documented several student responses to the impact of seeing (or not seeing) their own cultures represented in the archive (Tribbett, Dang, Yun, & Zavala, 2020). Unfortunately, affective impact may also manifest as trauma when interacting with painful histories or silences in the archive (see Sloan, Vanderfluit, & Douglas, 2019). Whether positive or negative, affective impact within the archives should not be ignored or erased. Acknowledging this impact may help students feel empowered or, in the event of trauma, heard and supported. Drawing from feminist and queer studies frameworks, research on emotional labor and affective impact within archives has emerged primarily from the literature on community archives (see Caswell, Cifor, & Ramirez, 2016) or from the perspective of the archivists or memory workers themselves (see Cifor, 2016). However, it is essential we also recognize and leave space for these experiences among students in academic repositories.

Like archives, library digital scholarship initiatives have a responsibility to become more equitable and inclusive in the ways we conduct outreach and support Latinx and other underrepresented students through our pedagogies. Tara McPherson outlined in the contribution to Debates in the Digital Humanities titled "Why Are the Digital Humanities So White?" ways in which histories of race and computing in the humanities have structured the very tools we use, in addition to the ways they privilege certain sources of knowledge and encode that knowledge in seemingly objective terms (McPherson, 2012). It takes an explicit commitment to teaching digital tools and methods through the lens of critical pedagogy to avoid reifying these tools' ability to privilege white, patriarchal ways of knowing at the expense of other, marginalized forms of knowledge. At the same time, equitable collaboration has been a topic of ongoing discussion among digital practitioners who are based in libraries. As Roxanne Shirazi notes, "power relations...are embedded in the hierarchies that make up academia, in both the social stratification of varying job ranks and the hierarchical classification of service and scholarship," calling for more nuanced approaches to both conducting digital scholarship and teaching digital skills and methods to younger generations of scholars (Shirazi, 2014).

From a sociolinguistic perspective, Latinx students are routinely exposed to micro- and macro-aggressions related to their use of language (Zentella, 1997; Mendoza Denton, 2008; Holguín Mendoza, 2018; among others). The variety of Spanish language in use in California, as well as that in use in other border areas, has been traditionally misconstrued as a transitional variety (Alvar, 2000) and at the same time without roots (Perissinotto y Moreno de Alba, 1998) and without future

(Silva Corvalán, 1994). More recent investigations shed light upon the solidity of the variety (Parodi, 2009) as well as its past (Lamar Prieto, 2018) and its future (Guerrero y Parodi, 2012; Carr, 2020). While this more recent research has begun to percolate into K-20 textbooks and mindsets, we have the responsibility to offer tools and resources to those who will be bilingual professionals in the future, as is the case for many of our undergraduate students.

Collaborative Instruction

Special Collections and University Archives

Materiality, and by extension tactile exploration, are key aspects of primary source instruction. The UCR Library department of Special Collections and University Archives (SCUA) supports hands-on, active learning activities during instruction so students can dive deeper into the materiality, history, and context of the collections. Direct engagement with archives helps students better understand the function, need, and wealth of potential within archival research.

However, due to the need for remote instruction at the time the Spanish 130 course was held, we suddenly had to select and digitize hundreds of pages from the Tomás Rivera collections without being able to properly search them on-site, in order to make sure that students had ample material to work with remotely. We also had to find creative ways to engage students in the archives without the tactile activities and lessons we typically focus on. To that end, we developed two virtual activities to conduct with students over Zoom. Our goals for this project were to introduce students to the history and legacy of Tomás Rivera, pique student interest in archival research, and help students develop the preliminary skills needed to engage in archival research. In addition, we wanted to empower students to conceptualize their own heritage and cultural knowledge as valuable tools and assets within their research journeys.

We chose to focus on only two documents from the Rivera archive to allow for deeper engagement and discussion. In a way, the Zoom platform provided an advantage to this type of individual analysis, since students could easily zoom in and out of the image and get a closer look without having to navigate around their peers to view a physical item. The first activity centered on Rivera's birth certificate and asked students to reflect on how this document demonstrates social or cultural norms that are generally quite distinct from our own. Through this activity, we also discussed with students the important considerations of archiving such personal documentation and what research value these types of documents may have. For the second activity, we selected a bilingual English/Spanish poem written by the Chicana activist and poet Angela de Hoyos for Concha Rivera, Tomás' wife. We chose this particular poem because it gives students the opportunity to read and learn about Rivera's Chicanx contemporaries and it introduces students to a woman's perspective and experiences within the Chicanx community (see Hoyos 1977). Inviting Spanish heritage speakers to engage with a bilingual Chicanx poem like this also opens the doors to new learning opportunities and cultural exchanges that might not have been possible with a different class. For instance, the poem contains several examples of code-switching and slang specific to Chicanx culture, so students needed to draw on their own cultural heritage and knowledge to translate and discuss the poem's full meaning. During the debrief discussion, students who were unfamiliar with Chicanx slang deferred to other students in the group who they felt had authority and knowledge to translate. Both of these documents highlight the nuance and intersectionality within Chicanx and Latinx experiences. It is our hope that activities such as this encourage students to value their own social and cultural repertoires on par with the skills and knowledge traditionally valued by western society.

Digital Scholarship

Collaboration is a central value for the UCR Library's Digital Scholarship Program, which aligned closely with Covadonga Lamar Prieto's pedagogical approaches and the course learning goals for Spanish 130. The two primary digital scholarship components that were integrated into this course were the transcription and creation of metadata around archival documents, using the online relational database Airtable, and the development of small digital exhibits to contextualize the archival documents, using the digital collections tool Omeka (specifically the multi-site version, Omeka S).

Covadonga Lamar Prieto regularly implements digital projects in her teaching. As such, she had created an Airtable template for each team to share. Students received a link to their team's Airtable and, in a guided activity, they learned how to use the database for inputting data. After that, they got access to the Tomás Rivera Archive and SCUA materials that had been assigned to their group. The selection of the materials for each group was done in consultation with the SCUA team, and issues of difficulty, total word count, and whether the document was a handwritten versus a typed manuscript were taken into account. They had the opportunity to annotate, translate, and transcribe handwritten letters, as well as to link image files of each document to its metadata. This process was collaborative in the sense that students were divided into small groups and shared access to a set of materials. They performed their translation, transcription, and metadata creation individually, and then shared it with their teams. Each team was responsible for the collaborative creation of a digital exhibit page for their materials.

Once the information was collected and described, the students could then begin to visualize how they would like to arrange those materials, describe them with longer-form narrative text, and share their own perspectives on them in the form of a small digital exhibit. Omeka S is an open-source digital publishing platform and one of the primary digital scholarship tools that is currently supported by the UCR Library. Rachel Starry and Krystal Boehlert formed the student-facing digital scholarship support team, but many of our library colleagues were involved in the broader systems support that made this project possible. Metadata preparation for the archival documents themselves was performed by Noah Geraci, the Metadata Digital Asset Management Librarian, and Omeka S server updates and maintenance were done by Scott Metoyer, our Lead Software Developer. Additionally, Spanish 130 course site setup and user management for the student accounts was managed by the library and handled primarily by Krystal. Supporting the students using digital tools in this course truly was a collaborative effort through every step of the process.

To provide students with essential information about using Omeka and to assess what level of technical experience the students were bringing to the course, the Digital Scholarship Librarian and Digital Initiatives Specialist facilitated a one-hour, in-class workshop about Omeka S for the Spanish 130 students. In addition to demystifying the tool interface and outlining its basic functionality, we also introduced students to the process of working collaboratively in the Omeka S system. Unlike other collaboration tools the students may have been familiar with, such as Google Drive and Google Docs, Omeka S is not designed for folks to work simultaneously to create items or exhibit pages. For this reason, we also spoke with them about the challenges related to metadata management and what the process would look like to migrate the information they had created in their Airtable database into the item records inside of Omeka S. We then walked students through some of the options for arranging and displaying that content, including examples of how they could juxtapose images of the archival documents and combine those with their own narrative text within an exhibit page. We also wanted to help the students envision the end product and how they might want to present their research. By exploring these options early in the instruction process, we hoped that they might ask different questions of the archival materials, or consider their audience when synthesizing what they had learned. Finally, we also addressed some of the common strategies they could use for troubleshooting when something did not work as they expected in the system. Demonstrating how to ask for help and where to search for answers is an important skill and one we wanted to emphasize, particularly since most of the students in this course had no prior experience with this particular digital scholarship tool.

Having learned that the students had mixed levels of comfort and familiarity with tools like Airtable and Omeka, we also offered one-on-one consultations with each of the small groups who would be working together on their final project for the course. Additionally, we created

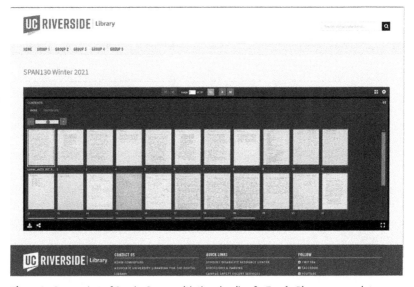

Figure 2   Screenshot of Omeka S page with thumbnails of a Tomás Rivera manuscript.

ad-hoc how-to videos for specific tasks as needed; this was particularly necessary when the Library's Omeka S version was updated in the middle of the quarter, changing some of the functionality. Following up the workshop with these short instructional videos allowed us to remain responsive to the specific needs of the students as they arose. As Spanish 130 was one of the first courses we supported using the Library's Omeka S platform, this had the added benefit of enabling us to learn what students found most challenging, so we could build support materials and technical documentation that addressed the most significant student needs and which could be repurposed and built upon in the future.

Reflections and Outcomes

One of the primary student learning objectives was to increase the linguistic self-esteem of this group of students. All of the students in this course were bilingual speakers of Spanish and English. As Spanish speakers in the United States, these students are often approached from a deficit model of thinking, where they are unfairly perceived as less capable or skilled as their monolingual English-speaking peers. There may be assumptions about their competence in English because they are bilingual. With this project we intentionally fought against that notion and aimed to create a space in which students could "own" their bilingualism. Bilingualism is a unique skill that these students have and brings a deeper understanding and linguistic knowledge to the subject matter. The goal of introducing students to the archival materials from the Tomás Rivera Archive was in large part to allow bilingual students to experience their bilingualism as a unique skill set and recognize it as an asset in their academic career. We found that the students were highly engaged with the materials because they could bring their own strengths and experiences into the research process, and we hope the students continue to draw on this confidence in their knowledge and expertise in their future endeavors.

Another course objective that we found to be successful was exposing the students to digital tools and methods and building their confidence in developing new skills and digital competencies. Creating and organizing metadata for archival documents played a central role in this project, as the students were responsible for both creating transcriptions or translations of the materials and summarizing information about people, places, and topics present in the texts in a structured format. We encouraged them to think about the eventual publication of their research, even research conducted on a smaller scale with a group of archival documents for a single course project. The final project asked them to experiment with the arrangement and display of those materials on a webpage–quite a challenge for students who were overall new to this form of scholarly communication. Because each small group of students would be responsible for a single page on the larger course exhibit site, they also had to consider a hypothetical user's navigation of those webpages. Troubleshooting collaboratively with their peers, using technical documentation and the larger Omeka S user forums, was another important skill we believed they could translate to technical projects in many other contexts in their academic careers.

The objective of introducing the students to archival research methods was also achieved, as students learned about both the process of conducting archival research and interacting with materials from the Tomás Rivera Archive, through the instruction session led by the University Archivist and the Special Collections Librarian. From the perspective of the classroom, the shift to a remote learning environment required changes in methodologies and modes of instruction and evaluation. At the same time, it provided an opportunity to reconsider the process of learning and acquisition of knowledge as a sequence of skills and competencies, and not as a memoristic exercise.

In addition to those successes, several challenges were met during this course. The first iteration of Spanish 130 took place during the early stages of the COVID-19 pandemic, which contributed to student stress for a multitude of reasons. While the full impact of the pandemic on the health and well-being of students, as well as faculty and staff working in higher education, has not yet been addressed by researchers, our experience was also one of extreme uncertainty and stress as the pandemic affected each of our lives in different ways. The closure of the library to the public during the pandemic also meant that archival material could not be accessed by the students in-person, so the SCUA team had to improvise and coordinate with minimal on-site presence to both research and scan materials in unprecedented ways.

Beyond the upheavals of the pandemic, the course faced the common challenge of finding a balance between teaching the disciplinary content and helping students overcome the learning curve of applying new technologies and digital skills in analyzing and reflecting on the course content. Combining this balancing act with the temporal compression of a 10-week academic quarter exacerbated the struggle. Even under the best circumstances, introducing students to new tools can be incredibly time-intensive, depending on their previous exposure to similar tools. On the one hand, students were almost all able to complete their annotation, transcriptions, and translations of their assigned archival documents within the Airtable database, and accomplish other non-digital course assignments. On the other hand, while many students were certainly able to begin their work within the Omeka S platform and envision the published end product, the digital exhibition portion of the final project was not completed by the end of the term. Finding the right scale for the technical components of a course with these particular learning goals is a challenge that we will need to continue thinking through.

Another aspect worth mentioning as a challenge was the shift to remote teaching. Neither the faculty nor the students were completely prepared for this new environment. While for the faculty it required a new understanding of pedagogies, remote learning brought to the surface many inequalities that we have been trained to ignore when teaching in person. Being isolated and having access to class only online exacerbated difficulties in gaining access to reliable internet connections, as well as general shelter and care inequalities that are not equally visible when in person. Navigating those, in the middle of a public health crisis that has been more harmful to low income individuals than the global majority, was–and continues to be–a matter of concern.

Additionally, we faced some technical issues related to our Omeka S platform that added to the challenges of teaching with this tool. Some of the Omeka S server updates and customizations happening on the back end turned out to be disruptive to the students using it and to staff teaching around the tools. Another way we hope to address some of the Omeka S issues moving forward is to more actively develop our instructional approaches and materials. Instead of teaching "to the tool" specifically, we believe there is value in revising our instruction to better enable students to build on their existing knowledge about sharing images and text online, perhaps using other web content management systems.

In future iterations of the project, we would like to bring in our colleagues who have complementary expertise to advise on the project much earlier in the process. Specifically, from the SCUA perspective, we had digitized hundreds of pages of archival materials so the students could access them virtually after the Library closed to visitors. Initially, we didn't think about how we would deliver the metadata about those documents alongside the actual files. We needed to bring in our colleague, the Metadata Librarian, to lend his expertise. He wrote a script that automated the process of linking document metadata and attaching that to the PDF files, allowing us to facilitate the transfer of that information to Covadonga Lamar Prieto and the students in the course. In the future, we would definitely want to bring colleagues on board earlier to promote transparency around staff labor and streamline our collaboration workflows.

Conclusion

Spanish 130: Digital Dialectology provided a unique and important opportunity to collaborate across departments and specialties in support of Chicano/a, Latino/a, and Hispanic students. While this course was embedded in the Department of Hispanic Studies, as a part of the 2020 Teaching with R'Stuff program at UCR Library it benefited from additional support by a team of academic staff from Research Services, Special Collections and University Archives, and the Digital Library along with staff at the Exploration Center for Innovative Teaching and Engagement at UCR. While this class was held during a time of significant stress and uncertainty due to the global pandemic, ultimately all parties came together to successfully plan and execute a course designed towards the unique strengths of Spanish heritage speakers. Amongst ourselves, we also learned and honed new skills, such as managing instruction through Zoom, in order to ensure the success of the course. Several aspects of this course, including the digitization of hundreds of documents from the Rivera archive, will have a lasting impact on the university as they increase preservation of and access to the materials for future scholars.

While the first iteration of this course is now complete, we aim to continue finding innovative ways to support Latinx students across campus. From the SCUA perspective, collaborating with BIPOC campus and community partners is a crucial part of our outreach strategy and has resulted in successful projects and events. One upcoming example of this is SCUA's partnership with Chicano Student Programs to develop specialized workshops for students to continue exploring Latinx representation across the collections and unpacking the impact of Latinx history on UCR itself. On a broader scale, SCUA is also creating asynchronous resources to support access, research, and engagement with BIPOC collections and materials, such as the research guide for BIPOC LGBTQ+ Representation in Special Collections (Enriquez, 2021) and African American Resources in Special Collections & University Archives (Hoff, 2021). The Digital Scholarship Program is also committed to seeking out opportunities to connect with and support Latinx students and scholars, and has plans to develop a summer training program that utilizes BIPOC materials from Special Collections and University Archives in the coming year. Spanish 130 is being offered again during the Fall 2021 quarter; current and future iterations of this course will build on what we learned from this experience, as well as incorporate student suggestions and comments. All in all, we believe this kind of collaboration is vital for higher education instruction, and we look forward to continuing to contribute to UCR's engagement of Latinx students.

References

Alvar, M. (2000). *El español en el sur de los Estados Unidos. Estudios, encuestas, textos.* Alcalá de Henares: Universidad de Alcalá de Henares.

Alvarez, A., Boehlert, K., Comerford, K., Enriquez, S., Geraci, N., Marshall, B., and Starry, R. (2020). UCR library digital scholarship working group (DSWG) report: Findings and recommendations for a digital scholarship program. eScholarship. https://escholarship.org/uc/item/39n4b1ht.

Adkins, D. and Hussey, L. (2006). The library in the lives of Latino college students. *Library Quarterly, vol. 76*(4), 456-480. https://www.journals.uchicago.edu/doi/10.1086/513862.

Brown, A. and Lopez, H.L (2015). Chapter 2: Latinos' attitudes about public libraries and library services. *Pew Research Center.* https://www.pewresearch.org/hispanic/2015/03/17/chapter-2-latinos-attitudes-about-public-libraries-and-library-services/.

Carolina, B. (2018, June 26). UC Riverside welcomes first full-Time immigration attorney. *UCR News.* https://news.ucr.edu/articles/2018/06/26/uc-riverside-welcomes-first-full-time-immigration-attorney.

Carr, J. R. C. (2020). Reframing the question of correlation between the local linguistic population and urban signage. In Gubitosi, P. & Ramos Pellicia, M. (Eds.) *Linguistic landscape in the Spanish-speaking world.* (pp. 239-265). Amsterdam: John Benjamins. https://doi.org/10.1075/ihll.35.09car

Caswell, M., Cifor, M., and Ramirez, M. H. (2016). "To suddenly discover yourself existing": Uncovering the Impact of Community Archives." *The American Archivist, 79*(1), 56-81. https://doi.org/10.17723/0360-9081.79.1.56.

Cifor, M. (2016) "Affecting relations: introducing affect theory to archival discourse." *Archival Science,* 16, 7-31. https://link.springer.com/article/10.1007/s10502-015-9261-5.

Cowan, J. (2020, August 5). Meet members of a historic University of California class. *New York Times.* https://www.nytimes.com/2020/08/05/us/university-california-latino-students.html.

Enriquez, S. (2021, July 29). BIPOC LGBTQ+ *Representation in UCR special collections.* UC Riverside Library. https://guides.lib.ucr.edu/bipoc.

Flores, E. and Pachon, H. (2008). *Latinos and public library perceptions.* Tomás Rivera Policy Institute. https://socialinnovation.usc.edu/trpi/archives/Latinos_&_Public_Library_Perceptions_Final.pdf.

Gilster, P. (1997). *Digital literacy.* New York: Wiley Computer Pub.

Hinojosa, R. (1988). Tomás Rivera (1935–1984). In V.E. Lattin, R. Hinojosa, & G. D. Keller (Eds.), *Tomás Rivera, 1935–1984: The man and his work* (pp. 64–65). Bilingual Press.

Hoff, A. (2021, Dec. 11). African American resources in special collections & university archives. *UC Riverside Library.* https://guides.lib.ucr.edu/c.php?g=1054443

Holguín Mendoza, Claudia. (2018). Critical language awareness for Spanish heritage language programs. *International Multilingual Research Journal,* 12(2), 65-69. https://doi.org/10.1080/19313152.2017.1401445

Hoyos de, A. (1977, August 6). *Concha Rivera.* Tomás Rivera archive, UC Riverside, Special Collections and University Archives. https://calisphere.org/item/ark:/13030/hb8p301110/.

Kolb, R. (1984, May 17). University of California Office of Public Information news bulletin. Office of Strategic Communications records, UC Riverside, Special Collections & University Archives.

Kravitz, R.R. (2003). Libraries, the FBI, and the USA Patriot Act: A chilling history. *Latino Studies,* 1(3), 445-451. https://www.journals.uchicago.edu/doi/10.1086/382843.

Lamar Prieto, C. (2018). Los californios : historia sociolingüística de California en el siglo XIX. Madrid: Iberoamericana.

Long, D. (2011). Latino students' perceptions of the academic library. *The Journal of Academic Librarianship,* 37(6), 504-511. https://doi.org/10.1016/j.acalib.2011.07.007.

Martinez, A.M. (1992). *Guide to the Tomas Rivera archive.* Riverside, CA: UCR Library: Special Collections & University Archives. https://oac.cdlib.org/findaid/ark:/13030/tf6r29p0kq/

McPherson, T. (2012). Why are the digital humanities so White? Or thinking the histories of race and computation. In Matthew K. Gold (Ed.), *Debates in the Digital Humanities.* http://dhdebates.gc.cuny.edu/debates/text/29

Mendoza-Denton, N. (2008). Homegirls: Language and cultural practice among Latina young girls. Massachusetts: Blackwell.

Moreno de Alba, J.G., & Perissinotto, G. (1998). Algunas consideraciones sobre el español de Santa Bárbara. *Nueva Revista de Filología Hispánica*, XXXVI (1), 171-291.

Olivares, J. (1986). In honor of Tomás Rivera. In J. Olivares (Ed.), *International studies in honor of Tomás Rivera.page numbers?* Arte Público Press.

Parodi, C. (2009). "El otro México: español chicano, koineización y diglosia en Los Ángeles, California." *Historia de la sociolingüística en México.* Ed. Rebeca Barriga Villanueva y Pedro Martín Butragueño. México: El Colegio de México.

Parodi, C., & Guerrero Jr, A. (2016). Los Angeles Vernacular Spanish. *Spanish Language and Sociolinguistic Analysis*, 8, 91.

Punzalan, R. and Caswell, M. Critical directions for archival approaches to social justice. *Library Quarterly: Information, Community, Policy*, 86(1), 25-42. https://www.journals.uchicago.edu/doi/pdf/10.1086/684145.

Rivera, T. (1984). Curriculum vita. In V.E. Lattin, R. Hinojosa, & G. D. Keller (Eds.), *Tomás Rivera, 1935-1984: The man and his work* (pp. 54-55). Bilingual Press.

Rodriguez, Joseph. (1982, November 2). 150 rip plan to dismantle UCR ethnic studies. Press-Enterprise.

Santa-Ramirez, S. (2021). A historical snapshot of Latinx student activism from 1960s to 1990s: A university archival analysis. *Journal of Hispanic Higher Education*, https://doi.org/10.1177/15381927211008681.

Santiago, D.A.. and Andrade, S.J. (2010). Emerging Hispanic-Serving Institutions (HSIs): Serving Latino students. Excelencia in Education. https://files.eric.ed.gov/fulltext/ED508202.pdf.

Shirazi, R. (2014). Reproducing the Academy: Librarians and the question of service in the digital humanities. https://roxanneshirazi.com/2014/07/15/reproducing-the-academy-librarians-and-the-question-of-service-in-the-digital-humanities/

Silva Corvalán, C. (1994). *Language contact and change.* Oxford: Oxford University Press.

Sloan K., Vanderfluit, J., and Douglas, J. (2019) "Not 'just my problem to handle': Emerging themes on secondary trauma and archivists." *Journal of Contemporary Archival Studies*, 6(20), 1-24. https://elischolar.library.yale.edu/jcas/vol6/iss1/20.

Soria, K.M., Fransen J., and Nackerud, S. (2013). Library use and undergraduate student outcomes: New evidence for students' retention and academic success. *Libraries and the Academy*, 13(2), 147-164. https://doi.org/10.1353/pla.2013.0010.

Tribbet, K., Dang T. V., Yun, A. E., and Zavala, J. (2020). Transforming knowledge, Transforming libraries: researching the intersections of ethnic studies and community archives. UCI Libraries. https://escholarship.org/uc/item/47c2h0dd.

University of California, Riverside. (2020, December 10). *First-time full-time frosh graduation rate–overall. Institutional Research.* https://ir.ucr.edu/stats/outcomes/grad.

University of California, Riverside. (2021, February 8). *Enrollments: Demographic. Institutional research.* https://ir.ucr.edu/stats/enroll/demographic.

University of California, Riverside. (n.d.). Teaching with R'Stuff. UC Riverside Library. https://library.ucr.edu/instructional-support/teaching-with-rstuff.

Vos, J. and Guzman, Y. (2019). Understanding my home: The potential for affective impact and cultural competence in primary source literacy. *Journal of Western Archives, 10*(1), 1-29. https://doi.org/10.26077/90a0-8629.

Warren, J.D.. (2021, September 21) It's a three-peat: UCR again tops social mobility ranking. *UCR News.* https://news.ucr.edu/articles/2021/09/12/its-three-peat-ucr-again-tops-social-mobility-ranking

Zentella, A. C. (1997). Growing up bilingual: Puerto Rican children in New York. Massachusetts: Blackwell.

Image Credits

Boehlert, K. (2021, October 15) Screenshot of Omeka S page with thumbnails of a Tomás Rivera manuscript. CC-BY 4.0

Tomas Rivera seated at desk. (c. 1979-1984). Office of Strategic Communications records, UC Riverside, Special Collections & University Archives.

Contributors

Archer-Helke, Caitlin E.

Dusting off the Stacks:
Building a Representative Library Collection in a Small HSI

Caitlin Archer-Helke grew up in a vanished corner of the South Side of Chicago and spent years running away from the family profession of librarianship, getting a Master's in Spanish literature focusing on very dead people before turning to libraries. She has worked as a Spanish TA, a public librarian, an academic librarian, and an interim library director at a small HSI, and is currently Acquisitions & Content Support Specialist at Dykema Gossett.

Arocho, Aníbal

Centro Library and Archival Resources for Students and Educators in Hispanic Serving Institutions

Aníbal Arocho is the Library Manager at the Center for Puerto Rican Studies Library & Archive, Hunter College, City University of New York where he manages library reference services, and a growing collection of over 18,000 items. He holds a Master's of Science in Library and Information Science from the Pratt Institute.

Avila, Beronica

Inclusive and Culturally-Enhancing Programming in the Academic Library:
The Día de los Muertos Celebration in Context

Beronica is an information professional, educator, and advocate. Her scholarly interests include how libraries can better serve: traditionally underserved students, academic and professional developments for first-gen individuals, and the experiences of BIPOC librarians. Her approaches to information science are deeply rooted in the inquiry of how we can center and reframe voices of those not reflected in the dominant culture. She earned her BA in Counseling Psychology from North Park University and a Digital Curation Certificate and MLIS at Dominican University.

Bambenek, Jill E.

Inclusive and Culture-Enhancing Programming in the Academic Library: The Día de los Muertos Celebration in Context

I was born and raised in Minneapolis, MN and started my career as a Children's and Young Adult Librarian. I am a passionate librarian with a deep commitment to providing inclusive and accessible collections, spaces, and events to the places I serve, whether it be a public or an academic library. I work to build community, and a sense of belonging for every individual who walks through the door.

Boehlert, Krystal

Transforming Digital Pedagogies with Heritage Speakers of Spanish: Collaborative Instruction and Lulinx Archives

As the Digital initiatives Specialist at UCR Library, Krystal develops digital content, tools and systems for the Digital Scholarship Program and Digitization Services. She holds an MLIS from San Jose State University, specializing in digital services, an MA in Art Criticism & Theory from Art Center College of Design, and a BFA in Visual Media from the Rochester Institute of Technology. She has previously worked with the Visual Resources Collections of UCR's Art History department and with the Collections Information & Access department in The Getty Museum.

Browning, Sommer

Introduction, Book Editor

Sommer Browning is the former Associate Director of Collection Management and Discovery at Auraria Library, the library for Community College of Denver, Metropolitan State University of Denver, and University of Colorado Denver. Her research focuses on creating equitable access to electronic research materials and the intersection of creativity and librarianship.

Camacho, Azalea

Archives, Libraries, and Pedagogy at the California State University, Los Angeles

Azalea Camacho is the Archivist and Special Collections Librarian at the University Library of California State University, Los Angeles (Cal State LA). She oversees the operations of the Special Collections and Archives department, which includes archival processing, instruction, reference, public services, collection development and maintenance. She has strengthened community partnerships and fostered student curiosity in the field by providing engaging opportunities for the campus community. Azalea holds an MLIS with a concentration in Archival Studies from San Jose State University, and a BS in Communications from Cal Poly Pomona.

Cruces, Lisa

Applied Care Work and Authenticity in Undergraduate Instruction and Outreach

Lisa Cruces is a first-generation college graduate who holds dual BA degrees in History and International Studies from Texas State University and a Master's of Science in Information Studies with specializations in archives and academic libraries from the University of Texas at Austin. Throughout her decade working in higher education and community organizing, Cruces' mission has been to empower students with critical thinking skills for lifelong learning, and through representation in higher ed. Before joining Texas State's University Libraries in early 2021, Cruces worked at peer Hispanic Institutions, the University of Houston, and San Jacinto Community College.

Davis Jr., Anthony

Collaborating through Collections: The Male Success Initiative, Fullerton, Men of Color Collection

Anthony Davis Jr. is the Copyright & Policy Librarian at the California State University, Fullerton Pollak Library where he serves as the campus intellectual property policy analyst. An American Library Association Spectrum Initiative Scholar, Anthony completed a post-graduate diversity residency at the University of Delaware Library. His research interests include fair use, Creative Commons, and library outreach to men of color. He received a B.A. and a M.S.I. degree from the University of Michigan.

Enríquez, Sandy

Transforming Digital Pedagogies with Heritage Speakers of Spanish: Collaborative Instruction and Latinx Archives

Sandy Enriquez is the Special Collections Public Services, Outreach & Community Engagement Librarian at UC Riverside. She holds an MA in Latin American & Caribbean Studies from New York University and an MLIS from Long Island University.

Fiedler, Brittany Paloma

Is it for Me?: Alienation, Assimilation, and Ambition in Academia

Brittany Paloma Fiedler is a Teaching & Learning Librarian at the University of Nevada, Las Vegas where she spends most of her time providing information literacy instruction to first-year students. She holds an MSLIS from UIUC and an MA (English Literature) and BS (Secondary Education) from UNLV. Before entering academia, she was a high school English teacher and middle school librarian. Her scholarly interests include how libraries can work with traditionally underserved students and the experiences of academic librarians of color.

Fletcher, Stephanie B.

Inclusive and Culture-Enhancing Programming in the Academic Library: The Día de los Muertos Celebration in Context

Stephanie B. Fletcher is the Head of Discovery, Metadata, and Technical Services at Illinois Institute of Technology. Prior, she was the Technical Services Librarian at Dominican University and the E-Resources/Reference Librarian at the Art Institute of Chicago, where she advocated for art librarian-caregivers and co-authored the article "Addressing the Gender Gap: Confronting Inequities in Librarians' Professional Advancement by Establishing a Conference Childcare Program." Stephanie served as the Conference Childcare Coordinator for the 2022 Art Libraries Society of North America (ARLIS/NA) conference in Chicago and co-moderated the ARLIS/NA caregivers' group for four years, where she worked to normalize caregiving, parenting, and breastfeeding in art libraries.

Fullmer, Niki Suki

Is it for Me?: Alienation, Assimilation, and Ambition in Academia

Niki Fullmer is the Educational Outreach Librarian at the University of Nevada, Las Vegas where she spends most of her time developing co-curricular outreach programming for the University Libraries. She holds an MLIS from Simmons University and a BA from UNLV. Her scholarly interests include student belonging in academic libraries and information literacy instruction for first-year students.

Gomez-Hernandez, Elizabeth V.

Coming Together as a Comunidad: Sharing Our Latinx Stories and Culture

Elizabeth Gomez-Hernandez is a 3rd generation Latina/ Chicana/ Mexican-American and first-generation college graduate. She received degrees in Criminology, Law and Society and Spanish from the University of California, Irvine and her MMLIS from the University of Southern California. She was formerly a Research & Instruction Librarian at Cal Poly Pomona.

Hoff, Andrea

Transforming Digital Pedagogies with Heritage Speakers of Spanish: Collaborative Instruction and Latinx Archives

Andrea Hoff is the University Archivist at UC Riverside. She is responsible for providing leadership in the selection, transfer, description and preservation of official University Records. Andrea serves the UCR community by helping people connect with UCR's unique history by providing access to historical materials in University Archives. Andrea earned her MLIS from St. Catherine University and a BA in Art History from the University of Wisconsin-Madison.

Lamar Prieto, Covadonga

Transforming Digital Pedagogies with Heritage Speakers of Spanish: Collaborative Instruction and Latinx Archives

Associate Professor and Faculty Director of the Mellon Mays Undergraduate Program at the University of California Riverside. Her research deals with the first generation born after a conflict: how do they make sense, they different forms of language and literature, of the new power dynamics in their societies.

Loera, Alyssa V.

Coming Together as a Comunidad: Sharing Our Latinx Stories and Culture

Alyssa V. Loera is a librarian and information technology specialist living in Los Angeles, California on the unceded, ancestral, and traditional territory of the Tongva/Gabrieliño peoples. She received her MLIS from the University of North Texas, and a B.A. in International Development Studies (with a minor in Film & Television) from UCLA. She works as the Digital Services & Technology Librarian for the California State Polytechnic University, Pomona and has been working in libraries and archives for 14 years, with most of that time spent in academic environments. Alyssa's research interests include information systems, scholarly communication, digital collections, digital repositories, and how technology pervades human and non-human life. Alyssa is also deeply interested in making, creating, building, and forming radical futures through the continued dismantling of supremacist structures (in libraries and beyond).

Mansfield, Molly

Inclusive and Culturally-Enhancing Programming in the Academic Library: The Día de los Muertos Celebration in Context

Molly Mansfield is the Library Success Director at LibraryIQ.

Méndez Irizarry, Alejandra S.

"Estamos para servirte": Enhancing and delivering online services to Hispanic and Latinx community college students.

Alejandra S. Méndez Irizarry (she/her(s)/ella) is a Puerto Rican Research and Instruction Librarian at Northern Essex Community College in Lawrence, MA. Her previous work experience includes working in K-12 and academic settings in Puerto Rico. She has an Ed.D. and a MIS from Universidad de Puerto Rico, Recinto de Río Piedras. Méndez Irizarry, along with her family are advocates for the decolonization of her country.

Ortiz Rodriguez, Raquel M.

Centro Library and Archival Resources for Students and Educators in Hispanic Serving Institutions

Dr. Raquel M. Ortiz is an Emmy nominated writer, anthropologist, educator, and award-winning children's book author. She is the author of El Arte de la Identidad (University of Granada, 2011) and director of the documentary Memories on the Wall: Education and Enrichment through Community Murals (2013). She wrote the script and a song for Cucarachita Martina's Musical Adventure, which was shown at the 2021 Tribeca Film Festival and nominated for a 2021 Emmy. Her academic writing and scholarship focuses on the visual arts, culture, literature, music, and identity and includes El Arte de la Identidad: Aproximación crítica al jibarismo puertorriqueño en la literatura, la música y las obras de arte (University of Granada, 2011). Dr. Ortiz consults for the state of Connecticut, NYC Department of Education, NYC's United Federation of Teachers Union, Behind the Book, Brooklyn Public Library, Literacy INC, Arte Público Press, Cleveland Public Library, Museo de Arte Contemporaneo (San Juan, PR) and the Hispanic Information and Telecommunications Network (HITN).

Ramirez, Mario H.

Archives, Libraries, and Pedagogy at the California State University, Los Angeles

Mario H. Ramirez is the Head of Special Collections and Archives at the California State University, Los Angeles. He received a PhD in Information Studies and a Certificate in Experimental Critical Theory from the University of California, Los Angeles in 2017. Previously, he has held appointments as Project Archivist at the Bancroft Library (UC Berkeley) and at the Center for Puerto Rican Studies (Hunter College, CUNY). From 2018 to 2019, he was a CLIR Postdoctoral Fellow in Data Curation for Latin American and Caribbean Studies at Indiana University, Bloomington.

Romero, Sally Najera

Coming Together as a Comunidad: Sharing Our Latinx Stories and Culture

Sally Romero is a Research & Instruction Librarian at California State Polytechnic, Pomona (Cal Poly Pomona). As a first-generation Latina college graduate, she believes in playing an integral role in the intellectual and cultural life of an institution by facilitating the transformation of information through knowledge using core values such as integrity, diversity, community inclusion, student focus, and life-long learning. She supports students, especially those from racialized groups, in achieving their educational goals and hopes to foster a student-centered environment of life-long learning that contributes to student success.

Rodriguez, Rosemarie

The NVC Zine Library: Teaching with Zines

Rose Rodriguez (she/her) is a queer Academic Librarian at Northwest Vista College in San Antonio, Texas. She holds a BA in Art from the University of the Incarnate Word, and an MLS from Texas Woman's University. She helped create the first-ever circulating zine collection at a community college in Texas in 2020. Rose's research interests include DEI, accessibility, zines, therapeutic journal writing, and outreach and engagement.

Santana, Nelson

Decolonizing the Library: Building a Collection that Reflects the Student Body at Bronx Community College

Nelson Santana is associate professor / deputy chief & collection development librarian at Bronx Community College of The City University of New York (CUNY). His research interests include Dominican migration in the United States and the role of libraries and archives in under-served communities. Nelson is a graduate of Baruch College with a bachelor's degree in English. He also holds a master's degree in the Study of the Americas from The City College of New York and a Master of Science in Library and Information Science with a concentration in Archival Studies from Drexel University.

Soto-Luna, Isabel

Hispanic, Latine, Latinx: How Monolithic Terminology Can Amplify and Erase Millions of Voices, Book Editor

Isabel Soto-Luna is the Business Librarian at the University of Nebraska Omaha. She is a 2017 -18 Spectrum Scholar and 2020 - 2021 ALA Emerging Leader. Her research interests include DEAI in education and community, Open Access, and Open Educational Resources.

Starry, Rachel

Transforming Digital Pedagogies for Heritage Speakers of Spanish

Dr. Rachel Starry is currently the Digital Scholarship Librarian in the Research Services department at the University of California, Riverside Library. Previously, she was the CLIR Postdoctoral Fellow in Social Science Data Curation at the University at Buffalo Libraries. Prior to UB, Rachel worked with both the Digital Scholarship program and the Special Collections department in Library and Information Technology (LITS) at Bryn Mawr College, where she earned her MA and PhD in Classical and Near Eastern Archaeology.

Taveras Rivera, Elizabeth

Centro Library and Archives Bring Resources for Students and Educators in Hispanic Serving Institutions

I am a K-12 teacher, bilingual education consultant, and teacher educator. I earned my doctorate at Columbia University and work with pre- and in-service teachers and administrators on issues related to culturally relevant pedagogy, curriculum development, special education, and home-school partnerships. My research explores the work-lives of Puerto Rican teachers and the role of culture in their retention. Concurrently, I am conducting a series of interviews with PR pioneers in the area of Bilingual Education and PR Studies.

Teoli-Thomason, Elizabeth

"Estamos para servirte" Enhancing and delivering online services to Hispanic and Latinx community college students

Elizabeth (Liz) Teoli-Thomason is the Library Director at Umpqua Community College in Roseburg, Oregon. She holds an MLS from the University of Hawaii at Manoa and has devoted her career to serving community college students, specifically those who are from underrepresented groups.

Terrones, Lettycia

Archives, Libraries, and Pedagogy at the California State University, Los Angeles

Lettycia Terrones serves as the Librarian for Ethnic Studies, Latin American Studies, Honors College, and EOP at Cal State LA University Library.

Williams, Jess

Applied Care Work and Authenticity in Undergraduate Instruction and Outreach

Jess Williams (she/her/ella) is a first-gen academic librarian doing her darndest to lead her team with empathy, be a better ally, and put students first. Jess currently serves as the Head of Information & Undergraduate Services at Texas State University Libraries, and she is passionate about student success, organizational culture, and creating spaces that facilitate authenticity and self-expression.

Index

Printed in the USA
CPSIA information can be obtained
at www.ICGtesting.com
CBHW041207240924
14814CB00005B/11